Those Gentle Heroes

A TRIBUTE

Gary Blackburn

Introduction and sage advice courtesy of
Lonnie M. Long

NEWMAN SPRINGS PUBLISHING
320 Broad Street
Red Bank, NJ 07701

First originally published by Newman Springs Publishing 2020

ISBN 978-1-64801-888-6 (Paperback)
ISBN 978-1-64801-889-3 (Digital)

Printed in the United States of America

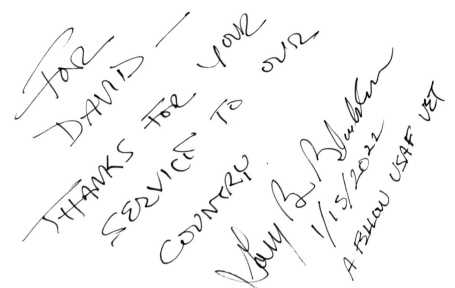

For David –
Thanks for your
Service to our
Country

Larry B Blubaum
1/15/2022
A Bluou USAF Vet

Be not ashamed to say you loved them… Take what they have left and what they have taught you with their dying and keep it with your own. And in that time when men decide and feel safe to call the war insane, take one moment to embrace those gentle heroes you left behind.

—Maj. Michael Davis O'Donnell
Shot down over Dak To, South Vietnam, while attempting
to rescue eight American soldiers trapped by attacking
North Vietnamese Army forces (New Year's Day, 1970)

Contents

Preface

It is my personal honor to recount the twenty-one stories in this book. My only intent is to honor these fine young men who sacrificed so much for their country and pay homage to over fifty-eight thousand other Americans who died in Southeast Asia.

Those of us who volunteered to serve during the Vietnam War years were very different from our peers on the left who always claimed to speak for us. In the words of Senator Jim Webb (D-VA), for us "Woodstock was a side show, college protestors were spoiled brats who would have benefited from working a few jobs to pay their tuition, and Vietnam represented not an intellectual exercise in draft avoidance or protest marches, but a battlefield that was just as brutal as those [our] fathers faced in World War II and Korea."

We were proud to be more like our parents' generation. We believed our mission to stop the expansion of communism was right and just, and we honored our fathers by trying to do as good a job as they had done fighting totalitarianism in the 1940s. Harris polls following the end of the war indicated 91 percent of us were glad we served, and 89 percent believed we were asked to fight a war the politicians would not let us win.

Two-thirds of the millions who served and 73 percent of those who died during the Vietnam War were volunteers. The heroes in this twenty-one-story salute were all volunteers who believed they were helping to make the world a better place. They represent all that was good and honest and brave in this country fifty years ago. We must never allow the world to forget them, or their brothers.

G. B. Blackburn
Oak Ridge, North Carolina

Foreword

From the author of *UNLIKELY WARRIORS: The Army Security Agency's Secret War in Vietnam 1961–1973.*

Nominated for the Henry and Ann Paolucci Book Award, 2014.

Powerful. Compelling. Insightful. Exciting—a much-needed historical account.
> —Col. David E. Servinsky,
> Executive Communications and Support
> NSA/CSS Colorado

This is a great book on the VN War and should be in every high school history class.
> —Maj. Marcus E. Michael,
> Former Commander
> 403rd SOD, Nha Trang, RVN

A great read about an important part of our military history.
> —Maj. Philip D. Rutherford, Ph.D.,
> Royal Australian Army
> New South Wales, Australia

Why have I not known about this book before?
> —Gen. Walter E. Boomer,
> Former Asst. Commandant of the Marine Corps

The stories in *THOSE GENTLE HEROES* recount actual events that occurred during the Vietnam War. The main protagonists and other primary figures were and are real people. Some of the peripheral characters, dialogue, and scenes, however, were created to preserve the integrity of the story line, while maintaining factual content. Family names of some characters have also been changed to protect the identities of those involved in the stories.

Technically, that makes these stories works of historical fiction, but this should in no way detract from the heroism of the main characters. All of their deeds and the main facts surrounding their heroism are factual. Some events may not correspond precisely with the memories of all those involved. Like witnesses to a crime, different individuals remember events differently, and time has a way of distorting the past, especially memories of traumatic events. I have used a variety of sources including personal interviews, news articles, official records, and after-action reports, and they vary significantly regarding the sequence of specific actions, the importance of particular episodes and the timelines when the events took place. I have simply tried to weave the stories together in ways that seem to be the most logical.

War drew us from our homeland
In the sunlit springtime of our youth;
Those who did not come back alive remain
In perpetual springtime—forever young;
And a part of them is with us always.

—Author Unknown

Glossary

AIT: Advanced Infantry Training
AO: Area of Operations
ARVN: South Vietnamese Army
ASA: Army Security Agency
CIDG: Civilian Irregular Defense Group
DEROS: Date Estimated Return from Overseas
DMZ: Demilitarized Zone
DSU: Direct Support Unit
ELINT: Electronic Intelligence
FAC: Forward Air Controller
FNG: F——king New Guy
MACV: Military Assistance Command, Vietnam
MCRD: Marine Recruit Depot
NVA: North Vietnamese Army
RRC: Radio Research Company
RRD: Radio Research Detachment
RRFS: Radio Research Field Station
RTO: Radio Telegraph Operator
RVN: Republic of South Vietnam
SOG: Studies and Observations Group
USAFSS: US Air Force Security Service

Introduction

Historical Perspective

It has often been said of Vietnam veterans that "they left Vietnam, but Vietnam never left them." This may be true of all veterans who served in any war, in Europe, the Pacific, or Korea, but I believe this has a deeper meaning to the Vietnam veteran. Vietnam was different on so many levels that it may never be fully comprehended. It was a war; it was a time of social and moral upheaval; it was a time of race riots, assassinations, drugs; and at the same time was proclaimed a time of peace and love. It was all those things and more. Vietnam dominated our lives. It seemed to never end. It was all-consuming of the American psyche from 1965 to 1975.

Actually, an American soldier had been killed-in-action in Vietnam as early as 1961. Spc. 4 James Thomas Davis of the 3rd Radio Research Unit was killed on 22 December 1961. Tom's unit had entered Vietnam earlier that year under secret orders from Pres. John Kennedy. Vietnam, that strange, far-away place, only came into the American lexicon around 1965 with the Gulf of Tonkin incident and the arrival of US Marines and US Army combat units. In one year (1965) the US involvement increased ten-fold to over 180,000 troops. By the end of 1968, that number would grow to 549,500.

The year 1968 was one of the most terrible years in US history. Described as "the year that shattered America," many of its events ripped at the very fabric of the American way of life. The US Naval intelligence vessel *Pueblo* was captured by North Korea in January. One American sailor was killed and eighty-two more taken prisoner by the communists. This was followed closely by the Tet Offensive, which US news media presented as a disaster for US forces in Vietnam. In April, Dr. Martin Luther King Jr., was assassinated in Memphis, and riots broke out in over one hundred American cities. Large sections of Washington, DC, Chicago, and Baltimore were burned to the ground. Two months later Robert F. Kennedy was assassinated as he campaigned for the presidency. That horrific event was followed in August by the Democratic National Convention, and Americans watched in dismay as Chicago police, Illinois National Guard troops, and war protestors fought pitched battles in the streets of Chicago. US casualties in Vietnam totaled over sixteen thousand that year, after the American public had been told by political and military leaders there was "a light at the end of the tunnel."

The Vietnam War had become a nightly television event in American homes, and the war impacted an entire generation. In his recent book, *Enduring Vietnam*, Dr. James Wright describes that generational impact: "Over 10 million baby boomers served in the armed forces in the 1960s and early 1970s. Nearly 27 million young American men reached 18, draft age, between August 1964 and March 1973. More than 2.2 million of them were drafted and 8.7 million enlisted in military services. Nearly 10 percent of the men in that generation went to Vietnam." It would be less than ten years before the dedication of the Vietnam Memorial Wall with 58,318 names engraved on it. It would seem more like decades to most Vietnam veterans. This book is a "slow salute" to those who did not return.

A Personal Note

In 2010, I approached Gary Blackburn with thirteen years of research on the Army Security Agency in Vietnam and eventually convinced him we should write our book. Actually, I convinced him he should write the book that I had researched. Gary and I met at Shu Lin Kou Air Base, Taiwan, in 1963 when, as a young Army Pfc., I was assigned to work with the Air Force for four months. At that time he was Airman 2nd Class Blackburn, Chinese linguist. Gary and I have an almost life-long friendship. Over the next three years as the book took form, it was obvious Gary gravitated toward the individual, personal stories of the men who had served. Being a history major, I leaned more toward the historical narrative. We worked out a balance and on Memorial Day 2013 we published our book, *Unlikely Warriors, The Army Security Agency's Secret War in Vietnam 1961–1973*.

Since publication, Gary and I have been invited to the National Cryptologic Symposium, Johns Hopkins University, given lectures at The US Army Intelligence Center of Excellence, Ft. Huachuca, Arizona, and the Intelligence and Security Command, Ft. Belvoir, Virginia. We also made a video for the Military Intelligence Museum at Ft. Huachuca. On two occasions we were invited to host book signings at the International Spy Museum in Washington, DC. We were recently honored with an invitation from the National Security Agency to attend a memorial ceremony at Ft. Meade, Maryland, for S. Sgt. Robert Townsend, an Army Security Agency soldier killed in Vietnam. A few months later, we were invited to give a presentation at the National Security Agency Center for Cryptologic History. This is heady stuff for two low-ranking enlisted guys, but what we are most proud of is the recognition we have generated for those unsung heroes who "Served in Silence."

Over the past five years, I have continued to research the intelligence war in Vietnam and Gary has continued to write. He developed a series of stories appropriately titled "Forever Young," dedicated to soldiers, sailors, airmen, and Marines in Vietnam who live on only in our memories. Those who read his stories kept asking for more, and from the original stories, *Those Gentle Heroes* was born. Vietnam veterans are bound together by their war experiences, but the strongest bond among all veterans from all wars is their love for those gentle heroes they left behind.

Lonnie M. Long
Davidson, North Carolina

1

John Francis Link

Johnny, We Hardly Knew Ye

John Francis "Johnny" Link

Johnny Link was born and raised in an Irish Catholic family in Ottumwa, Iowa. Surrounded by thousands of acres of Iowa farmland, Ottumwa is located in the Des Moines River Valley and is one of the larger cities in Southeastern Iowa. With John Morrell & Company meat packing, John Deere, a major farm implement manufacturer, and dozens of smaller plants and businesses, the city was a major source of employment and a mecca for shopping, dining, and entertainment. It was a good place to grow up in the 1950s.

Johnny's father and his four uncles were all soldiers in WWII. His dad, John, did not like to talk about the war. He had been a technical sergeant (E7) in the Army and had come ashore at Anzio with the expeditionary forces commanded by Gen. John Lucas in 1944. The Battle of Anzio was literally "hell on Earth." The months-long stalemate resulted in British and American losses totaling seven thousand killed, thirty-six thousand wounded or missing, and forty-four thousand hospitalized for various non-battle injuries and illnesses. The siege finally ended on May 23, 1944, when the Allies launched a breakout offensive. After John Sr.'s death, the family would find a Silver Star, a Bronze Star, and a Purple Heart among his possessions. They had never known "Dad" was a hero.

Those long months in Italy had exacted a toll on John's health. In the mid-1950s he developed full-blown tuberculosis and had a lung removed to keep the illness from spreading. At that time, a person had to be confined to a sanitarium for the duration of the recovery period. Johnny and his younger siblings, Terry and Jane Anne, had to have a TB Tine test every few months. Sunny Slope Sanitarium in Ottumwa was their father's home for the next two to three years, and the children could only see him through a screen on the outside of his room, if they could visit him at all. With grit, determination, faith, and most of all, love, their mother, Anne, kept the family together, housed, clothed, fed, and educated. John would get a furlough to come home for a weekend visit every six months or so, and Johnny's baby sister, Jody, was born in August 1957.

Johnny and his brother, Terry, attended St. Patrick's Catholic Grade School and then moved on to Walsh High School. Walsh was a four-year, all-boys school located in an old mansion in Ottumwa and was ruled by the Sisters of the Congregation of the Humility of Mary. Sister Mary Louise was the "iron-fisted" principal (nicknamed "Shanks" by the boys), and few challenged her authority and lived to tell about it. There were fewer than a hundred boys in the school, so there were not many places to hide from the eagle-eyed vigilance and stern discipline of the nuns in the classrooms. Johnny's bright red hair, freckles, and a crooked, mischievous grin seemed to merit special attention, and he always looked guilty, whether he was or not. In those days, if the boys were in trouble at school, they were also in trouble at home, but always with love.

Summers were a time for both work and play. Johnny and Terry played Little League and Babe Ruth baseball and made all-star teams as catchers. Johnny worked as a life guard at the municipal swimming pool and as a soda jerk. He put up hay on a local dairy farm and worked part-time in a military surplus store. That's where he got his first exposure to military equipment and bought his first gun, a Browning sixteen-gauge semiautomatic shotgun. He enjoyed hunting pheasant, quail, rabbit, and squirrel during the various local hunting seasons. It was a rite of passage for a young man growing up in Iowa.

Following high school, Johnny was accepted at Northeast Missouri State Teachers College in Kirksville, Missouri, but after a less than stellar year there, he decided to quit school. Several of his friends had taken jobs with Coors Brewing Company in Golden, Colorado, and being a fan of Coors Beer, he decided to join them. A few months later, he made the decision to enlist in the Army.

Johnny read everything he could find relating to the "Green Berets" and their creation in June 1952. John F. Kennedy (the first Irish Catholic president) had been very keen on Special Forces, and that may have played a role in Johnny's decision to enlist. He was going to become a Green Beret.

After completing basic training in 1965, young Link headed to Ft. Bragg, North Carolina, where he underwent the lengthy, intensive training required to become a full-fledged member of Special Forces. Then, he headed to Vietnam for his first tour.

Vietnam was everything he had expected, and more. He was based at Nha Trang and was working with South Vietnamese Rangers and Montagnards in the Mike Force units. Every day was a new challenge, and he believed deeply in the work they were doing. He decided to sign up for a second tour.

Heading back to the States on leave in December 1967, Johnny enjoyed the cold Iowa weather and his first Christmas with his family in two years. On New Year's Eve, he went out with a group of old high school friends who were home for the holidays. His leave was nearly up and he would be returning to Vietnam, so Johnny's buddies decided to celebrate the New Year by throwing him a "going away" party at one of their old hangouts. The group had a good time, enjoying the food, telling "war stories," and having a great deal to drink.

Sometime after welcoming in the New Year, "Joey" one of Johnny's smaller friends got into a fracas with a large stranger who was as drunk as Joey. Little Joey had always prided himself on being able to drink as much as the rest of the gang and usually ended up "shit-faced" as the others laughed at him. Hearing the altercation above the loud music, Johnny went to investigate and discovered a table-full of strangers just as big and drunk as the man Joey was berating. Inserting himself between his irate buddy and the big man, Johnny broke into his most engaging grin and tried to calm the situation. Before he could speak, or his own friends realized what was occurring, Link and Joey were surrounded and beaten to the floor. The affair was over in seconds. The strangers disappeared in the crowded tavern as bouncers and John's friends came to break up the melee. Johnny was taken to the hospital with a broken jaw, and his departure date was delayed. His jaw was still wired shut when he finally flew out for his second tour at Nha Trang. No one was more loyal to his friends than Johnny Link, especially if they were in trouble. He would fight to the end, against all odds.

In March 1968, members of an elite Special Forces Detachment B-52 (Project Delta) recon team (precursor of the current "Delta Force") were serving as advisors to the ARVN 81st Airborne Rangers. The units were engaged in Operation SAMURAI IV, and their mission was to prevent reinforcements and supplies coming down the Ho Chi Minh Trail from reaching the NVA offensive in Huế. This was a continuation of the Tet Offensive, which had begun in January, and the men had been involved in nonstop action in the A Shau Valley for weeks.

On March 29 the Rangers and their American advisors came under heavy attack as their helicopters landed near A Luoi. Several of the choppers were destroyed, and there were many dead and wounded. Maj. Jim Morris, a former Green Beret working as an Army public information officer, was along on the mission and told of encountering a "redheaded trooper" in the middle of the firefight.

"The trooper looked to be about twenty-three or so," Morris said, "and following him was a slender, clean-cut kid with black hair."

The redhead called to some Vietnamese Rangers who had sought cover among the trees. He told them he and the kid needed help hauling about fifteen wounded men out of a bomb crater. Morris followed the two young soldiers back through the trees as the redhead led the way, calling for help as they went. The fighting had been brutal—the machine guns and B-40 rockets were relentless, and no one volunteered. The ARVN Rangers sat and stared vacantly as if they had not heard. The two soldiers came to a steep embankment that overlooked the landing zone. From the hillock, Morris could see the crater filled with wounded Rangers, Green Berets, and US Marine chopper pilots. They were pinned down by enemy machine guns firing from bunkers across the open field.

"There was scarcely a twig or blade of grass between us and the crater," the major recalled. The redhead stopped and looked back at the lone young man behind him. He shook his head and then broke into a lopsided grin. Scrambling down the steep earthen bank, he broke through the trees with the kid on his tail. There was thirty yards of open space between the tree line and the bomb crater.

The two Green Berets made a broken-field run toward the crater with machine-gun rounds kicking up sprays of red dirt all around them. "I didn't see them get hit," Morris said, "but if they weren't, it was a miracle."

The two made it to the hole and dived in, but they were not going to make it back without covering fire. There was a destroyed helicopter behind the crater, but an NVA machine gun in the trees on the edge of the jungle to their right had a clear shot. The enemy gunner would sporadically rake the entire area with a hail of deadly fire and then sit like a coiled viper, waiting to strike at anyone or anything that dared to move across the barren patch of ground again.

Maj. Morris and another Green Beret opened fire on the machine gun as the redhead and his buddy began to move the groups of wounded men across the clearing. The first group made it across and into the cover of the trees, quickly followed by the rest. Finally, there were only two left to climb the dirt embankment, and both were wounded.

"C'mon, let's go!" Morris yelled as he continued to fire. He had only one clip of ammo left. They needed to hurry.

"Sir, I'm too weak to make it up," the dark-haired kid said. "You've got to pull me up."

The boy was wounded in the legs and struggling to stand. The redhead had his arm around the young man's waist and was holding him up. They were attempting to climb the steep sandy rampart, but kept sliding back to the bottom.

Morris knew if he stopped firing on the enemy machine gun, the gunner would open up again, but both young soldiers were bleeding, and their strength was waning. He had to help.

"I'll try and push him," the redhead said. "See if you can pull him up."

Morris lowered his weapon and reached down to grab the youngster's outstretched hand. As the two men strained to lift the kid up the incline, machine gun rounds sliced through the brush and struck all around them, sending out sprays of shredded leaves and bark. Morris could see the pain and fear in the boy's dark eyes; sweat streaked the smudges of dirt and camouflage paint on his face. Morris pulled with all his strength, but could not lift the young man. Then he realized the redhead had stopped pushing. He had leaned in—cradling the younger man in his arms and was protecting him from the machine-gun rounds with his own body.

Suddenly Morris felt a massive blow to his lower arm and he was thrown onto his back. Losing his grip on the outstretched hand, the wounded men dropped out of sight. Looking at his arm he saw a large black hole spurting blood. Bleeding profusely, there was nothing more he could do. The 7.62mm round had severed an artery in his forearm, and without help he would bleed out in minutes. Calling for a medic, Morris sought help and sent others to assist the two young soldiers.

"I couldn't have helped them if I'd stayed," he said sadly, "and I'd have died. But I still felt rotten. Beret or no beret, we were just guys. There are no supermen and damned few heroes—almost no live ones."

Later that night, team medic Roland Meder struggled to save Morris's arm, and told him the two young soldiers he had tried to rescue were John Link and Albert Merriman. Link was the redhead; Merriman was the dark-haired kid.

Dulled by shock and morphine, Morris was suddenly alert. "Did you get them up?" he asked.

The medic nodded. "Yeah, Link's got three slugs in the back. He's unconscious. Merriman's got three in the legs."

Morris asked if they would make it; Meder was silent a moment and then replied, "Merriman will—we're not so sure about Link."

By early next morning, the various allied units had regrouped and prepared to withdraw, led by the Delta Recon team. Troops had straggled in all night from around the destroyed LZ, and many were wounded. The date was March 30.

Moving quietly through the misty jungle, the lengthy convoy headed for a nearby stream that weaved its way in the general direction they needed to go. Jungle-covered mountains towered high above them. Airstrikes had been called in to conceal their departure, and they could hear distant explosions as the unit moved toward a more secure LZ where they could be extracted. The seriously-wounded and dead were carried in poncho liners strung like hammocks from bamboo poles and borne on the shoulders of troopers as they sloshed along the rocky creek.

Morris's arm was swollen three times its normal size and he was in a great deal of pain as he trudged along with the other walking-wounded. The procession left the stream and moved into a thick forest of bamboo and tree ferns. Doc Taylor, another of the team medics, came by to check on Morris, and he took the opportunity to ask about the two young soldiers he had tried to help.

Bowing his head and closing his eyes, Doc took out a handkerchief to wipe his face, and then replied softly, "Johnny Link died this morning, just as we left out. Bert Merriman's going to make it okay."

"I felt depressed," Morris said. "Not guilty, just bad."

"No, that's bullshit!—I felt guilty as hell! I felt like I'd let those boys down."

The group finally reached the new landing zone late in the day. They had pushed their way through miles of dense jungle and had managed to avoid additional enemy contact. The Recon team had stayed in contact with their forward air controller, and additional harassing air attacks had been launched during the day to keep the NVA at bay. The disparate crew of Vietnamese Rangers, US advisors, Marine pilots, and dozens of wounded were exhausted. There were many who could not walk. The men settled wherever they could to await the arrival of the CH-46 transports. Light was fading under the thick jungle canopy, lending a somber note to the scene as the dead were hauled in, tightly wrapped in their bloodstained ponchos, followed by the rear guard. The two troopers carrying Johnny Link's body reverently lowered it to the ground about eight feet from Morris.

A grim-faced Green Beret walked over and knelt beside Link's body. Removing his striped boonie, the soldier bowed his head and closed his eyes. He looked up after a few moments and patted the bamboo pole the body was slung from. "Well, Link, old buddy," he said softly, "Goddammit! This is f——kin' bullshit!" Then, he got up, put the hat back on his head and walked away in silence.

For a brief moment, there was only the sound of the wind in the treetops, the squawks of jungle birds, and the incessant hum of insects. If the choppers did not arrive before dark, the men would have to spend another night in the jungle, and if that happened, more would die. And Jim Morris would lose his arm.

Bert Merriman's litter had been lowered to the ground a few feet from Link. His eyes were closed as he quietly smoked a cigarette. Releasing the blue smoke softly out through his nose and the corner of his mouth, it slowly spiraled upward through the heavy jungle air as if searching for the light. The boy's tiger fatigues had been cut open to above his knees and his legs were wrapped in heavy bandages. Much of his uniform was black with dried blood, both his and Johnny Link's, but he was not aware of it. He was numb with shock and a combination of morphine and Demerol.

Light-headed from shock and his own blood loss, Morris staggered to his feet. Clutching the sling holding his injured arm, he slowly made his way over to the young man and stood looking down at his face. At thirty-one years old, Morris was a grizzled, battle-hardened veteran, and after the past thirty-six hours, he felt old. He had earned three Purple Hearts before the Marines landed at Đà Nẵng in 1965.

Merriman looked so young. Though deeply tanned by the sun, he was pale from his trauma. Morris knew this kid had to be tough as nails, but tonight he appeared small and fragile. There were still smudges of green and black camouflage paint along his jaw line. With some slight hesitation, Morris spoke. "Hey, listen," he said. "I feel rotten about leaving you guys like that."

Merriman opened his eyes, removed the cigarette from his mouth and turned his head slightly, trying to focus his gaze on Morris. Finally realizing who he was, the boy slowly shook his head from side to side.

"Forget it, sir," he mumbled. "You had to go. I saw what happened."

"That made me feel a little better," Morris said, "but not much." He paused for a moment, as if trying to decide whether he wanted to know the answer to his next question. Then, staring at the ground, he asked softly, "How long before they got you out?"

With a slight frown on his face, the boy seemed to struggle recalling and sorting through the terrible ordeal he had endured. Reclosing his eyes he sighed deeply and tried to swallow away the lump in his throat. Then in a husky whisper he said, "Fifteen minutes, sir."

"My God," Morris exclaimed. "That long?"

Merriman opened his eyes once again and nodded, blinking away tears. "Yes, sir," he said, "but we'd already taken the rounds while you were there. Johnny and I just laid there quiet, and he didn't fire anymore."

Johnny Link's funeral mass was held at St. Patrick's Catholic Church in Ottumwa, Iowa, on April 17, 1968. It was a gorgeous spring day in Iowa. By order of the city council, all US flags in Ottumwa flew at half-staff for the first time since the war began. St. Patrick's was standing room only. Johnny Link had come home.

> Proud, dignified, ancient imperial fortress, Hué,
> Dank, sweltering, house of pleasure,
> Innocent, willowy coeds with long raven black hair,
> Heaven, 13 k's from hell.
> Matt Cain's—a bit of Ireland,
> Glasses raised high among friends,
> Young red-haired man, savoring, taking, living life,
> Proud, dignified, braggart, Green Beret under epaulet.
> Pawn of nationalism, conflict of ideas, a friend,
> Unrelated.
> Coming of the New Year, "Tet,"
> Spring, monsoon, life,
> The same heaven, now a hell.
> Medic! Medic!
> The cross, symbol of sacrifice now a target,
> "Duty, honor, country,"
> "The last full measure."
> Why?
>
> "Requiem"
> —Lonnie M. Long

Sgt. Link was recommended for the Medal of Honor and posthumously awarded the Distinguished Service Cross (second only to the MOH) "for extreme gallantry" and the Purple Heart. He was twenty-three years old.

"The president of the United States takes pride in presenting the Distinguished Service Cross to John Francis Link, Sergeant, US Army, for extraordinary heroism in connection with military operations involving conflict with an armed hostile force in the Republic of Vietnam, while serving with Detachment B-52, 5th Special Forces Group (Airborne), 1st Special Forces.

"Sgt. Link distinguished himself by exceptionally valorous actions on 29 March 1968 as Special Forces advisor to a Vietnamese platoon conducting a combat operation in enemy territory. The unit had just completed a helicopter assault into an exposed landing zone when it was subjected to automatic weapons, rocket, grenade, and mortar fire from an enemy force occupying positions on three sides of the landing zone.

"Braving a withering hail of hostile fire, Sgt. Link raced across the open clearing and removed equipment from two helicopters which had been shot down by the savage fusillade. He placed fierce fire on the enemy and assisted wounded comrades to the relative safety of a rise of ground at the edge of the landing zone. Continuing to expose himself to the barrage, Sgt. Link fearlessly left his unit's hasty defensive perimeter numerous times throughout the raging battle to treat casualties and pull them to cover. He was thrown to the ground and wounded by rocket and mortar fire, but got up and courageously resumed his lifesaving efforts. While shielding the body of a fallen soldier from the ravaging enemy fire, Sgt. Link was mortally wounded."

The war in Vietnam took the lives of thousands of young Americans. Inexplicably, out of those tens of thousands, the death of Johnny Link has been chronicled in at least four books about the war and in *Soldier of Fortune* magazine (August 1981). Such was the force of his personality.

In his book *Mike Force*, Lt. Col. L. H. "Bucky" Burruss wrote: "Back in Nha Trang, I learned that Delta's Ranger battalion had gotten into a major battle when they went into the area of the NVA road. Several of the Marine CH-46 helicopters which took them in were hit by rocket-propelled grenades as they flared for landing, and there were heavy casualties. One of those killed was Specialist 5

John Link, a fine young demolitions specialist who had been on my first A Team at Fort Bragg. He was killed while rescuing a wounded comrade from the fire-swept LZ, shielding the other man with his body when he was taken under machine-gun fire, for which he was posthumously awarded a Distinguished Service Cross.

"John link had been one of my favorite soldiers, a good-natured kid with no business amidst the death and destruction of war, but who believed strongly in what we were doing. Confronted with the twisted reporting of the week-old news magazines and the photos of Link's civilian peers protesting the war in their all-too-similar 'individual' hippie uniforms, I sat down in my hootch and wrote about my young friend in a poem."

Look here.
Have you ever seen a soldier cry?
I weep
Because I lost a friend today—
Not some 'comrade-in-arms'—
But a fine, young friend.
You'll never understand
Why he died,
Nor why I grieve for him,
Because you never even understood
Why we came.
I knew. He knew.
Perhaps someday, like you,
I'll forget—
If I live that long.
Link
KIA—1968
Ranger Valley, RVN

—Bucky Burruss

Johnny Link (far right) and friends, 1967

2

Larry Leonard Maxam

Life to the Max

Larry Maxam

Larry Maxam was not the typical Southern California pretty boy; although his mother, Alice, once described him as her "husky beautiful boy," and his little sister's friends all had crushes on him. Larry was more the smart, handsome, athletic type who would rather spend his days on a Scout hike than waste time lying on a beach. An avid outdoorsman, he explored the California hills with his friends and once hiked twenty miles from Burbank to Monrovia. He had become an Air Explorer Scout by the time he reached high school and was inducted into the Order of the Arrow, Scouting's National Honor Society.

Maxam's first two years at Burbank High were "okay." He liked being on the football team and studied hard. Still, he yearned for more. His father had died years earlier, after a long illness, and Larry had grown up fast, spending much of his childhood helping his mother raise his younger brother and sister, Robin and Linda. Now mature beyond his years, Maxam wanted to do something for himself, and midway through his junior year, he made a decision that would change his life.

He told a friend from the football team: "There's nothing else for me to learn here. I'm moving on and joining the Marines." He left school at the end of the semester and enlisted in March 1965. He had just turned seventeen, but had such a commanding presence and air of quiet self-confidence most people assumed he was much older.

Everyone joins the Marines in search of something. It might be adventure or a place to belong, for the challenge or just the uniform. It is certainly not for the pay or lavish accommodations. Whatever Maxam was searching for, he found in the Corps. He completed basic training at MCRD San Diego, combat training at Camp Pendleton, California, and Marine aviation training in Jacksonville, Florida, by February 1966. Then, over the next eighteen months, he continued to train and gain experience at Camp Lejeune, North Carolina, Marine Corps Base-Quantico, Virginia, and Camp Garcia in Vieques, Puerto Rico.

By July 1967, Maxam had risen to the rank of lance corporal and arrived in South Vietnam. He was assigned to Company D, 1st Battalion, 4th Marines as rifleman, radioman, and squad leader, and was promoted to corporal in October. At nineteen years of age, he was already a seasoned Marine.

In November, the 3rd Marine Division launched Operation KENTUCKY south of the DMZ in Quảng Trị Province. This was another operation to secure the Cồn Tiên area from the North Vietnamese Army units that controlled it. The KENTUCKY Tactical Area of Operations included Firebase Gio Linh, Cồn Tiên, Cam Lộ Combat Base and Đông Hà Combat Base—the area known to Marines as "Leatherneck Square," and the Marines saw action throughout the area for the remainder of 1967.

On January 9, 1968, "Max" and the Marines from his squad celebrated his twentieth birthday in style. He was their leader and their friend, and his buddies wanted to be sure their "Hollywood Marine" had a party he would remember the rest of his life. The Tet holiday was approaching—maybe they would get some downtime and could catch up on their rest, at least as much as the Corps would allow. The men had seen almost continuous action for over two months. This was not the Air Force—Marines never really got a day off.

"Other guys'd go out, get rowdy, whatever, but not him," said Larry Cline, who shared a fighting hole with Maxam. "He was quiet, always looking to help new guys coming into the platoon."

Maxam's buddies described him as a friendly guy who wore his Mormon religion on his sleeve right next to his corporal stripes. No one envisioned the quiet, religious kid from California as a hero.

Part 2

During the weeks following the birthday party, Marine recon patrols began to see evidence of large enemy troop infiltrations near Cam Lộ, a sprawling hamlet eight miles south of the DMZ. There had been local rumors of an enemy attack on Cam Lộ for some time, and there had been recent encounters in the area between the Marines and troops from the 320th NVA Division.

Intelligence reports coming in from the 1st Radio Battalion (the Marine communications-intercept branch of Naval Security Group) and Army Security Agency intercepts along the DMZ also indicated an attack was imminent. Normally, the only defense available at Cam Lộ District Headquarters was a half-dozen US Army advisors and a "Combined Action Unit." The CAUs were counterinsurgency groups comprised of a thirteen-man US Marine rifle squad, a Navy corpsman, and a less-than-reliable Vietnamese Popular Force militia platoon of older youth and elderly men from the local hamlet. As tensions increased, the commander of the 2/9th Marines assigned an understrength platoon of two squads from Delta Co. 1/4th Marines, along with two US Army M42 "Duster" tanks to reinforce the headquarters defenses. Cpl. Tim Russell and Cpl. Max Maxam were the two Delta Co. squad leaders.

On the night of January 29, the so-called "Tet cease-fire" exploded with a Việt Cộng attack on Đà Nẵng. The next day, Huế was attacked, and then Quảng Trị City. By 31 January, nearly every major city, provincial capital, and military installation throughout South Vietnam was under assault by the Việt Công, North Vietnamese Army units, or both. The 1968 Tet Offensive had begun.

As evening approached on February 1, darkness came early in Cam Lộ. The sky was overcast and threatening. It had rained earlier in the day. Temperatures were in the seventies; the dew point was also in the seventies and mosquitoes were swarming up from the nearby river. Conditions within the headquarters compound were "miserable" as the motley assortment of Marines, US Army soldiers, and South Vietnamese militia settled into their assigned defensive positions for the night.

The Marine contingent consisted of the D Company platoon, led by Lt. Mike Steck and S. Sgt. Don Sellers, and the CAU, commanded by Capt. Pete Haines. There was also a minesweeping team from the 11th Engineers, with their Marine security squad and two quad 50s mounted on deuce-and-a-half Army trucks, and a small squad of Echo Co., 2/9th Marines who had found their way into the compound looking for a safe place to bed down.

The Army advisory team consisted of the Cam Lộ senior advisor, Maj. James Payne; his deputy, Capt. Raymond McMaken; OPs NCO, Sfc. Robert Hidinger; S. Sgt. "Doc" Bradley, the medic; John Cleary, a civilian advisor to the US Army; and Warrant Officer Frank Branson of the Australian Army.

The first day of February was Maxam's third night at Cam Lộ. His Delta Co. Marines were combat-experienced grunts, and tonight, they all shared the same uneasy premonition: "there was gonna be a shit-storm before morning," and they would be right

GARY BLACKBURN

in the middle of it. Marines had been assigned to cover the most critical positions, and Delta was assigned to cover the defensive perimeter along the northern end of the compound. They had done everything they could to prepare. The platoon had been reinforced with two M60 machine guns and an M20 bazooka team. The Marines had piled sandbags a little higher; dug their fighting holes a little deeper; cleaned and oiled their weapons; and deployed Claymores. All they could do now was watch and wait. "Kind'a like sittin' in the Alamo, waitin' for Santa Anna," Max thought with a wry smile. His history teacher would be proud.

After evening c-rats of ham-n-whatever, Maxam sprawled on his poncho against a sandbagged bunker, opened a can of warm Foster's beer and lit a cigarette. Not a leaf was moving on the broken trees in the dilapidated compound. Blowing out a ring of smoke, he watched it lazily float upward in the dim light. Any breeze they had enjoyed earlier was gone with the last bit of day-light. He tugged a stained rag from around his neck and casually swiped the sweat that had begun to trickle its way down the side of his close-cropped head. Damn it was hot—too hot to sleep. Daydreaming about home and the cool breezes that flowed down from the San Gabriel Mountains, he pulled another cigarette from the crumpled Camels pack in his lap and lit it with the butt he had just removed from his mouth. He took a swallow of the foamy tepid beer and looked at the faces around him—his hard-chargers, his buddies. Some were writing letters to their girls; most were just quiet. God, he loved these Marines. How many of them would still be alive by tomorrow night?

Sometime after midnight, as thick fog swirled up from the Cam Lộ River, two battalions of enemy infantry and a sapper company from the 48th Regiment, 320th North Vietnamese Army Division, silently approached Cam Lộ. The NVA commanders, expecting an easy coup, had brought along a bright new communist flag to hoist after their victory. They had promised their troops a stockade defended by only boys, old militiamen, and a few US advisors—what the Người Mỹ (Americans) called a "sitting duck." But what the North Vietnamese soldiers were reaching out

36

to grab hold of in the murky darkness of that moonless morning was a very different animal—one with steel teeth, a mean streak, and attitude.

The headquarters compound at Cam Lộ was comprised of eight crumbling French colonial structures, surrounded by an earthen berm and several belts of concertina wire. There were bunkers and sandbagged fighting positions located between the buildings and around the compound's defensive perimeter. The southern perimeter was covered by the 11th Engineers and their Marine security squad. The northwest defensive perimeter was defended by the CAU Marines, US Army advisors, and the squad of 2/9th Marines. Lt. Mike Steck had placed his two Delta Co. squads along the northern and northeastern perimeter.

Part 3

Shortly after 2:00 a.m., on February 2, the compound was hit by a barrage of mortar, rocket, and recoilless rifle fire. Those Marines and troops who were sleeping outside immediately moved into their bunkers and fighting holes and prepared for the ground attack they knew would follow. Maj. James Payne, the senior Army advisor, hurried to the tactical ops center to contact Đông Hà for artillery support. While making the call, a recoilless rifle round made a direct hit on the fortified bunker, seriously wounding Payne and two of the local militiamen who had accompanied him.

As Doc Bradley, the Army medic, fought to save Payne, Capt. McMaken took command and began relaying artillery fire adjustments to Đông Hà. The first NVA ground attack hit the southern end of the compound and broke through into the motor pool. Enemy rocket propelled grenades made quick work of the Army trucks and the quad-50s were destroyed before they fired a shot. Spotting the breach, the Marine squad unleashed a hail of small arms and automatic weapons fire into the ranks of the enemy troops, forcing them back out through the wire just as a barrage of

US artillery began to ring the compound. The NVA took cover and the attack was stopped for a brief time.

Lance Cpl. Lawrence Eades, a company clerk with the CAU, saw that the Popular Force militia had abandoned a section of their perimeter defense, and NVA troops were about to breach the wire. Summoning the Navy corpsman and three Marines from his unit, Eades ran to stop them. Grabbing a .30-cal machine gun and using their M16s, the five-man team stopped the assault, in spite of being wounded by grenades and small arms fire. Two dozen NVA died in the wire as they retreated.

At the onset of the night attack, Maxam's Delta Co. partner, Tim Russell, was knocked unconscious by a rocket explosion. When Russell awakened, he struggled to clear his head and assess his status. He was bleeding heavily from shrapnel wounds on his arms and had blood trickling from his nose and ears due to the blast, but refused medical attention. He would not leave his men in the middle of a fight. Russell stayed with his squad, shouting encouragement, directing their fire, and leading them in a fierce counterattack when NVA troops attempted to break through the northeast perimeter.

Further north, Max Maxam had his hands full, too. He had finally drifted off sometime after midnight, but his sleep had been troubled. He had rarely felt such a sense of foreboding and had jumped instantly awake with the first rocket burst. Rallying his Marines, they had quickly fallen into their assigned places and awaited his signal.

The assault on Delta's end of the compound began about 3:00 a.m. with a firestorm of mortars, rockets, recoilless rifle and heavy machine gun fire. That was followed by the usual tinny bugle call as some two hundred NVA launched a human wave attack on the thin Marine line. Unaware they were facing battle-tested Leathernecks and expecting only light resistance, the communist infantry charged forward with abandon. Waiting below their fortifications until the last possible second, the fire team leaders ordered "fire!" and in a stunning surprise to the enemy commanders, dozens of charging NVA troops went down en masse, having never fired a shot. Marine Pvt. 1st Class Marlin Resinger, who had been on watch in the compound's guard tower, fired round after round from his M79 grenade launcher down into the attacking force. The massive assault slowed to a stumbling halt momentarily before pressure from those in the rear forced it forward again.

As the fight ensued, Maxam spotted a section of the perimeter defenses the mortars had destroyed. Beyond that were a large number of enemy troops preparing to breach the wire near an abandoned machine gun post. Leaving his fire team assistant in charge, Max ran to cover the breach amid a hail of small arms fire. Suddenly there was a blinding flash, and the young Marine was thrown through the air, crashing into a bulkhead adjoining a bunker. His helmet was blown off, and he landed awkwardly on his left shoulder still clutching his M16. For a few seconds he lay stunned, unable to move. The roar from the mortars, rockets and machine guns sounded miles away. Moaning, he slowly got to his knees. He was bleeding freely from shrapnel wounds, and the sleeves of his uniform were shredded. Gathering his strength, Maxam grabbed his helmet, rose to his feet, and made his way to the abandoned position. Only a few minutes had elapsed, but it seemed much longer. With rounds striking all around him, he began to fire the machine gun, instantly killing a dozen of the nearest NVA who were trapped in the wire.

When the enemy commanders saw the American firing the gun, they directed maximum fire power against him. He could do more damage with that one weapon than all the rest of his squad combined. Still feeling the effects of the grenade blast, Max struggled to clear his head. He had to focus on keeping the enemy away from the broken sections of wire. If they breached it, they would flank his Marines, and that would be fatal. Checking to ensure he had adequate ammunition, he continued to fire into the horde of troops who were still emerging out of the smoky blackness, illuminated by exploding rockets and mortar rounds.

Then, without warning, the machine gun position exploded. There was a tremendous flash and bang, and a huge ball of flame.

The bunker surrounding the gun had taken a direct hit from a rocket propelled grenade. Max was blown backward out of the sand-bagged fortification. He felt blistering heat and a smashing blow to the side of his face, then there was only blackness.

Maxam's Marines had seen the blast and were watching to see if he was still alive, as they continued to fire at the enemy. Max was spread-eagled on his back. Most of his flak jacket and blouse had been blown away; his face and chest were smeared with a mixture of blood, sweat, and sand. His legs were covered with debris from the shattered gun emplacement, and he was not moving.

Then, slowly Max's head rolled to the side, and several of the Marines nearest to him began to fire a barrage of rounds over him and directly into the NVA troops beyond him. They had to provide cover for him. There was no way any of them could get to him, but he was alive, and they had to keep the enemy from overrunning his position.

Max struggled to his knees and huddled behind the fortified position. He knew he was seriously injured. He laid his cheek against the wet sandbags feeling the cool roughness against his hot skin. It helped to ease the pain. Running his tongue over his cracked lips, he realized he was incredibly thirsty, and although sweat continued to streak the blood on his bare chest, he felt cold. He was bleeding profusely from severe wounds to his right shoulder, neck, and face, and he was blind in his right eye. Wiping away the gore from the left side of his face, he slowly turned to his right, easing far enough around to clearly see his men with his good eye. He needed to see their faces. What he saw was their grit and courage, and their determination to do what they had to, for him and for each other. Then he turned away, blinking back tears and thinking of his family back home.

In great pain, Maxam pulled himself up and crawled in behind the machine gun, testing it to see if it would still fire. Finding the weapon in working order, he loaded more ammo and began to fire methodically. Without his flak jacket, he was more vulnerable, but he was beyond caring. He was struck several times by small arms, but continued to fire with such ferocity he forced the enemy troops back through the concertina wire to positions of cover.

In a desperate attempt to silence this American "ác quỷ" (devil) and his terrible weapon, the North Vietnamese threw hand grenades and directed recoilless rifle fire against him, inflicting additional wounds. Max was becoming more and more light-headed and was having difficulty focusing his vision. And then there was the cold chill that was gradually moving up his arms and legs. His heart was racing and his breathing had become very shallow. Stifling a dry cough, he shook his head again, trying to clear away the cobwebs. He had to stay alert. He had to protect his men.

Finally, too weak to reload the machine gun, Maxam crawled back out of the destroyed fortification and collapsed into a prone position alongside the bunker with his M16. He had always been a crack shot with an instinct for hitting what he aimed at, and he began to deliver deadly fire, one shot after another. It had been one and a half hours since he left his squad. He had been hit repeatedly by small arms fire and shrapnel from exploding grenades, but the NVA had been unable to stop him.

Now, the enemy soldiers began to turn around; first in twos and threes, pushing their way toward the rear as the Marine continued to pick them off. He was running low on ammo, but the mass of brown uniforms he had seen in front of him for so long was moving away. He heard one final bugle call, and the mob melted into the darkness, leaving in their wake mounds of dead piled high within the encircling rings of concertina.

Maxam rested his head against the cool, smooth stock of his M16, took a deep breath—and closed his eyes for the last time. He had successfully defended half the perimeter almost single-handedly.

The Marines from Maxam's squad slowly rose from their fighting holes and made their way to him, kneeling beside his body. They were still there, watching over him, when the first Navy medics arrived sometime later. All of the Marines were wounded but refused treatment until the "docs" had tended to their squad leader and friend. No one spoke as they assisted the medics in moving him onto a stretcher and escorted the body in toward the center of the compound. The fog and mist had begun to clear, but the sky was still dark.

To the north, the NVAs bedraggled companies were attempting to regroup at an abandoned airstrip for another massed attack against the Marines' compound. As the enemy commanders prepared to move their units out, Marine artillery exploded across the strip, tearing the heart out of the assembled force and any remaining will to fight as well.

At 4:30 a.m., a 9th Marines relief force left Fire Base Charlie-3 to assist Cam Lộ. Two platoons from Foxtrot Co., 2/9th Marines, supported by two M50 Ontos self-propelled multiple-recoilless rifles and three tanks moved through Cam Lộ village and broke out into the open paddies northeast of the compound. Alerted that Marine armor and infantry were charging their way, the remaining NVA units south of the compound broke off their attack and fled north across the Cam Lộ River.

Three miles to the north at Fire Base Charlie-2, Alpha Co., 1/4th Marines had formed up in the predawn darkness with a sense of urgency. They had been told Delta One-Four was in danger of being overrun and needed help. The determined Marines, loaded with all their fighting gear and ammunition, began a forced march southward. When they were near enough to hear the sounds and see the flashes of the conflict, they broke into a near run. Negotiating their way through the rugged countryside in the darkness, they arrived in time to set up a blocking position north of the headquarters compound and intercepted the retreating NVA. There were few enemy survivors.

A third relief force of tanks and infantry departed 9th Marines HQ at Đông Hà and arrived at the Cam Lộ compound at daybreak. The relief-force Marines were stunned by what they found. Much of the compound was destroyed, scarred and blackened by the brutal violence of the night, and there were NVA bodies everywhere they looked. They would not soon forget the scene—vicious coiled wire, tangled with its nightmare collection of enemy dead, riddled by Marine bullets and flying shrapnel. One Marine said, "It was like looking straight into the gates of hell."

Maj. Payne died of his wounds, along with nine other soldiers and Marines—a total of ten Americans. Nearly all of the US survivors had been wounded, some several times, and were tended to by Navy corpsmen. Twenty-three were seriously wounded and had to be medevaced. A number of South Vietnamese militiamen also died defending their headquarters. Capt. McMaken, who had survived his wounds, supervised the burial of enemy dead and counted 156 NVA bodies at the compound as they were placed into a mass grave near the motor pool. Fifty-three enemy troops had been captured, along with a bright, new communist flag, found on the body of a dead NVA officer.

The defenders of Cam Lộ had not only survived, but had triumphed against nearly impossible odds. Fewer than fifty Marines and combat engineers, plus a handful of US Army advisors, had held off and defeated at least two battalions of NVA regular infantry and a sapper company.

"The Marines just stacked them up on the wires," McMaken stated later. "They were magnificent!"

Delta Co. Marine Don Jackovac said, "I wouldn't be alive today if it wasn't for Maxam's defense at Cam Lộ that night. I never thought I'd see the sun rise. I never got a chance to thank Max."

"He sacrificed his life to defend the line," Gunnery Sgt. Danny Whyte said.

The heroic fight at Cam Lộ did not make news in the States. Battles were raging all over Vietnam, and ten US dead at some remote village no one had ever heard of were not enough for the media to notice. For most Americans, Cam Lộ never happened. But for a few good men and their families, it is still remembered, and many were officially recognized for their valor that night.

Among the medals awarded: Marine Cpl. Timothy Russell, Squad Leader, D Co., 1/4th Marines and Marine Lance Cpl. Lawrence Eades, Cam Lộ CAU, each received the Navy Cross, the nation's second highest award for "extraordinary heroism";

US Army advisor, Capt. Raymond McMaken, and Marine Lt. Michael Steck, D Co., 1/4th Marines, each received the Silver Star for "gallantry in action"; Meritorious Unit Commendations with "V" for valor were awarded to the 1st and 3rd Platoons, D Co., 1/4th Marines, and to the 1st Squad, 3rd Platoon, E Co., 2/9th Marines.

Cpl. Larry Maxam was laid to rest in the National Memorial Cemetery of the Pacific, located at Punchbowl Crater in Honolulu, Hawaii. Back home in Burbank, the news barely made a ripple. Young Americans were dying by the hundreds in Vietnamese villages and jungle ten thousand miles from home, in a war that was increasingly unpopular. Only Maxam's family and friends understood the terrible loss his death represented.

Some months after Larry's death, Alice Maxam made the decision to move to Australia. The Maxams had always been a deeply religious family, and she was unhappy with the direction she saw society moving in the Los Angeles area. She was afraid without Larry's influence, her younger son would get in with the wrong crowd. In a letter Larry had written her from Vietnam, he had told her he was looking forward to going to Australia on R&R, and that had planted the seed. She was ready for a fresh start, so she took Robin and made the move. Somehow, for some reason, it made her feel closer to the son she had lost. Her daughter, Linda, joined them a year later.

On April 20, 1970, Alice and Robin Maxam flew from Australia to Washington, DC, for a special ceremony and Vice Pres. Spiro T. Agnew presented them with Larry's Medal of Honor. His other medals included the Purple Heart, the Vietnam Military Merit Medal (the highest military award bestowed to enlisted personnel by the Republic of Vietnam), and the Vietnam Gallantry Cross w/Palm, bestowed by the Republic of Vietnam in recognition of deeds of valor or heroic conduct while in combat with the enemy.

Maxam was twenty years and twenty-four days old on the day he died.

The proud young valor that rose above the mortal,
And then at last was mortal after all;
The chivalry of hand and heart that,
In other days and other lands,
Would have sent their names,
Ringing down in song and story!

"Through Blood and Fire at Gettysburg"
—Gen. Joshua Lawrence Chamberlain

On April 17, 2010, Pacific Park in Burbank, California, was officially renamed "Larry L. Maxam Memorial Park" in honor of the City of Burbank's only Medal of Honor recipient. Robin Maxam and Linda Maxam Clark flew from Australia to Burbank for the dedication.

"Larry Maxam Avenue" is located at Miramar Marine Corps Air Station, near San Diego, California.

"Maxam Hall," a dining facility at Marine Corps Base Quantico, Virginia, was dedicated in memory of Cpl. Larry L. Maxam on May 26, 2011.

"Battle of Cam Lo," is a song about Larry Maxam and the defense of Cam Lộ, written and recorded by "Doc" Ken Walker, April 29, 2013.

3

Leonard Ray St. Clair

Junior Superhero

Leonard St. Clair

Leonard St. Clair was never the typical Texas school boy. Whether he was involved in church, or academics, sports, or socially, he always gave everything he had to give. He was active in Scouts and worked as a roughneck in the oil fields during the summer. That stood him in good stead for football at South Park High School in Beaumont. He was on the varsity team his junior and senior years from 1962 to 1964.

Leonard had a distinctive deep voice and was an active member of South Park's award-winning National Forensic League team, which won both regional and state debate competitions. He was also a lead character in numerous school plays that were produced for parents and students.

And then there were the girls—"Leonard was a real ladies' man," one of his Beaumont friends said. "We had some great times double-dating in high school and at Lamar College. Leonard had that bass voice and a smile that just melted the girls' hearts. He wore his hair slicked back like Marty Robbins and had a red '56 Chevy two-door hard-top with all the bells and whistles. The ladies adored everything about him."

After a year of college, Leonard dropped out of school. He loved country music and idolized Ernest Tubb, Hank Williams, Marty Robbins, and Patsy Cline. He and another buddy briefly aspired to careers as country and western singers, but decided they liked to eat too much to stick it out for long. The term "starving artist" did not fit into Leonard's future career plans. The war in Vietnam was cranking up and the draft along with it, so he enlisted in the Marine Corps.

After completing boot camp and ITR, St. Clair was assigned to India Company, 3rd Battalion, 5th Marines, and his unit deployed to Vietnam in June 1966. India Company was located near Chu Lai, South Vietnam, and his squad was out in the field, away from any of the comforts of home (or base) for two weeks at a time. It was tough, dangerous work, not to mention hot and dirty. When the men returned to their base camp, they took off their flak jackets, literally peeled off their utility uniforms, scrubbed down in the showers and were issued new utilities. They burned their old uniforms, and then headed for the "club" (beer tent), looking for some Carling's Black Label beer. That was usually all they had, and it was warm, but it was better than any of the local brews.

One of St. Clair's fellow squad members said, "After a few beers, we'd go to the squad tent and try to pick a fight with the northern guys, since we were from the south—'Saint' was from Texas, and I was from Tennessee. A couple more of our fellow Marines were also Southerners. It was all in good fun. We'd all be back in the field together a few days later and always had each other's backs."

In August, St. Clair and a couple of his buddies were transferred to Mike 3/1. They had volunteered to join a new CAC unit (later called CAP), a Combined Action Platoon comprised of a thirteen-member Marine rifle squad, with a US Navy corpsman and a South Vietnamese militia platoon of older boys and elderly men. The unit was located in or near a rural Vietnamese hamlet, thus preventing the village from being used as a sanctuary for the Việt Cộng. Then in late November, he was transferred back to India Company. He had been promoted to corporal and was to take over a squad as squad leader, "because of his leadership skills."

St. Clair had been involved in operation after operation for six straight months, from DECKHOUSE I and NATHAN HALE in June 1966, through Operations HASTINGS and DECKHOUSE II in July, COLORADO and JACKSON throughout the month of August, MUSTANG in the fall, and Operation CORTEZ in early December. He and his squad were totally exhausted and in need of some R&R.

Leonard flew home to Texas for Christmas 1966 and enjoyed visiting with family and friends, although the weather was not ideal. After months of tropical heat, the unusually cold December weather in Beaumont was a shock to his system. It was twenty-eight degrees on the morning of December 24 and Christmas morning dawned dark with pouring rain and a temperature of thirty-four. St. Clair was not ready to return to Vietnam, but he was ready for warmer climes.

There was supposed to be a cease fire in Vietnam over Christmas and New Year's, but that never really happened. Returning to RVN in January, St. Clair was immediately ordered back into the field with his Marines in Operation DESOTO II. They were operating in Quảng Ngãi Province, in the area surrounding Đức Phổ (about 100km south of Đà Nẵng), and most of the action was against insurgent VC forces utilizing bunker complexes and dry paddy dikes for fighting positions. The rice paddies provided the enemy with clear views of anyone approaching their defensive line from any direction, and well-constructed caves in the surrounding hills furnished them with living quarters and logistical support. Artillery smoke rounds were used to assist the Marines in crossing the wide-open paddies against heavy resistance, and the fighting was bloody. As always, the Marines fought with great valor.

Part 2

Early in 1967, Leonard wrote a fan letter to Stan Lee, the creator of *Spider-Man*. When *Spider-Man* first appeared in the early sixties, teenagers in superhero comic books were usually relegated to the role of sidekick to the hero. *Spider-Man* comics broke new ground by featuring Peter Parker as a teenage high school student (and secretly the hero, *Spider-Man*) with whom young readers could relate. Marvel's superhero comics were welcome diversions for the fighting men in Vietnam and passed from man to man until they were dirty and dog-eared.

The Letter

Dear Stan,

I thought I had left comic books somewhere in my past, but once again, I find myself reading them. It would surprise (shock!) many people back in the states to learn that so many service men read them. Especially the Marvel Comics Group which is sold in every P.X. I've been in over here. And it always makes us mad to miss an issue! We don't have much time for reading here in Viet Nam although we usually are able to squeeze in enough time to read your Marvel's. Spider-Man is, by far, my favorite, although all of your super-heroes are really something. We sure could use them over here, but I guess we'll just have to rely on our own "talents." It may be a coincidence, but we think of ourselves as "junior super-heroes." If you get a chance, send one over here to give us a hand! But, to be serious for a second, thanks for providing a lot of us with some good action-packed reading material. We really enjoy your series. They, like letters from home, help take our minds out of Viet Nam for a while.

Cpl. Leonard R. St. Clair
FPO, San Francisco, Cal. 96602

Stan Lee's Response

In that case, Len, even if they serve no other purpose, we'll still keep turning 'em out to the best of our agonizin' ability! Unfortunately, we can't actually send any of our costumed characters to the field of battle, but we can always do the next best thing—so watch for the first issue of the complimentary subscription which we're winging your way, with our sincerest best wishes to you and your battle-honed buddies. May you all successfully and safely complete your tour of duty, and soon be able to latch onto your favorite mags merely by walking to the corner newsstand.

Stan Lee

Follow-Up

Cpl. St. Clair's letter was published in the July 1967 issue of *Amazing Spider-Man*, and appeared with a note: "We recently received a letter which affected all of us very deeply. We are printing it, in its entirety, with no comment—save one."

> Dear Stan,
>
> Since all of us in the headquarters section of India Company are Spider-Man fans, we regret to inform you that Corporal St. Clair, whose letter will be printed in SPIDER-MAN #50, was killed in action on 28 February 1967. [The correct date was February 26th.] He was a squad leader in our 3rd Platoon when his patrol was ambushed southwest of Da Nang. Your comic SPIDER-MAN is the most sought after piece of literature and art work in this company. Keep up the good work; you're a real morale booster.
>
> India Company 3/1 3rd Bn., 1st Mar.
> 1st Marine Div. (REIN) FMF, FPO

> Comments from Stan Lee:
>
> "God rest you, soldier. And God bless you all. As a mark of respect to Corporal St. Clair, and all others who have given the last measure of devotion for their country, we are omitting our usual 'Coming Attractions' paragraph this issue. We prefer, instead, to express the fervent hope that the day will soon come when men in every land will walk together in peace—and brotherhood."

One of Leonard's buddies said, "I got the news the day after his being killed in action while on patrol. Saint was hit by a sniper. A few days later, I hitched a ride into Da Nang to look up another close bud of Saint's who was serving as part of a guard unit, to commiserate with him the news of our fallen friend. I also composed a letter to his folks to share with them my thoughts and feelings about their son—Semper Fi, Saint—Semper Fi!"

Leonard St. Clair was twenty years old.

> The spiders of weariness come on me
> To weave wide webs on my brain.
> I must go to the night and the sighing sea
> And the drive of the drifting rain.

> "The Spiders of Weariness"
> —Robert Ervin Howard

4

Dale Eugene Wayrynen

Always the Best

Dale Wayrynen

For Dale Wayrynen, being the best at whatever he opted to do was not a choice; it was just understood from the outset. The oldest of four brothers in a tight-knit northern Minnesota household, Dale was born in Mooselake and grew up in tiny McGregor, population 275. He was a natural leader and an outstanding athlete by any standard. During his final year at McGregor High School, he was quarterback and co-captain of the football team, as well as co-captain of the basketball and baseball teams. He was a member of the student council, a class officer and received all-conference honors in football and baseball. The village of McGregor would not soon forget Dale Wayrynen.

During his senior year he began talking about Vietnam. His father, Eugene, had been a "waist gunner" on a B-17 during WWII. His plane had been shot down and he finished the war in a German POW camp. Now, the younger Wayrynen was feeling the pull to do his part in his war, and after graduation in May 1965, he joined the Army. He applied for jump school and became a proud member of the 82nd Airborne Division at Ft. Bragg, North Carolina. In March 1967, he volunteered to go to Vietnam and was assigned to the 101st Airborne Division, the "Screaming Eagles."

As his parents drove the 130 miles to the airport in Minneapolis/St. Paul, Dale stared out the car window at the snowy countryside. He never tired of seeing the beauty that had surrounded him his entire life—the rocky hills, the dense forests, the hundreds of crystal-clear lakes. He had been in North Carolina for almost two years; he had missed the deep snow and icy stillness of the sub-zero winter mornings, and the spectacular beauty of the northern lights. Now he was headed for tropical Vietnam and a world unlike anything he had ever known.

Dale looked down at his youngest brother who was riding in the back seat beside him. John was six years old and had no understanding of where Dale was heading or what he was heading into. He had a new coloring book and was carefully selecting the crayons he wanted to use. Dale slid over closer to the boy and placed his arm around the youngster's narrow shoulders He then picked up one of the bright crayons and began to help him color the picture on the page.

Today was going to be a difficult day. He had been training and preparing for this day for well over a year and was confident in his own abilities, but he knew his parents and his two middle brothers were concerned to see him go. He had talked late into the night with his brothers, trying to allay their fears with his bravado and had walked them out to catch their school bus that morning. Dave, who was just finishing high school, was already planning to join up when he graduated. He wanted to fly helicopters. Dale hated "goodbyes." As painful as it would be, he would be glad when he was on board the plane and had all of this behind him.

Six weeks later, Wayrynen was beginning to settle into his new unit. He had been assigned to Company B, 2nd Battalion, 502nd Infantry. First Brigade, 101st Airborne, and they were stationed near the town of Đức Phổ in Quảng Ngãi Province. Known as "Battlin' Bravo," the company motto was: "They've got us surrounded, the poor bastards."

In May 1967, several thousand First Brigade soldiers were conducting operations around Đức Phổ, and much of it was jungle patrol. Danger was everywhere: landmines, booby traps with trip wires, and camouflaged pits bristling with sharpened punji stakes were a constant threat, not to mention poisonous snakes and other natural threats. Nearly every operation resulted in casualties.

On 18 May, units of North Vietnamese regular infantry attacked First Brigade patrols on what was known as Hill 424. When the attack began, Dale Wayrynen was several miles away with other soldiers from his Bravo Company 2/502 platoon. They were patrolling separately from the main body of troops and received news of the attack by radio. The Bravo Co. squad immediately set out to assist and ran several miles, fighting their way through outlying NVA units as they moved toward Hill 424.

Bill Gunter and Don Singleton were with Dale Wayrynen that day. "When we got to the base of the hill we could hear gunfire," Gunter said. "And then we walked slowly up the hill until we reached the company. There was wounded all over the place and some killed." The NVA had broken off their attack and retreated into the thick jungle growth taking their dead and wounded with them.

Among the friendly casualties were a number of Montagnard soldiers who had been helping the Americans. The platoon made stretchers to move the wounded off Hill 424 and started down a jungle path in single file as darkness fell. The path was going in the general direction the platoon leader wanted to go; Bill Gunter was walking point. Directly behind him was Dale Wayrynen, followed by Don Singleton and the rest of the troop column.

Singleton was a young black trooper from Richmond Hill, Georgia. "It took nerve to set foot in the jungle," he said. "Think about you goin' out into the woods to hunt deer or hunt rabbit or whatever. And all the deer and all the rabbits, all of 'em got weapons. I mean it was, you know, nasty, dirty, wet, hot, snakes, leeches; it was the jungle, man. It was tough. We went out to kill people and you know, if you're out there killin' people, chances are you may get killed too."

Gunter led the platoon a short distance into the tall grass and jungle growth. He moved hesitantly and then slowed to a stop. The sky was covered in thick clouds, and as night closed in, it quickly became dark. Gunter was struggling to follow the narrow path. The only light came from occasional flashes of distant lightning. There was a thunderstorm somewhere beyond the horizon. The unit radioed for illumination flares and waited. Wayrynen squatted down behind Gunter in the dark. He could hear the rumble of thunder, or maybe it was big guns firing miles away. The intermittent rumbles continued, followed by the flashes of light. They called it "heat lightning" back home in Minnesota. Intense thunderstorms would move across the lakes during the short summers there and put on a light show that rivaled the Fourth of July. God how he missed home—especially his mom and the boys—and his tour had only begun.

It was miserably hot. Dale could feel the sweat seeping from under his helmet liner and running down the sides of his neck, soaking into the soggy collar of his fatigues. It gave him a slight chill and he shrugged it off. "This sure ain't Minnesota," he thought to himself, smiling. Lightning flickered again, briefly illuminating the anxious faces of the soldiers crouched behind him and providing a momentary glimpse of the surrounding jungle. Then they were plunged back into total darkness. He could hear the breathing of his buddies near him and the incessant buzzing of swarms of insects, but he could see nothing.

"I turned around to say something to Dale, and then I turned back and looked at the trail," Gunter said. "There was a slight burst of lightning, and I was looking dead into the face an NVA soldier. I could reach out and touch him, and there were several more behind him.

"Holy shit," Gunter continued, "I just screamed and started firing."

The American platoon had blindly stumbled onto a heavily fortified NVA bunker complex in the jungle, and an enemy patrol had nearly walked into them in the dark. Alerted by the gunfire and Gunter's warning yell, the North Vietnamese soldiers in the bunker immediately swept the area with automatic weapons fire, probably hitting their own patrol.

Gunter was hit and fell to the ground. As he struggled to crawl into the cover of the tall grass, another NVA soldier charged toward him, illuminated by muzzle flashes from the weapons of the Airborne troops who were firing at the bunker. As Gunter attempted to turn and defend himself, Dale Wayrynen leapt over him and killed the attacking enemy soldier. Wayrynen then grabbed Gunter by his shoulders and dragged him down the trail where the rest of the squad had hastily formed a defensive line.

"I was wounded in the right lower leg and knocked down," Gunter said. "So Dale jumped out and helped me back to where some of the other guys were, and they started firing."

At that moment, the illumination flares burst overhead, bathing the area in brilliant light. Despite the injuries to his leg, Gunter lay down in a prone position and resumed firing at the enemy. NVA rounds were striking all around them, and there were explosions from enemy hand grenades.

Suddenly, amid of the wild melee, a body came flying through the air. Gunter grunted in pain as someone sprawled across his injured legs. That was followed by an immediate violent, but muffled explosion. An NVA hand grenade had landed in the middle of the tightly grouped Americans, endangering the entire squad and the platoon leader who was crouched nearby. It had exploded at Gunter's feet. Dale Wayrynen had shouted a warning, pushed another soldier out of the way, and thrown himself on top of the grenade at the moment it exploded, taking the full force of the blast with his chest.

"At the time I didn't know where Dale was," Gunter said. "All of a sudden, someone landed on my legs and ka-boom!"

Bill Gunter had additional injuries to his legs, but if it had not been for Wayrynen, he would have died at that moment. "Or I'd not have either one of my legs," Gunter said later. Don Singleton was injured by the same grenade, but Dale Wayrynen had also saved his life and the rest of the squad.

Wayrynen lived for several hours. Then, as the fighting subsided and the sounds of battle were replaced by the moans of the wounded and the hushed tones of those caring for them, Dale Wayrynen died.

The unit spent the remainder of the night on Hill 424, patching up the wounded with their limited supplies and guarding against a counterattack. The dead and wounded were evacuated by helicopters at daybreak.

"I came out on a Huey chopper," Don Singleton said. "I was the only guy on that bird that was alive other than the crew. They had bodies just stacked across the chopper."

On October 15, 1969, Eugene and LaVerne Wayrynen were flown to Washington, DC, to receive Dale's Medal of Honor in a White House ceremony. The event was hosted by Pres. Nixon and Army Chief of staff, Gen. William Westmoreland. Westmoreland had previously served as the Commanding General of the 101st Airborne Brigade.

The MOH certificate reads in part: "His deep and abiding concern for his fellow soldiers was significantly reflected in his supreme and courageous act that preserved the lives of his comrades." Dale Wayrynen was twenty years old.

> They shall grow not old, as we that are left grow old:
> Age shall not weary them, nor the years condemn.
> At the going down of the sun and in the morning
> We will remember them.
>
> "For The Fallen"
> —Laurence Binyon

Dale E. Wayrynen Recreation Center, Fort Campbell,
Kentucky (Dedicated October 30, 1974)
Dale E. Wayrynen Memorial, McGregor,
Minnesota (Dedicated July 4, 1976)
Dale E. Wayrynen Veterans Memorial Gymnasium,
McGregor High School (August 19, 1995)
Dale Wayrynen Memorial Highway (MN-210 in
Aitkin County) (Dedicated July 4, 1996)
Dale E. Wayrynen American Legion
Post 23, McGregor, Minnesota

5

John C. Borowski

Sky Warrior

John "Ski" Borowski

It was the mid-sixties in Evergreen Park, Illinois, a predominantly white bedroom-community southwest of the Chicago Loop. With a population of twenty-five thousand, thirteen churches, one of the earliest shopping malls in the country and little industry, Evergreen Park appeared to be Middle America's idea of the ideal place to live and raise a family. However, for one young man, life was not easy.

John Sak spent as much time as possible away from the home where he had lived since the age of six. He had friends at Evergreen

Park Community High School, but only a few of his closest friends knew he was adopted. The Sak family was prominent and well-liked in the community. It is difficult to know exactly when the problems began, or how physical they were, but John Sak was a troubled teenager. One of his best friends said, "John had a very bad foster home life. In fact, he spent more time staying at my parents' home than with his foster parents."

Good-hearted by nature, the young man discovered at an early age that "volunteering" was the easy way to get out of the house. Whether it was a trip to the grocery for a sick neighbor or extra work with his Boy Scout troop, if a volunteer was needed, John Sak was always the first to volunteer.

In November 1964, John turned eighteen and legally took charge of his life. He had already spoken with Army recruiters and knew exactly what he wanted to do. Dropping out of school midway through his senior year, he enlisted in the Army, with the promise of "jump school" after basic. In one final act of rebellion, Sak signed up using his birth name. From that day on, the world would know him as "John C. Borowski."

John liked everything about the Army from his first day at Ft. Benning. He had a clean slate, and for the first time he could remember, he felt he was being treated with respect. As long as he performed to the best of his considerable ability, everything went well, and Borowski was a happy young man. Each skill he learned opened new doors for him, and the future seemed limitless.

Army Airborne School was even better. The training was three weeks long with ground training the first week, followed by tower training, and finally "jump week" when he got to jump out of real airplanes. Borowski had to complete five jumps successfully, including a night jump, to graduate from the program. Guests and family members were invited to attend the graduation ceremony and participate in awarding the parachutist wings to the soldiers, but there was no one there to pin on John Borowski's wings. He departed Fort Benning the next day for his first duty station. He had been assigned to the 101st Airborne Division at Ft. Campbell, Kentucky.

"The Army was John's home," a friend said. "He loved it. I can remember vividly how proud he was when he graduated jump school and was a member of the 101st Airborne. He wrote to me sometime after that to tell me he was going into an elite unit, the 173rd Airborne."

The 1st and 2nd Battalions, 503rd Infantry, 173rd AB had deployed to South Vietnam in May 1965. Then, the 4/503rd left Fort Campbell in August 1966 to join them.

In the spring of 1967, John Borowski went home on leave. Upon his arrival in Chicago, he learned several vicious tornadoes had struck northern Illinois a few days before. The southern suburbs had been especially hard hit by the twisters, and they had left a path of death and destruction across the communities. The following day, Borowski went to a volunteer station and spent most of his leave time helping to clear debris from the storm ravaged areas.

At the end of the month, he flew out of O'Hare Field for his next duty assignment: machine-gunner with Alpha Company, 4/503rd Airborne Infantry in Vietnam. Within a week he was in combat near the Cambodian border.

Part 2

During the summer of 1967, heavy contact with NVA forces in the Central Highlands near Đắk Tô prompted the launching of Operation GREELEY. It was a combined "search & destroy" effort by elements of the US 4th Infantry Division, the 173rd AB, and the ARVN 42nd Infantry and Airborne.

In a letter to James Sak, his foster brother, Borowski described in vivid detail numerous Việt Công atrocities he had witnessed. "The American people are kidding themselves if they think communism is a form of government," he wrote. "The VC are insane, and we need to stop this madness here."

Đắk Tô was located on a valley floor surrounded by ridges that rose into peaks. The mountains then stretched to the west and southwest toward the tri-border region where Vietnam, Laos, and

Cambodia came together. A few miles southwest of Đăk Tô was a 2,700 ft. mountain referred to as "Hill 830" and it sat astride a major access point to the Ho Chi Minh Trail.

At 7:10 a.m. on the morning of July 10, 1967, Bravo Company, 4/503rd Infantry was ordered to move out and began ascending Hill 830. Bravo was leading the regiment, followed by Delta Company, then the TAC Command Post. Alpha Company was the rear guard. About 3:45 that afternoon, as the four companies neared the crest of the mountain, they were struck by a barrage of small arms and machine gun fire, and blasted by rockets, RPGs, and mortars, making advance or retreat nearly impossible. Alpha Company had been investigating a fresh trail up the mountain when its lead platoon began taking heavy small arms and automatic weapons fire from two bunkered light machine guns. The enemy force, initially thought to be an NVA rifle company, was entrenched in well-fortified positions approximately 115 feet in front and northwest of Alpha.

The 1st Platoon leader, Lt. Dan Jordan, was ordered to maneuver his men in a flanking attack on the enemy position in an attempt to ease the pressure on the lead platoon. Because of poor radio reception, Jordan was forced to run through heavy enemy fire, back and forth between his men and his commander to report progress and receive instructions. He then moved among his men, calming and encouraging them as they advanced to assault the NVA machine gun position. Ski Borowski and his assistant gunner, Doug Rutledge, were the M60 machine gun team for Jordan's platoon.

Another Alpha Company officer, Lt. Mercer Vandenburg said, "Despite the terrain, terrible weather, and additional weight he carried with his M60, Ski never complained and always kept a great sense of humor. After humping up some of the worst mountains, he would comment how it was still better than being with his family in Chicago."

Borowski's squad was on the left flank when the machine guns opened up. There was heavy brush on all sides, and the rounds were slicing through the leaves like swarms of angry hornets. "It sounded like a thousand firing lines," Doug Rutledge said.

"Horrible!" Ski had his right shoulder shoved into the soft red dirt of the mountain and could feel the dampness soaking through his uniform. It rained every day in these damned mountains. It was not as hot up here, but it was sticky as hell. He had all twenty-four pounds of his M60 "pig" cradled in his right arm, along with a rucksack and extra belts of ammo slung over his left shoulder, so for the moment, he was content to hug the mountain. As the enemy machine guns continued to chew the tops off the brush over his head, Ski kept low and waited for the order to move out.

A few minutes later, there was a call from back down the line of troops. One of the lieutenants had been hit and needed help. Rutledge, who had been trained as a medic ditched his rucksack, grabbed his first-aid kit and crawled back down the trail. The young officer had a clean through-and-through wound to his right shoulder, which Rutledge quickly cleaned and bandaged.

As he was tending to the officer, Rutledge noticed he had a better, if somewhat less safe, view of the machine gun positions. Calling out to Borowski, he began yelling fire directions. Ski got his pig set up just above a rocky outcropping and began firing in the direction he was told. To eliminate the need for his assistant gunner, whose primary job in combat was to keep the belts of ammunition coming, Ski had wired a c-rat can to the left side of the gun just below the feedway so the belts would not bind up and jam the works. He could not be dependent on someone else in a fight. He was no longer John Sak; he was Ski Borowski and he had learned to be self-reliant.

As Borowski turned his head, reaching down for a band of ammunition, machine gun rounds began to strike all around, zeroing in on his position, and he felt a searing slap across the back of his head. He dropped to his knees, and his chin sagged to his chest. Closing his eyes, he fought to stay conscious. Cold sweat broke out on his forehead and upper lip, and a wave of nausea grabbed him by the throat. Struggling to keep from vomiting, he took hold of a small tree growing out of the bank, steadied himself, and grabbed the back of his head under his helmet. His hair was wet with blood, and it was running in streams down both sides of his neck, soaking into his shirt. Calling for a medic, Ski released his grip on the sapling and settled down onto his haunches, holding his head.

Hearing his partner call for a medic, Doug Rutledge came quickly, crawling on all fours. He laid Borowski back against the embankment, and carefully removed his helmet; there was a lot of blood. Head wounds always looked worse than they actually were, but the young soldier was barely conscious. Ski was his best friend in the squad, so he hoped it was not serious. Opening the bloody flak jacket and shirt, Rutledge made sure he wasn't injured anywhere else, and then cleaned and dressed the deep graze on the back of his head. Rutledge assured Ski he would survive, telling him he had incurred worse head-wounds shaving.

Lt. Vandenburg came crawling down the line checking on the men, and seeing Borowski's blood-soaked hair and uniform, inquired how he was. Looking a bit like the bandaged fife-player in "The Spirit of 76," Borowski opened his eyes, gave the officer a weak smile, and replied, "Sir, ya can't kill a Pole by shooting him in the head."

Rutledge moved back down the trail to assist other wounded, and Ski remained slumped against the muddy outcropping where he had been hit. He lit a cigarette and rubbed the side of his throbbing head. Taking a long drag on the cigarette, he appeared to be in deep thought. Slowly rising, he stepped on the cigarette butt and carefully placed the helmet on his bandaged head. Then, picking up his machine gun and a supply of ammo, he began to make his way up the mountain.

Part 3

Obviously playing it safe had not worked for Borowski or the rest of his company. Disregarding his own safety, he moved from cover to cover, firing eight to ten-round bursts as he ran. Regaining his strength, he soon found himself within sixty-five feet of the enemy guns and their camouflaged bunker.

Ski had been taking rounds the entire time he was moving up the hill, and as he prepared to make another run, an enemy round hit the side of his M60, smashing the barrel and jerking it out of his hands. Hunkering down behind a clump of trees, he stared at his pig lying in the dirt, and strains of the old barracks ditty ran through his mind: "This is my rifle; this is my gun; this is for fighting, this is…" Shaking his head, he tried to refocus on his mission. Obviously his hard Polish head was feeling some effects from the grazing.

Pulling his .45 out of its holster, he checked the clip, crouched low, and ran on to the nearest point of cover, firing several shots as he ran. He wasn't sure how many clips he had, but maybe the pistol could get him close enough to toss in a grenade. Zigzagging back and forth, Borowski managed to advance another thirty feet toward the enemy position before a grenade came rolling down the hill.

Ski saw it coming and dived for cover but the explosion was staggering. He had managed to escape the full force of it, but had numerous shrapnel wounds and was dazed by the blast. He was covered in red dirt and shredded leaves, which clung to his sweaty face and blood-soaked uniform and caked in the blood oozing out of his many wounds. Finally realizing he was going to require more than a .45 to destroy the machine guns, Borowski began to crawl back down the mountain. He had spotted a small squad of Alpha Company troopers who were pinned down behind some logs to one side, and he needed to rearm.

Reaching the soldiers, Borowski jumped down in their midst and asked for any weapons they could spare. The men just stared at him. Then, a medic crawled forward offering to help him and dress his wounds. Covered in blood, mud, and bandages, Borowski looked ghastly, but most of it was on the surface. He pushed the "doc" away, saying he didn't have time; he would "take care of it later." The soldiers immediately provided him with an M16, an M79 grenade launcher, and ammo for both, then Ski began to crawl back up the hill. The Alpha troopers looked at each other and followed him. As the squad reached the crest of the hill, they fanned out and concentrated their fire on the enemy bunker. Obviously well supplied, there were a number of additional NVA troops within the fortification, along with the machine gun teams, and they had not stopped firing for over two hours. Two of the Alpha soldiers, including Sgt. Charlie Smith, had already been hit.

There were other NCOs in the squad, and Borowski was only a private first class, but at this point in the battle, he was leading the attack. None of the soldiers wore any rank on their uniforms, and Borowski was a natural leader. He forged ahead, and other men wanted to follow him. Waving the squad members around to the left as a diversion, Borowski swung right in a flanking movement and crawled behind a log, moving ever closer to his objective. Rising up, Borowski fired the grenade launcher, and saw the bunker housing the machine guns explode in a huge fireball. As he settled back, a single bullet hit him in the throat, just above his larynx. An expression of surprise flashed across Ski's face, but he made no sound as the blood filled his throat, and he fell back behind the log. Rising again, he clutched at his throat and fell onto his back, silently clawing the air.

Doc scrambled to Ski, screaming for him to "stay alive," but he felt helpless as he tried to save the drowning man. Using every skill he knew, the medic attempted several times to resuscitate Borowski before collapsing across the still body of his young patient. The other members of the squad had risen and were watching, silhouetted against the smoldering hulk of the NVA bunker. Finally Doc rose to a sitting position and sat staring at Borowski. He was only twenyty-five, but suddenly he felt very old. Looking back at the others with tears in his eyes, he shook his head and said, "It ain't no f——king good!" Then turning away, the medic looked up at the ominous clouds, and rain began to fall.

As darkness settled over the mountain, all was quiet. The battle had ended as suddenly as it began. Doug Rutledge said, "Around dusk someone hollered 'Pull back!' and as the few left on our flank crawled downhill, Ski and Sgt. Smith were going to be left behind. I tried to get others to get them, but none would, so they covered me, and I went alone. When I reached Ski he was on his back with a large hole in his throat and dead. I left him and crawled to Sgt. Smith, who was about twenty-five feet past Ski.

Smith was still alive. I left my weapon behind because I knew I couldn't drag him and shoot at the same time. I dragged Smith about fifty feet and put him on the back of a guy who crawled down the hill with him. Ski was recovered the next day." Sgt. Smith survived.

It was determined later that the 4/503rd Airborne Infantry had been ambushed by the North Vietnamese K-101D Battalion of the Doc Lap Regiment. The four 503rd companies spent the night on Hill 830 as the rain continued to fall and dense fog moved in. Their medics were caring for sixty-two wounded, some seriously, and they had twenty-five dead. The next morning, the mountain remained weathered in, making it impossible for choppers to medevac the wounded or transport the dead. The battalion commander sent out patrols, and the North Vietnamese had gone. The bodies of nine NVA soldiers were found on the mountain, along with one wounded NVA, who was taken prisoner.

The weather cleared after two days, and Rutledge helped load Ski's body aboard one of the slicks. He did not know the circumstances surrounding Ski's death, and it didn't matter. He knew he had lost his buddy. He put in for a transfer and volunteered as a door gunner with the 173rd Assault Helicopter Company. With Ski gone, he needed a change.

On July 12, after taking the hill, Delta Company discovered a network consisting of sixty bunkers with supporting foxholes. In short order, two more bunker complexes were discovered. The fighting on July 10 cost twenty-five American lives; eleven of the dead on Hill 830 were from Alpha Company. Lt. Jordan, the First Platoon leader had also died trying to save his men. Pfc. John "Ski" Borowski and Lt. Daniel Jordan both received the Distinguished Service Cross, second only to the Medal of Honor, for "extreme gallantry" and "extraordinary heroism." John Borowski was twenty years old and had been in Vietnam for ten weeks.

Back home in Evergreen Park, Illinois, there was a funeral mass for Borowski at Holy Redeemer Catholic Church, followed by burial at Saint Mary Catholic Cemetery. John's best friend from high school attended the service, but had no contact with the Sak family and never knew John had died a hero. Most of John's class-mates did not even know he had died in Vietnam. They had fin-ished high school two years before and moved on with their lives: college, marriage and Vietnam. His death was announced in the local newspapers, but none of them had ever heard the name "John Borowski."

It was thirty-five years before his closest friends discovered John Borowski had earned a Distinguished Service Cross on Hill 830. "We never knew how he died." One of them said, "We never knew he was a hero."

In a final bit of irony—one of the sergeants in Ski's company said, "You did good John. If only I'd had a son like you."

> Rid of the world's injustice, and his pain,
> He rests at last beneath God's veil of blue:
> Taken from life when life and love were new
> The youngest of the martyrs here is lain,
> Fair as Sebastian, and as early slain.
>
> "The Grave of Keats"
> —Oscar Wilde

> I do not fear an army of lions, if they are led by a lamb.
> I do fear an army of sheep, if they are led by a lion.
>
> —Alexander the Great

6

Harold Ray Reeves

They Called Him "Shorty"

Harold "Shorty" Reeves

He didn't weigh much over a hundred pounds, soaking wet. Harold Ray Reeves was often described as "a big man in a little man's body," although those who knew him never thought of him as small. The family moved frequently when Harold was growing up. His dad, Jimmy, worked for an oilfield service company and was constantly being transferred from oilfield to oilfield, all over Texas. The one constant in Harold's life was spending summer vacations at his grandparents place in the country near Gainesville. He would turn berry-brown from the Texas sun and rarely went in the house. With several siblings and assorted cousins, Harold would tear around barefoot, "kickin' up dust" and being a rotten little boy. He got into his share of mischief, but no one could stay angry with Harold Ray for long. He had eyes the color of Texas bluebonnets, and they could melt any heart. Those eyes would stand him in good stead with the fair sex a few years later.

In the early sixties, Jimmy Reeves went into business for himself as owner/operator of R. J. Rig Sales, and the family settled down in Odessa. Harold sailed through junior high and moved on to Permian High School. Odessa had a long history of great football teams in a football-crazy state, and Odessa-Permian, a new 4A high school, was eager to build its own reputation. In 1965, Permian won the Texas State 4A Football Championship, and Harold decided he was going to be on the team. Every boy in West Texas wanted to play football for Permian, but Harold was determined to make it happen. When Coach Mayfield held tryouts in the spring of '66, Harold was there, all five feet of him, and he gave it everything he had. He did not make the player's roster, but impressed the coaches with his drive and determination. That fall, when the Friday-night lights came on at Permian High, and the defending state champion Panthers took the field, no one stood taller than their new student manager. Harold had made the team.

Young Reeves also enjoyed his social life. He was the oldest boy in his family, and aside from being somewhat smaller than most guys his age, he held his own. With an older sister, Barbara, and another one a bit younger, Valerie, there were always plenty of girls around, and Harold had those blue eyes. Most of the girls didn't seem to mind if they were taller than he was. He was cute, and he could dance. One of his female cousins said, "He always had a smile on his face, and those eyes, what he could do with those eyes."

By Harold's junior year, he had a steady girlfriend. "He made me laugh and his attitude was always happy and positive," Kathy said, "and his eyes were the prettiest blue I had ever seen." Midway through the year, Harold became increasingly bored with school. He felt he was not being challenged and needed to take the next step in his life. He and pal Ricky Ray talked about foregoing their senior year and joining the Army on the buddy plan. Harold had to persuade his parents, but they finally agreed on the condition he would get his GED and go to college after he finished his enlistment. No one could resist Harold's powers of persuasion for long.

Harold was truly excited. Mr. DeBary's health class was his first class of the day, and he was there early the next morning. With a broad grin, he announced to all his friends that he and Ricky Ray were "joining-up." However, there was still a minor problem. Harold had to meet the minimum physical requirements for the Army to accept him. Stretching to his maximum height, he could barely reach the required altitude, but he struggled to gain weight.

"He never let his size stop him," Barbara said, smiling, "not in life, not in football, and certainly not in the military. He ate three dozen bananas before he went to weigh in, and it was enough to get him into the Army." He was too happy to care about how sick he was later.

At the end of their junior year, Harold and Ricky made the four-hour bus trip to Fort Bliss in El Paso. Harold had turned seventeen only a month before. The two remained together on the buddy plan through basic training, but separated for advanced infantry training at Fort Polk, Louisiana. After AIT, Harold left for his first duty assignment at Fort Ord, California. He was still seventeen, so he could not go to Vietnam. Army regulations prohibited anyone under eighteen from serving in combat. Harold spent almost a year at Ft. Ord and completed the requirements for his GED. Late in the summer of 1968, after his eighteenth birthday, he was reassigned to Vietnam.

Harold went home on leave and then reported for duty on September 19, 1968. He was assigned to Alpha Company, 5/12th Infantry Regiment, 199th Light Infantry Brigade, called the "Redcatchers." Apache Company operated out of Fire Support Base Stephanie, five nautical miles southwest of Saigon. Charged with aggressively patrolling and protecting the various approaches and infiltration routes into the Saigon/Biên Hòa/ Tân Sơn Nhứt area, the 199th area of operations consisted of some of the harshest terrain in Vietnam. Known as the "Redcatcher Warriors," the Apache 5/12th platoons patrolled endless miles of rice paddies, swamps, nipa palm groves, triple canopy jungle, and rivers. The patrols lasted as long as two weeks, and hostile contact with Việt Cộng and NVA troops was frequent. Booby traps and IEDs were a constant and deadly threat.

It didn't take Harold long to make friends with the "Warriors" in his Apache platoon. It was impossible not to like him. He was every guy's little brother, and the men not only welcomed him, they adopted him, nicknaming him "Shorty." In Vietnam, everyone was called by their last name or a nickname. Most of the men had no idea what the other soldiers' first names were. They were part of a brotherhood and the stress and strain of almost daily combat forged deep friendships in a short period of time. Shorty was soon taken under the wing of Hippo Rodriguez, and they became very close. Hippo was an "old timer" having been in Vietnam seven months, so his experience and know-how was a welcome resource for the "newbie." Hippo was as big and easygoing as Shorty was little and determined. They made a great team, and the Warriors rarely saw one without the other.

Shorty had many friends, even in other platoons. He always had that big smile and lit up any room he walked into. Larry was a friend from AIT at Fort Polk. He was another one of the "little guys," and they had become friends during infantry training. Larry was based not far from Shorty, and the two were planning to meet before Christmas and have a few beers, as they had done at Polk the year before. "We shared a commonality during our school years of what some would call diminished vertical reach," Larry recalled with a wry smile, "but neither of us would allow an indication of any limitations. I would fight, but Harold would show you the enormity of his heart. You had to relent, to give in to his bigness. Harold had an inner power beyond reproach, an innate ability to express his bigness, without even a blink, just a twinkle in those blue eyes, and that twinkle was always there. To measure a man you need a yardstick..." But you could not measure Harold's heart.

Since arriving in Vietnam, Harold had written home as often as he could. He knew his mother worried and waited eagerly to hear from him. He also wrote to Kathy. He was able to get to a PX at Thanksgiving and picked up a few Christmas cards. A friend wrote to tell him Ricky Ray, his basic training buddy, might come to Vietnam, so he sent her a card and a note. He asked her to tell Ricky not to worry; he would take care of him if he came to 'Nam. He also told everyone not to worry about him; he was so little, he could never be hit. His tour would be over soon, and he was eager to get home. He would be barely twenty when he got out of the Army, and he was going to college.

Living conditions at Stephanie were not too bad; they received three hot meals a day. The water didn't taste good, but many of the men received Kool-Aid and instant coffee from home to mix with it. They could get warm Cokes and Carling Black Label beer at their "club," and sometimes they traded with the local villagers for ice, but they didn't have it otherwise. It seemed like it rained almost every day, but they slept reasonably secure in their sand-bagged hootches.

Conditions on patrol were tough and highly dangerous. The second week of December, Shorty, Hippo, and the Apache 1st Platoon headed to Five Fingers on ambush patrol. Five Fingers was a large area known to include major NVA infiltration routes into the region around Saigon. Their hazardous mission was to set up night ambushes of VC and NVA troops moving toward Saigon, and on this trek, they were exploring new territory. So far, there had been no enemy contact.

Late in the afternoon, the unit crossed a fifty-foot-wide canal, which was particularly harrowing for someone of Shorty's stature. Weighed down with sixty pounds of equipment and his M16, the youngster stepped into a hole and sank completely underwater. Hippo was nearby and came to his rescue, dragging him to the surface sputtering and laughing. Upon reaching the other side, the platoon leader discovered little dry ground anywhere in sight. It was getting dark, so the soldiers were told to make camp. They would spend the night on the rice paddy dike. They set up M60 machine guns on each end of their narrow encampment, placed claymores for added protection, and posted guards with a starlight scope that would allow them to see in the dark. No one expected to sleep much; the area was just too dangerous.

"Shorty" Reeves

As twilight settled over the camp, a slight breeze came in off the water, and it was almost cool. Frogs were croaking a loud chorus, and swallows were swooping and diving over the water snapping up flying insects. Undressing briefly, the men began a systematic check of themselves and each other for leeches, and nearly all of them had several of the blood-suckers acquired during their canal crossing. Using the "bug juice" they had been issued, they quickly divested themselves of the leeches and maybe discouraged a mosquito or two in the process.

Shorty and Hippo finished their c-rats, spread their ponchos on the ground, and leaned back against the sloping bank of the dike. As usual, Shorty talked and Hippo listened to him ramble on in his soft Texas twang. Shorty told him about camping along the Red River near Gainesville during those hot summers when he was a kid; just him, his cousins, and his "Paw-paw," out under that big Texas sky, full of stars. Then he trailed off, alone with his thoughts.

Shorty took off his helmet, placing it on the poncho beside him, and laid his head back, closing his eyes. The breeze off the water tousled his sandy hair, and he could almost smell the sweet scent of the mimosa trees along that broad river so far away. Hippo heard Shorty chuckle softly and saw a trace of a smile creep across the boy's tanned face. Smiling to himself, Hippo laid back and remained silent. Shorty had obviously gone to some other place, and if he could do that, even for a few moments, why would any true friend want to bring him back to 'Nam?

Morning dawned gray and foreboding, with misty drizzle and layers of fog slowly moving across the canal and rice paddies. The frogs were still singing and the mosquitoes were still biting. It was the sixteenth of December, nine days until Christmas. The warriors collected their equipment and weapons, and headed out across the paddies. Reaching solid ground at mid-morning, the platoon moved into dense jungle, tangled with vines, bamboo, and thorny brush. The air was thick with swarms of small flies and heavy with the smell of rotting vegetation. The soldiers cut their way through the thicket with machetes, catching flashes of brilliant blues and yellows as exotic birds flushed ahead of them. If the map was correct, they should reach a clearing in about an hour and would stop to rest and heat c-rats. There was still no sign of the enemy.

As the platoon neared the clearing, the point man eased his way in and surveyed the area. Seeing no sign of an enemy presence, he signaled the unit to move ahead. Some of the soldiers had already stepped out of the jungle into the open when there was a loud boom and a blast that knocked several men down. The rest of the platoon hit the ground with their weapons at the ready. Twigs, leaves, and small debris sprinkled down through the trees as frightened jungle birds squawked in protest. There were moans from a few stunned soldiers; otherwise, it was deathly quiet.

Hippo jumped up looking for Shorty, who had been ten yards ahead of him. All he saw was brush and a swirling cloud of thick smoke. Hurrying forward, he found the youngster lying on the ground, and there was so much blood. Screaming for a "doc,"

Hippo pulled a towel from around his neck and frantically tried to staunch the bleeding. Laying on his back and slightly propped by bags of gear, Shorty's eyelids fluttered, and he slowly raised his head. He opened his eyes and looked at Hippo. He could see Hippo's mouth moving, but there was only silence, and tears streaming down Hippo's face. Shorty tried to move, but nothing seemed to work. He felt very tired—and it was so quiet.

Doc Zeitler was there in seconds, shoving Hippo aside. Zeitler had only been with the 5/12th for two months, but was combat-experienced and knew immediately Shorty had devastating wounds. The young soldier had tripped some type of explosive device resulting in major injury to his feet and lower legs, along with third-degree burns. The medic applied tourniquets to both legs, administered morphine, and tried to make the boy as comfortable as possible. The platoon leader had called for medical transport. There was little more the "doc" could do in the field. They had to get the young man to a hospital as quickly as possible. Per SOP, the troops had been widely spaced as they moved through the jungle, so aside from minor wounds and ringing ears, no one else was seriously hurt.

Hippo and some other buddies moved back near Shorty's head and removed his helmet, the heavy ruck sack, and other equipment attached to the young man's body. Shorty appeared to be fading in and out of consciousness. He opened those startling blue eyes, searching the faces of the men who knelt beside him, speaking only with his eyes. Then he faded and his body grew limp. He did not appear to be in pain, but the warriors around him were distraught. This was their little brother.

Within minutes, the men heard the sound of the chopper. The platoon leader popped a purple smoke grenade to mark the LZ, and the bird was soon on the ground. Two medics jumped out before the "slick" touched down and came on the run with a stretcher. They quickly loaded Shorty on board, and as the Huey lifted off, they were already administering intravenous fluids and working feverishly to save him.

For a moment everything was silent, and then several of the warriors began to collect Shorty's belongings. Hippo picked up his helmet and slowly turned it in his hands. Neatly printed on one side was the name "Fayrene," Shorty's mother, and on the other side was the name "Kathy." He held it to his chest for a moment, and then quietly slipped it into his ruck sack. He prayed Shorty made it, but if not, the folks in Texas would have this helmet. No one in the platoon was hungry, so after a brief radio call to headquarters, the platoon leader turned the Apache Warriors around, and the solemn cortege slowly made its way back toward Stephanie.

Two days later, 1st Platoon was notified Shorty had passed away. The trauma was too extensive and the blood-loss too great for him to survive the extensive surgery his injuries required. He had fought valiantly for forty hours but gradually lost the battle and closed his eyes for the last time. The news spread quickly from platoon to platoon. Shorty had only been in Apache Company for ninety days, but the warriors in the other platoons all knew him, and in a place with so much death and destruction, they stopped for a moment to consider the death of this one special young man.

On December 20, Texas time, an Army Master Sergeant from Midland knocked on the front door of the Reeves home on Hanley Street and notified the family Harold had been killed in action. His family and friends were heartbroken. They had received his Christmas cards the day before.

Funeral services for Harold Ray Reeves were held at the Rix Funeral Home Chapel in Odessa on December 29, 1968. He was buried with full military honors at Fairview Cemetery in Gainesville on New Year's Eve, just a few miles from where he had spent those carefree summer days with his Pawpaw. He was awarded posthumously the Army Commendation Medal for heroism and the Purple Heart. "Shorty" Reeves was eighteen years old.

Among the belongings sent home from Vietnam was his helmet, with the names of his mother and Kathy neatly inscribed on the camouflaged cover.

And the little gray hawk hangs aloft in the air,
And the sly coyote trots here and there,
And the black snake glides, and glitters and slides
Into a rift in a cotton-wood tree;
And the buzzard sails on—
And comes and is gone—
Stately and still like a ship at sea.
And I wonder why I do not care
For the things that are, like the things that were—
Does half my heart lie buried there
In Texas, down by the Rio Grande?

"In Texas, down by the Rio Grande"
—Frank Desprez

7

Kenneth Alan Luse

Sunward I've climbed and joined the tumbling mirth of
sun-split clouds and done a hundred
things you have not dreamed of
—wheeled and soared and swung high in the sunlit silence.
Hovering there I've chased the shouting wind along and
flung my eager craft through footless halls of air.

—Laughter-Silvered Wings*

Kenneth "Ken" Luse

Maybe it had something to do with that incredible Iowa sky, the
deepest azure blue, which appeared to go on forever. Or it might

have been growing up on the northern prairie, equally as majestic, in its own way. At night, Kenny Luse would lie on his back in the soft, sweet grass and dream. He could feel the cool dampness and smell the fragrance of the rich black soil he rested upon, but his heart was in the heavens. He yearned to be up there, among the brilliant stars splayed across that immense, velvety dome. He could almost reach out and touch them—someday, he would.

If there is such a thing as a "flying" prodigy, that was Kenneth Luse. For Ken, flying was like breathing, or eating or any of the other functions he required for survival. He begged his parents to join the Cedar Rapids Civil Air Patrol as he entered high school, and he never looked back. He won a scholarship for glider training in Elmira, New York, when he was sixteen and earned his glider pilot's license. He returned home filled with ideas of buying a glider and catapult and training his own CAP "glider squadron." By the next year, he had moved on to powered aircraft and began taking flight lessons. He had his private pilot's license by the time he was seventeen and was soon promoted to cadet commander of the Cedar Rapids CAP squadron. Under Ken's leadership and with a great deal of hard work, Cedar Rapids won the state drill competition, and the Air Force flew the squadron in a C-119 to the Air Force Academy for the national competition.

In the winter of 1966–67, the commander of the Iowa Wing of CAP set up an intensive program to train senior cadets in ground search & rescue techniques and wilderness survival. The program was known as the Civil Air Patrol Special Service Corps. Ken Luse was one of the first members of the "Blue Berets" and demonstrated the same leadership abilities at the state level he had in his own squadron.

Graduating from JFK High School in 1968, Luse had only one path open to him. Civil Air Patrol was sponsored by the Air Force, but he could not be an Air Force pilot without four years of college, and he wanted to fly. He would enlist in the Army warrant officer program and become a helicopter pilot. When he reported to the Armed Forces Examination Station in Des Moines for his Flight Aptitude testing, he ran into an old acquaintance.

Jim Spencer was from Iowa City, and the two had known each other through CAP. The young men discovered they had more in common than just flying, and became close friends. After basic training at Fort Polk, Louisiana, Ken and Jim moved on to Fort Wolters, near Mineral Wells, Texas, for primary helicopter training. They thought they had experienced hot summers in Iowa, but soon discovered "Texas hot" meant something entirely different. Some days were so hot they could not get a chopper off the ground with both student and instructor on board.

As graduation day approached, Jim's parents decided to make the trek from Iowa City to Texas and watch the boys graduate. Ken's parents would wait and see them get their wings at Fort Rucker, Alabama. The ceremony at Wolters was standing-room only, and as they announced the superlatives for the class, the commander read: "Honor Graduate—Kenneth Luse; for Best Academic Achievement—Kenneth Luse." Then, the officer paused and said, "You might as well stay here, because Kenneth Luse gets the Best Flight Achievement Award too." Ken had earned three of the highest awards out of five and finished at the top of the class.

In 1968, the anti-war movement had reached its peak, fueled by the news media and brutal clashes with Chicago police during the Democratic Convention. Ken and Jim had a break over Christmas and flew home. As the young soldiers changed planes, they were pursued by a trio of war protesters who ran toward them screaming, "The Army sucks!" Polished and spit-shined to perfection, Ken turned to the scruffy trio with his direct, honest bearing and said, "So do smart-ass civilians."

Arriving in Alabama early in 1969, Ken and Jim learned to fly Hueys at Fort Rucker and were trained in additional skills, such as formation flying. The school was tough, but Ken enjoyed every second in the air, and the weeks passed quickly. The training class at Wolters had begun with 188 students; 144 received their wings at Rucker, and Ken finished third in the class. This time, Ed and Deloris Luse were there to watch the ceremony, and his parents were so proud of him. Ken's mother pinned the new wings on Ken and Jim and gave each a kiss. Then Ken asked her if she would do the same for another friend. Gary Swinson, one of their buddies through Wolters and Rucker, was a fellow Iowan from Ames and had no family present. Ken had told him it was unlucky not to have his wings pinned on by a woman. Deloris was honored to do so and gave Gary an extra kiss for good luck. The new Army aviators celebrated that night with a formal dress blues banquet at the officers' club.

Jim, Gary, and the majority of their class headed home for thirty days leave and then on to Vietnam. Ken, however, spent the month of August at Ft. Stewart, Georgia. Because of his intellectual and flying abilities, he and the other top graduates in his class were about to join an elite group. They would be trained to fly the AH-1G "Cobra," the Army's high performance attack helicopter. This was the "brass ring" all had strived to reach; Ken and his peers at Ft. Stewart had grabbed it.

Ken finished Cobra school in September. He went home for thirty days before deploying to Vietnam, and Iowa had never been more beautiful. After spending over a year in Louisiana, Texas, Alabama, and Georgia, Indian summer along the Cedar River was wonderful, and the family enjoyed doing the things they had always done. Ken hung out with Paul and Glen, his two younger brothers. They had grown tall in his absence. He also spent hours working on his old Triumph Spitfire. He enjoyed several immense "thresher" dinners with his grandparents and extended family and visited with high school friends. Shortly before leaving, Ken visited a CAP squadron meeting to tell the cadets about his experiences and the helicopters he had learned to fly. No one wanted to think about his departure, but the day arrived all too soon. Family and friends gathered to see him catch his Ozark flight, chatting and making small talk as they watched the minutes tick off the clock. Ken's mom and dad were uneasy about him going but tried not to show it. His brothers were more confident—Kenny always came home.

Luse was assigned to Troop B, 1st Squadron, 9th Cavalry, 1st Cavalry Division, known as the "Bullwhip Squadron," and was sold on it from the first day. He was involved in all facets of flying. He flew as observer on OH-6A "Loaches" and right seat on

UH-1C Huey gunbirds. The gunbirds were somewhat more dangerous than flying Cobras, but the excitement was well worth it.

Ken's flight school buddies were scattered all across Vietnam. Gary Swinson, from Ames, was with the 4th Infantry Division. Bill Wall and Mike Garner had gone through Cobra school with Ken and had become two of his closest friends. Mike was in the 9th Cav, but he and Ken were in different troops. Mike stopped by one day and saw Ken sitting in a "Charley" model (UH-1C) with his feet propped up. He had an M16 laid across his lap, casually smoking a cigarette, and was gazing out over the rows of Hueys like a king surveying his domain. Mike ran up and surprised him, and they laughed and talked. The crew chief on Ken's chopper was re-arming the rockets and "chunkers" (grenade launchers). The C-model carried a gunner and crew chief with M60s, and the pilot used an M16. During an operation, the aircraft commander fired the rockets and chunkers, and the other three would cut loose with their weapons, producing a formidable force. In the vernacular of the day, "It was a gas!" Ken was always the first one on the bird, raring to go. Death was a calculated risk in the job—but for him, and most of his cohorts, the job was worth it. This was what they had been trained for, and they were damned good at it.

In November, Luse was assigned to fly the gunner seat on a Cobra and accepted his new job with enthusiasm. Most of the younger pilots drooled over Cobras, and Ken was no exception. The AH-1G was the "hot rod," the Army's version of a "cheap jet fighter," and only the best pilots earned the privilege of flying it. The Cobra was the first helicopter engineered to be a true gunship. Long, lean, and mean, it bristled with weapons. The aircraft flew nearly twice as fast as the Huey gunbirds with a top speed of over 200 mph and possessed a system of electronic flight stabilizers that increased the accuracy of its weapons. The gunship would fly directly toward its target during an attack, and the target was usually shooting back. The Cobra's advantage was that although it was forty-five feet long and thirteen feet tall, its fuselage was barely three feet wide. It was a difficult target to hit. As one Cobra pilot said, "We could come in lower, stay longer, and get down dirtier."

The gunner normally operated the turret on the front of the Cobra, which included a minigun and a 40mm grenade launcher. Tracers in the minigun provided the gunner with an accurate idea of where the rounds were going, and he could flex the weapon up to 230 degrees to adjust the aim as he desired. He had only a general idea, however, where the grenades were going to land until they made impact. All the weapons systems could be fired from either the front seat (gunner/X-ray) or the back seat (AC/aircraft commander); however, the back seat could not fire the turret weapons in the flexed positions, and the front seat did not have the ability to arm the weapons systems by himself. In an emergency, the AC could fire the turret in a fixed-forward position, and the X-ray had simple flight controls that allowed him to fly the machine from the front if the situation required it.

The 1/9th Cobras were operating as the "muscle" part of the 1st Cav "Pink" teams, a combination of Red teams (Cobras) and White teams (Loaches). The Loaches flew as low as possible searching out the enemy. If they were shot at, they called in the Cobras to attack. If the Loach was shot down, a Blue recon team was called in to secure the site and aid in the extraction of the White team and helicopter. In the worst-case scenario, the Blues were called to recover the remains of the lost team.

Luse had not been assigned to a permanent team, but filled in as needed, and flew frequently with Larry Babyak, (call sign "Saber 22"). Babyak appeared to be everyone's idea of the laid-back Southern Californian. With his tanned good looks, easy manner, and ready smile, it was easy to assume he spent his free time enjoying the good life; however, that obscured his true nature. Larry Babyak was a devout Catholic, had joined the Knights of Columbus while in flight training, and spent his free time working to ease the life of hundreds of Vietnamese orphans. At twenty-four years of age, he was five years older than Ken Luse, was married, and had been an Army pilot for over two years. He was on his second tour in Vietnam. Ken knew he could learn a lot from Larry Babyak. The prodigy and the veteran aviator; fate had brought them together.

Lawrence "Larry" Babyak

Part 2

The 1st Cavalry Division had partnered with the Army Security Agency for two years in a highly classified and highly effective search & destroy operation called "Project Left Bank." Helicopters and pilots were provided by the 1st Cav, and their ASA direct support unit, the 371st Radio Research Company, provided Morse intercept operators. Left Bank birds were JUH-1H Hueys, configured with top-secret antenna and airborne radio direction finding systems. Their crews consisted of two pilots and two ASA ops, and their mission was to track the enemy by intercepting their radio transmissions, then fixing their location with triangulation. The Hueys were unarmed due to the weight of their equipment; when they had a fix, they called in Pink teams to pinpoint the location and do the killing.

On November 29, 1969, a Left Bank Huey (call sign "Jaguar Yellow") was operating near LZ Buttons, a few miles from Sông Bé. There was speculation that the enemy was tired of being pounded whenever the helicopter with the strange antenna appeared, so they set a trap. The Morse ops picked up an enemy signal, and as the aircraft commander flew closer, the sky exploded with a hail of .51 caliber machine gun and small arms fire. The pilot of the unarmed craft attempted to gain altitude, but as the Huey turned away from the deadly fire, a rocket propelled grenade smashed through the chin-bubble and exploded inside. The supporting pink team responded immediately, flying in to help facilitate a rescue. The call sign of the Cobra gunship was "Sabre 22."

Babyak and Luse heard the call on the radio: "Jaguar Yellow down!" and were on the scene in a matter of seconds. The narrow Cobra cockpit was arranged with Larry Babyak, the AC, sitting directly behind and slightly above Ken Luse, the X-ray (gunner). From his elevated position, Babyak had sufficient visibility to maneuver the aircraft as the situation demanded. Luse had a better view of the ground immediately in front of the aircraft and was focused on locating the source of the enemy attack that had brought down the Huey.

Cruising into the area, Babyak saw the burning hulk of the Left Bank bird in a valley surrounded by brush and jungle.

"Firing," Luse called on the intercom, and he fired several bursts from the turret minigun into the thick foliage. Spotting muzzle flashes in the trees near the burning wreck, he called, "flashes at ten o'clock," and lobbed several 40mm grenades as the Cobra overflew the area and circled for another run. X-ray and AC communicated about the possible location of the enemy force as they climbed over a thousand feet in the air.

"Running in!" Babyak called, and he nosed the ship back over into the valley, ripple-firing pairs of rockets into the dense vegetation as Luse fired three-second bursts of suppressive fire along the treeline. A platoon of 1/9th Bravo "Blues" was moving in, and the Cobra crew had to dampen enemy fire so the troop-carrying Hueys could land.

Each all-volunteer Blue platoon had 21-men and carried almost as much firepower as a 140-man infantry company. The platoon was divided into three six-man squads plus a headquarters element and was armed with six M60 machine guns, six 40mm grenade launchers, and fifteen men with M16s. They were called "recon teams" but were some of the finest fighting units in Vietnam.

As the Cobra started to recover from the firing run, it was hit by an intense barrage of .51 caliber machine gun and automatic weapons fire. Luse saw bright tracers streaking past the ship, and there were loud thumps as rounds hit the underside of the aircraft.

"Taking fire! Taking fire!" Babyak yelled into his helmet microphone. Suddenly the plexiglass exploded with a loud roar as another burst of .51 cal fire raked the ship along its left side.

Luse felt a jarring blow and sharp pain to his left shoulder, and the Cobra began to roll to the right. He yelled at Babyak on the intercom, but got no response; grabbing the cyclic stick to his right, he soon brought the Cobra under control. His maneuvering capabilities were limited from the forward seat, but Ken Luse could fly anything.

Luse yelled at Babyak repeatedly, but got no response. He could not see the AC's seat above and behind him. However, looking in the small rearview mirror above the forward windscreen, he could see part of Larry's right shoulder. He was not moving. Ken could also see blood splattered across the top of the canopy, and it was not his. He assumed his AC was either dead or badly wounded.

A .51 cal round had penetrated the Cobra above Luse's head, spraying him with sharp shards of plexiglass. His helmet had protected his head, but he had been wounded in his left shoulder at the edge of his chicken plate body armor, and he was bleeding freely from the injury. Blood had saturated his sleeve, but he could still use his left hand. The last burst of fire had blown a larger hole in the plexiglass panel next to the AC's seat behind him and had also knocked out the radios, so he had no contact with anyone. It was all up to him.

As the Cobra soared skyward, the wind came blowing through the broken canopy. Ken unfastened the chin strap on his helmet and with some effort managed to pull it off his head, enjoying the coolness of the breeze on his hot face. Sweat was trickling down the sides of his head and soaking into the scarlet "Bravo 1/9" bandana tied around his neck. He swiped his hand across his face to clear his eyes, and then over his close-cropped hair. His shoulder throbbed, but he had to focus on his next attack. There was a sizeable VC force in the jungle below. He needed to take out as much of their firepower as possible with his next pass. He might not get another chance.

Climbing to nearly two thousand feet above the ground, Luse leveled off and surveyed the majestic scene before him. He could see the beauty of Núi Bà Rá in the hazy distance, and for a brief moment, he wished he were back home, lying in the grass on a warm summer night, dreaming of touching the stars. Brief glimpses of his parents and brothers flashed through his mind, and a smile flicked across his face. He could feel their love a world away. Then, he eased the Cobra over and began another shallow rocket run.

Plunging at nearly 200 mph, Luse began to fire pairs of rockets at the treeline below him and saw the jungle convulse with deadly explosions. The sky filled with a hail of RPGs, small arms and machine gun fire. He could feel and hear the rounds slamming into the Cobra as it sliced its way toward earth, and he felt a sense of fulfillment.

"Everything I have done in my life has prepared me for this moment," he thought, "at this place."

Then there was a flash of brilliant white light…

Pilots in other 1/9th aircraft in the area watched in stunned silence. The Cobra pitched upward, as though someone had yanked back hard on the cyclic. In a slow-motion ballet, the main rotor hit the tail boom and separated from the mast. The beautiful aircraft made a long, slow roll to the inverted position; the nose lowered and the ship impacted the ground with a horrific explosion.

Part 3

December 3 was Paul Luse's eighteenth birthday. Paul and fifteen-year-old Glen were in the basement watching the *CBS Evening News* and listened as Cronkite solemnly reported the number of Americans killed in Vietnam that day. Mom called for them to wash for supper, and as Glen ran up the stairs, the doorbell rang. He answered the door and found two Army officers in dress greens standing on the porch. They asked if Mr. and Mrs. Luse were home, so Glen called his dad and told him someone was there to see him and Mom. Mothers always know when something is wrong, and Deloris Luse detected something terrible in Glen's voice. The soldiers were from the ROTC unit at the University of Iowa and had been sent to inform the family Ken was missing-in-action. His helicopter had been shot down and burned near Sông Bé, South Vietnam, on 29 November. Due to heavy enemy presence in the area, his unit had been unable to investigate the crash.

The term "missing-in-action" was so vague the family was not certain what to feel. It seemed unlikely Ken had survived, but "MIA" still left a glimmer of hope for some kind of miracle. Should they prepare for his funeral, or was it possible he might be a prisoner of war? They felt so helpless, but by the next day, extended family and a wide circle of friends had appeared to lend support, pray, and bring in food. They would all wait, together.

On the tenth day of December, an Army captain came to the house and informed the family a 9th Cavalry reconnaissance team had recovered remains believed to be Ken and his fellow crewman, Lawrence Babyak. As soon as the Army had made positive identification, the family would be advised. There was still no final word, and for the youngest Luse, the wait was almost overwhelming. Glen idolized his oldest brother, and Kenny always came home. That night, with tears in his eyes, Glen said a prayer: "Please God, dead or alive, let my family be together for Christmas."

A few days later, Ed and Deloris received a letter from Ken's buddy, Mike Garner in Vietnam. "Mr. and Mrs. Luse," the letter began. "Ken died the morning of the twenty-ninth here, the thirtieth Stateside. I was working a mission about ten miles east, and being in a different troop, I had no commo with any Saber (B Troop) aircraft. I saw the crash and found out that night it was Ken."

Mike continued by telling the family about their job and how much Ken loved it. He summed it up by saying, "We lose so few cobras that when we do lose one, all the harsh realities suddenly come to the surface and slap pretty hard. ...Ken enjoyed the work, as most of us do, and I'm sure he wouldn't have traded jobs or places with anyone in the world... Don't feel sorry for Ken. I don't. He wouldn't want anyone to, and I don't want anyone crying over me if and when it happens to me. Death is a calculated risk in the job—the job is worth it."

Mike also told them about a "Boots and Saddles" memorial that had been held in the battalion chapel that day. "I cried at the services," he said. "I couldn't help it. I hate to see anyone cut off in their prime, but the fourteen months I knew him, Ken lived hard, all the time. We all did. Twelve months in flight school is, in level of experience, worth four years of college and two on the job. Two months over here under fire is worth more than that."

"What hurts the most," he concluded, "is the personal loss, the loss of a friend, someone who knew you. When you lose one, you lose that part of yourself and the identity gained from it. I think John Donne had that in his brain when he wrote that poem-essay on the nature of man. No man is an island entire to himself, but all a part of mankind. And everyman's death diminishes me. Ask not for whom the bell tolls—it tolls for thee. Ken will live in my memory. I'll miss him. I compliment you on raising a man of his stature. I sympathize with you, as I hope you do with me, Bill, and all Ken's other friends."

The captain returned ten days later to advise the family Ken Luse was coming home and asked if there was someone they wanted to serve as escort. Ed and Deloris wanted Jim Spencer, but were hesitant to ask him, fearing it would be too difficult for him emotionally. The next day, Deloris received a call from Faye, Jim's mother, and as they talked, Glen brought in the mail. There was a letter from Jim in Vietnam, and Glen opened it. Jim had written that he knew about Ken's death, and asked if he could escort the body home. When Deloris told Faye what Jim had requested, she replied softly, "Bring our boy home."

Jim met Ken's coffin and escorted it through all the plane changes, getting off the aircraft, supervising the unloading of the coffin, checking to make sure the flag was tightly secured, and then escorting his buddy across the tarmac to the next plane in Denver and Chicago. The two of them had been through so much together: Civil Air Patrol and Army basic, plus warrant officer candidate school and helicopter training. Somehow, he had never envisioned it ending like this. On the night of December 30, Jim and Ken arrived in Cedar Rapids, together, on Ken's last flight.

Ed and Deloris waited outside the terminal with their two younger boys and Jim's parents. The weather was mild for Iowa at New Years, but as the group watched the Ozark DC-9 taxi in, Glen began to shiver uncontrollably. Faye thought he was cold and reached over to hug him, but the chill was inside, and he continued to tremble. The green and white aircraft pulled up to the terminal and Jim deplaned first. When Glen saw him, he stopped shaking. The young pilot's uniform was immaculate; his shoes, brass, and the wings on his chest gleamed and glittered in the lights from the terminal, and the boy knew everything would be okay. Jim moved to the cargo hold to supervise the offloading of the coffin and the transfer to the hearse. Then he rode with it to the funeral home. Later, he was driven to the Luse home by the funeral director.

After dinner, the family, along with Jim and his parents, left for the visitation. The viewing room was small and dimly lit. A soft spotlight was focused on the flag-draped coffin, and Jim took his place beside it at parade rest. The room was banked with sprays of flowers and beautiful floral wreaths. Deloris wondered where so many flowers could have come from in such a short period of time. Glen stepped forward, took his mother's hand, and squeezed it softly. There was soft music playing in some distant place, and the room was very peaceful. It was only five days past Christmas, and his family was finally all together.

At 1:00 p.m., on New Year's Eve, the Luse family arrived at St. Andrew Lutheran Church for the funeral. The main sanctuary was standing room only as they were escorted to the choir area, which was partially secluded. The service was beautiful. With Ken's favorite hymns and a touching eulogy, there were few dry eyes among the assembled multitude. After the service, the family watched from their limousine as a US Army honor guard carried the flag-draped coffin along the walkway lined full-length with saluting Civil Air Patrol cadets.

The funeral procession from the church to the cemetery at Cedar Memorial Park was over three miles long. Jim stumbled over a few words as he presented Deloris with the flag from Ken's coffin, and she could hear the emotion in his quiet voice. This was so difficult for him. She wanted to reach out and comfort him, but she could not. Tears flowed again during "Taps," and Glen shuddered with each volley of the twenty-one-gun salute. Deloris placed her arm around him and squeezed Paul's arm on the other side. This is almost over she thought, closing her eyes. Then in the distance, she heard the faint drone of aircraft engines.

Ken had been one of the first CAP Blue Berets and had been well-known in squadrons across the state of Iowa and beyond. As the graveside service concluded and the last M14 volley echoed across the Cedar Valley, the Iowa Civil Air Patrol paid final tribute to the former cadet commander of the Cedar Rapids squadron and saluted his love of flying with a mass flyover of the cemetery. In perfect formation, they came by the dozens. And somewhere, Kenny Luse was smiling.

Chief Warrant Officer 2 Lawrence Joseph Babyak was buried with full military honors at San Fernando Mission Cemetery in San Fernando, California. His posthumous medals included a second Silver Star Medal, the second Oak Leaf Cluster to the Bronze Star, the twelfth Oak Leaf Cluster to the Air Medal, and the Purple Heart. These men were true heroes of the first order.

Several months later, Ed and Deloris Luse were invited to Fort Leonard Wood, Missouri, to receive Ken's medals. In a solemn and beautiful ceremony, the commanding officer began to read the certification for his Distinguished Flying Cross, "for heroism while participating in aerial flight...above and beyond the call of duty." As Ed and Deloris listened, the officer related how Ken had "distinguished himself by exceptionally valorous action...when his unit was on an air assault mission and although wounded, with complete disregard for his own personal safety," had flown his aircraft back into the area in an attempt to engage the enemy position and mark it so other gunships and Air Force jets could destroy it. They had always known how special their eldest son was. Now, many others knew it as well.

In addition to the DFC, Ken Luse was awarded his second Bronze Star, with "V" device for valor, the Air Medal, second through fifth Oak Leaf Cluster, with "V" device for valor, and the Purple Heart. He had been in Vietnam exactly eight weeks and was nineteen years old.

> Up, up the long delirious burning blue
> I've topped the wind-swept heights with easy grace,
> where never lark, or even eagle, flew;
> and, while with silent, lifting mind I've trod
> the high untrespassed sanctity of space,
> put out my hand and touched the face of God.

(From "High Flight," a sonnet written by John Gillespie Magee Jr., an American pilot who flew with the Royal Canadian Air Force during WW II. Magee was killed in a mid-air collision in England on December 11, 1941. He was nineteen years old.)

Author's Note

I wish to thank Jeremy Hogan of the "Bravo Troop, 1st Squadron, 9th Cavalry" Facebook page (Jeremy's father served with Bravo 1/9), George "Scotty" Scott (Saber 16), formerly of Bravo Troop, 1/9, 1969–1970, and especially James "Jim" Kurtz, a former Cobra pilot with Apache Troop, 1/9. I was an Air Force Security Service Chinese linguist; Jim Kurtz literally flew me, step by step, through the Cobra attack segments of this story. Without his expertise and patience, the story would be much less interesting and far less accurate. Jim and Scotty: I am in awe of the job you men performed in Vietnam. Thank you for your service (GBB).

8

Ralph Judson Mears Jr.

Bright Light

Ralph "Juddy" Mears Jr.

From his early days in Tidewater Virginia, tossing copies of the *Virginian-Pilot* onto neighbors' porches, through his years in the Boy Scouts, everyone knew it. Ralph Judson Mears Jr. was special. With a wild shock of blonde hair and an impish grin, "Juddy" had a way with people, a maturity, and a respect for others that was far beyond his years. He was a described as "a bright light" and was hard to forget. Maybe that inner strength and maturity had something to do with being the son of a Norfolk homicide detective, or maybe it was just Juddy. He played hard, and he worked hard. He became an Eagle Scout two weeks after he celebrated his fifteenth birthday.

Juddy was a natural athlete and spent much of his free time working out. He lifted weights and enjoyed time on the boxer's speed bag in the garage. He lettered in shot put at Granby High School in Norfolk, and there was usually a group of his friends playing basketball in the driveway.

Ralph Mears Sr. had joined the Marines during WWII and served as an antiaircraft gunner aboard the aircraft carrier USS *Franklin* in the Pacific. The *Franklin*, called "Big Ben," was the most heavily damaged US carrier to survive the war. Kamikaze attacks in March 1945 resulted in the loss of over eight hundred crewmen, and Ralph Mears was awarded two purple hearts for combat wounds he incurred during his duty on board the ship.

Juddy was very proud of his father's military service. He was unsure what he wanted to do after graduation from Granby in June 1967, so he discussed his future with his dad. The war in Vietnam was raging, and drawn to serve his country, the young man enlisted in the Army.

After basic training, Mears went through ten weeks of additional combat medic training and then on to jump school at Ft. Benning. The Army needed to fill the airborne divisions in Vietnam, and the combined classes of officers, NCOs, and enlisted men were huge. Mears' class consisted of over a thousand men. The training facilities at Benning were sufficient to handle that number, but that maximum number began to decline after the first week. The training was extremely physical, and class members began to leave, some voluntarily, some not so voluntarily, and others due to illness and injury. The men double-timed everywhere (the DIs called it the "airborne shuffle"); they were dropped for pushups constantly, and the training was nonstop. At the end of the first week, they had to pass a PT test in order to advance to the second week of training. Always in excellent physical condition, Juddy had no problem moving on.

Week two was spent on the thirty-four-foot tower. Each man in turn was strapped into a parachute harness which was attached to a steel cable. The cable ran from the tower to the ground and was designed to train the men how to exit an aircraft. It also allowed them to feel the hard, physical jerk when their chute opened, especially in the groin area. If he did not have the straps positioned and tightened correctly, a man could be in for some serious pain.

On the day of their second jump, the soldier ahead of Mears had not tightened his leg straps properly. The release plate across his chest was yanked upward when he jumped and cut a deep gash in his chin. Even worse, the young man had bitten down hard and nearly cut off the end of his tongue, which was bleeding freely. Juddy came down immediately behind him. The young man was standing dazed. The front of his uniform was covered with blood, which continued to stream from his mouth. Juddy had the youngster on the ground and was swiftly administering first aid before the DIs got to him. Recognizing Mears obviously had medical training and knew what he was doing, the instructors stood back and allowed him to tend to the soldier until medics arrived on the scene and took over. Juddy considered that incident one of the highlights of his jump school experience, and he talked about it for days.

By the third week, the trainees had moved to the 250 foot tower and then on to a series of actual jumps from airplanes at an altitude of 1,250 feet over various drop zones. Upon graduation from jump school, Mears was assigned to the 3rd Brigade, 82nd Airborne Division at Ft. Bragg, North Carolina. On 12 February 1968, in response to the Tet Offensive, his unit was deployed to South Vietnam, and there Ralph "Juddy" Mears realized his true calling. At eighteen years of age, he was a combat medic with Alpha Co., 1/505th Infantry, 82nd AD.

The 505th Infantry arrived in Chu Lai as part of Task Force JAMESON. After several days of in-country orientation and training, the unit was airlifted to Huế/Phú Bài on 23–24 February where it would operate under operational control of the 1st Marine Division. With the launch of Operations CARENTAN I and CARENTAN II (from 9 March through the end of April), the entire brigade was involved in combat operations.

Over the next couple of months, Mears continued his training. There was much to absorb, and lives would depend on how well he mastered his craft. As always, he wanted to be the best, and he learned quickly. He spent most of his time in a battalion aid station, learning firsthand how to treat the wounds of soldiers medevaced in from the field and how to treat the ever-prevalent skin diseases. His fellow medics enjoyed working with him and were awed by his talent. He was born to be a healer, but he looked so young. They called him "Baby-san."

"Baby-san" (left) with a buddy

But that was not where the young medic wanted to be. He was driven to be where he could do the most good—in the field with the troops he had come to help. Soon, Mears began going out on field operations.

The third week in March saw the transition to CARENTAN II. Moving east on Highway 552, Alpha Company encountered heavy enemy contact. The unit was then ordered to conduct "extensive recon-in-force in the area north of Song Ba and west of the Perfume River." The troopers cleared and secured Highway #1 and then secured the An Lo Bridge. The fighting was some of the bloodiest and most intense Mears had experienced, and he was in the middle of it. While carrying a wounded trooper to safety, he almost died. Struck in both legs by rounds from an NVA machine gun, he nearly bled to death before his fellow medics got him to a field hospital. It took eighty-one stitches to close the terrible wounds in his legs, but the medical staff would not keep him down for long. He saw the steady influx of wounded, and they needed his help. With the assistance of crutches, he was soon working nearly full time in the hospital as he recuperated.

One of his fellow medics said, "Doc Mears was one of the first who reached out to me when I arrived in May 1968. I was placed with Charlie Co. 1/505th as the 1st Platoon medic and was trying to keep up with my end of everything. The confidence and spirit from Doc Mears helped me get through my time in the war, and I am forever grateful."

By mid-1968, Doc had turned nineteen and was the senior medic in Alpha Co. Ed Burke, one of his fellow soldiers said, "We called him 'Doc'—no one knew his first name. I was a Pfc. when I first met him, and as a typical A Co. grunt I had to walk point." That was the most dangerous place to be.

"Doc Mears would voluntarily walk point with me at night. As head company medic he wasn't required to," Burke continued. "He was supposed to be in the middle of the column of men, so he could get where he was needed as quickly as possible, but Doc was right there with me more than once. He knew the danger, but he was a good friend and had the natural courage of the brave."

In November, Mears was wounded again. During daily patrols, he walked with the lead platoon, because he assumed that was where he would be needed first, if fighting broke out. He always ran toward the action. There were four other medics, but he was the senior man. He had trained all the others, and they deferred to him. This time, he was struck by shrapnel as he tended to an injured man during a fire fight twelve miles northwest of Saigon. As the fighting raged around him—with blood streaming down the side of his face—he calmly continued to work, directing the other medics, taking care of the wounded and refusing treatment for himself until the fight was over, and all his boys were taken care of. That was Doc Mears. He had built a reputation as one of the best. Even the battalion surgeon said there was "no one better."

At the end of his first tour, Mears signed up for a second tour and went home to Virginia on thirty days leave. It was late February 1969. Daytime temperatures in Norfolk were in the mid to upper forties, with a stiff breeze coming in off Chesapeake Bay. After a year in Southeast Asia, Juddy thought it was cold, and his mother fussed about how thin he was. She was determined to put some weight back on him, and he thoroughly enjoyed having her cook all his favorite meals. He spent time with his brother, Andrew, his girlfriend and other high school friends, and especially his dad. He even deigned to don his uniform for a visit to the Norfolk Police Detective Bureau early in March, so his father could show him off and brag on him a bit. His family was so proud of what he was doing.

Shortly after his return to Vietnam, Doc Mears was back in the field and back in the middle of the action with his men. On March 24 Capt. Jack Hamilton, his commanding officer, was wounded, and Mears treated him in the field, caring for him until he could be medevaced out to a field hospital. "Mears was a very brave soldier," Hamilton said, "and a great medic. Nothing shook him up. He was unarmed, as all medics are, but wasn't afraid to do what was needed to help the soldiers in his unit."

Eight weeks later, Alpha Company was on patrol in Hậu Nghĩa Province, west of Saigon. "We couldn't patrol because of a Vietnamese holiday," Lt. Bill Culp said. "We were instructed to move into the nearest village and not be on patrol. We always had to follow the rules you know."

The company holed up in an overcrowded ARVN stockade a few miles south of Củ Chi. The fenced-in area was large enough for about fifty men, with approximately one hundred ARVN and US soldiers crammed into it for the night. The front gate was chained together, but there was a wide gap in the center of the gate when it was closed.

"We shouldn't have been in that crowded ARVN compound that night," Lt. Culp continued. "We were very vulnerable, and we weren't even dug in. Most of the men were just lying on top of the ground, and the dirt was hard as concrete."

During the night, as the soldiers slept, the compound was attacked by the Việt Công, and the quiet night erupted in total pandemonium.

"B-40 rockets came in through the gap in the gate," Culp recalled. "They hit that hard ground and exploded in all directions. Doc ran toward the wounded like he always did without any regard for his own safety."

Rockets and mortars were exploding all over the compound as the troops ran for cover. There were bodies everywhere as Mears ran into the melee. Kneeling beside one of his Airborne troopers, the young medic knelt down to assess his wounds. As he leaned forward, placing his ear against the man's chest to check for a heartbeat, another B-40 round exploded about forty feet behind him, and he pitched forward on top of the soldier. Most of the wounded were much nearer to the blast. In the darkness and ensuing chaos, no one knew Doc Mears had been hit. When the attack was over, his fellow medics found him, unconscious. At first glance, there did not appear to be any visible injury.

"The wound appeared so slight we didn't notice it at first," Ed Burke said, "but it was at the base of the brain."

Medevaced to Japan, it was initially thought Mears would recover, although he had remained unconscious. His uncle, Lloyd Mears, was working for the US Government in Japan and rushed to his nephew's bedside. From the first optimistic days, through his turn for the worse, and finally his death on May 30, Lloyd never left Juddy's side.

"No records are kept of such things," Lloyd Mears said later, "but there is no doubt that many boys are alive today for no other reason than Juddy helped them. The parents of those boys will never know of him, but they have every reason to be forever grateful to him."

In his last conscious moment, Juddy Mears was doing what he loved to do—tending to the men he was called to serve. During his fifteen months in Vietnam, Ralph Judson Mears Jr. earned three

Bronze Stars, all with "V" device for valor, two Army Commendation Medals, one with the Combat "V," three Purple Hearts, and was recommended by his commanding officer for the Distinguished Service Cross, the nation's second highest award for "extraordinary heroism." He died one month past his twentieth birthday.

Epilogue

Body Escort Detail, 1969

Spc. 5 William Locke had served in the 82nd Airborne Division in Vietnam. After completing his tour in August 1968, he returned home, reenlisted, and was again assigned to the 82nd at Ft. Bragg. The following is a portion of a letter he wrote some years later:

> "I went to 'Nam with the 1/505 3rd Brigade in February 1968 I was RTO for Lt. Col. Jamison and Major Cincotti in the Battalion Command Post. After re-enlistment, I was sent back to Bragg.
>
> "One Saturday morning after a barracks inspection, I was in a softball game, and the company clerk came with a message for me to report to the 18th Airborne Corps Headquarters that afternoon. I reported and was told to be on a flight Sunday to Oakland, California, for a body escort detail.
>
> "I arrived at Oakland and was given a few hours of instruction over two days and a small manual. I reported to San Francisco International Airport and picked up my body. I put the American flag on the casket and rode the baggage carrier with the body across the tarmac to the aircraft; removed the flag and boarded the aircraft to Chicago. At Chicago the procedure was repeated in reverse. Body was

removed from the aircraft; I put the flag on, and rode the baggage carrier across the tarmac to our next flight. I arrived at Norfolk and was met by the funeral home personnel.

"The body was put in a small room, and I positioned myself outside. When there were visitors present, I stood at parade rest at the door. I would run to the latrine, get a drink, or eat, but I never missed being there when the door to the funeral home was opened by anyone. I met the family and realized the deceased soldier was from the 3rd Brigade 82nd Airborne, my old unit. He did not have the proper medals or jump wings, so I made a trip to the PX before the funeral home opened the next day. I had the funeral home director open the casket and tried telling him how the medals and wings should go, but finally had to do it myself. I participated in the rosary, visitation, and burial services. When the color guard arrived, I instructed them on how I wanted their participation to go. The burial officer that was sent to receive the flag and present it to the family was not comfortable doing it, so I accepted the flag and presented it to the soldier's mother.

"I arrived back at Fort Bragg, and several weeks later a letter arrived to the 18th Airborne Corps, which was forwarded to me. It was from the director of the funeral home stating they had done many military funerals, but the conduct of the military personnel involved and me in particular was the best he had ever been a part of.

"Everything went the way a fellow trooper
killed in battle deserves. It is the proudest thing
I have ever done in my life."

(William Locke)

This was the funeral of Spc. 5 Ralph Judson Mears Jr. He was buried with full military honors in Norfolk's Forest Lawn Cemetery on Sunday, June 8, 1969.

In a vision of the night I saw them,
In the battles of the night.
'Mid the roar and the reeling shadows of blood
They were moving like light,
With scrutiny calm,
And with fingers patient as swift
They bind up the hurts
And the pain-writhen bodies uplift,

This light, in the tiger-mad welter,
They serve and they save.
What song shall be worthy to sing of them…
Braver than the brave?
[Medic! Medic!]

"The Healers"
—Laurence Binyon

The one-hundredth anniversary celebration of the Tidewater Council, Boy Scouts of America, was dedicated to Eagle Scout Ralph Judson Mears Jr. (October 16, 2010).

9

Christopher Joseph Schramm

Man of Steel

Christopher Schramm

Chris Schramm was one of eight children in a big, close-knit family of Pennsylvania steelworkers. He was the middle son in a group of siblings that ranged in age from thirty-three to five years old, so it would have been easy for him to fade into the background, but that was not his style. Everyone who met him knew he was a special kid. Kind and generous to a fault, his first thought his entire life was always of "the other guy," not himself.

Chris was unsure of what he wanted to do with his life. After graduating from Bishop Egan High School in 1965, he followed the family tradition and took a job with US Steel at their Fairless Works. His father, John, was a locomotive repairman there, and Chris was working in the "sheet and tin" department, but that was not the future he saw for himself. He wanted to make a difference in other people's lives. He was drawn to serve his fellow man in some way.

Chris seriously considered the priesthood and enrolled in a Catholic seminary, but it took only a few months for him to decide that was not his calling. He loved children and wanted a family of his own sometime in the future. He quit school, and believing in the US effort to stop the spread of militant communism, he enlisted in the Army in October 1965.

After exhaustive testing and very high scores, Schramm was selected for the Army Security Agency. That elite group was comprised of the top 10 percent of Army enlistees, and those fortunate enough to qualify for inclusion in the unit worked directly under the direction of the National Security Agency.

After basic training, Chris moved to Ft. Devens, Massachusetts, for specialized electronic warfare training. He was trained to operate radio direction finding (DF) equipment and employ advanced identification techniques (AIT) to recognize, identify, and locate foreign radio transmitters;. He also learned how to do basic analysis of the information obtained from the use of DF and AIT. After several months of school, he was assigned to Taiwan (then called "Nationalist China"). He served there for a year, monitoring communist military communications on the Chinese mainland, which was some 110 miles away across the Formosa Strait.

As time neared for Schramm to return to the States, he faced the same dilemma and had to make the same difficult decision as other Army Security Agency soldiers. ASA had few assignment options on the US mainland. He could return to the States, which probably meant duty in a regular Army unit or transfer to another foreign post in order to remain in ASA. In late summer 1967, a call came out for volunteers to go to Vietnam, and Chris was the first to volunteer. One of his buddies took the other slot "because Chris did." In a letter to his parents, Chris wrote, "I volunteered for Vietnam because there's a job to be done. I owe it to my family and my country to do what I can to make this a better world."

Originally assigned to a land-based unit, Schramm later transferred to the 371st Radio Research Company, ASA's direct support unit for the 1st Cavalry Division. The 371st was operating a highly classified joint project (with the 1st Cav) called "Left Bank," and he would be serving as one of the radio intercept/DF operators in the back of a Huey chopper. The operators located enemy targets by intercepting their communications and pinpointing their location using triangulation. The Hueys worked in conjunction with 1st Cav attack teams, and those operations provided Chris an opportunity few other ASA soldiers had. He could do his job and then actually see the results as the Loaches and Cobras, acting on information he and his team had provided, moved in for the kill. It was dangerous, but with Project Left Bank, Chris Schramm was on the front lines and could see firsthand the difference he was making.

On March 25, 1968, Capt. John Casey, the twenty-three-year-old commander of the 371st RRC was killed by mortar fire. The 371st had been hit several times, and after Casey's death, the decision was made to move the unit headquarters to a more secure location.

Chris had gone directly from Taiwan to Vietnam. He had been there for over six months, so he had taken no leave time for some nineteen months. He had put in for R&R and was going to fly back to Taiwan for a week to visit friends. His crew was short-handed, and he had been working long hours. They were normally scheduled for four-hour flights, but Chris had been flying eight hours a day, and he was exhausted. He desperately needed the "rest and relaxation" his leave would provide.

On May 13, the 371st convoy headed out. They were en route from Phú Bài to Camp Evans, a distance of some twenty-two miles northwest. Chris had only two days until his leave started, so he was eager to get to the new base. He wanted to get moved in to his new quarters and unpacked before he left on his trip.

He was also looking forward to his DEROS date (return from overseas). He had written a friend that he had less than six months to go, and he would be coming home. It would be two years since he had seen his family. He had really missed them, especially Tommy, his youngest brother, who was five, and his three younger sisters, Eugenia, Dorothy, and Betty Ann. He knew they had really grown up while he was gone. They would have a lot of catching up to do.

In South Vietnam, it was always a bad sign if there was no apparent activity by the local people. It indicated there was enemy activity taking place in the area by either the VC or NVA, and the locals wanted no part of any military action that might take place. As the line of trucks made its way through the countryside in Thừa Thiên Province, the road was completely deserted. There was not an ox cart, or a pedestrian, or a child anywhere in sight. It was eerily quiet—almost spooky.

Suddenly, without warning, two of the lead vehicles exploded with a loud roar. Schramm was in a vehicle toward the end of the convoy. He opened his door and stepped out to see what had happened. Dirt, rocks, and shrapnel had shot high into the air and continued to rain down on most of the other vehicles in the convoy. The lead trucks had driven into an NVA mine field sown with Soviet TM-46 mines.

Schramm could see a large plume of black smoke and fire from burning fuel. Wounded and bleeding soldiers were struggling to escape the flames in the burning vehicles amidst a loud uproar of screams, yells, and curses. The scene was total chaos.

Without any thought or concern for his own safety, Schramm went running forward to assist his fellow soldiers. As he reached the first of the destroyed vehicles, he grabbed hold of the door handle and yanked the door open, stepping back to allow the occupants to escape. There was another violent explosion, and

Schramm was thrown through the air into an adjacent rice paddy. He had stepped back onto another mine. He died instantly.

In a *Philadelphia Inquirer* article dated May 18, 1968, his father was quoted as saying, "He was to have gone on a seven-day leave to Taiwan on May 15. Another day and a half and he might have made it." The family requested their son's body be accompanied home by his cousin, Sgt. Joseph McFadden who was stationed in Japan with the US Air Force.

Chris Schramm was awarded the Bronze Star for heroism with "V" device for valor, two Air Medals with twenty Oak Leaf Clusters "for meritorious service while participating in aerial flight," and the Purple Heart. He was twenty-one years old.

One of his nieces said, "He wanted to go to Vietnam to help save other soldiers' lives. Chris lost his life when he leapt from his vehicle to go to the aid of other soldiers... His life ended way too soon and has left an emptiness in our family that is still felt today. We miss him very much."

An Army buddy said, "Chris was too good, too decent for this world, but he showed us how to live in it."

In the beauty of the lilies Christ was born across the sea,
With a glory in his bosom that transfigures you and me;
As he died to make men holy, let us die to make men free,
While God is marching on.

"Battle Hymn of the Republic"
—Julia Ward Howe

10

Oscar Palmer Austin

Honor and Sacrifice

Oscar Austin

Oscar Austin was born in Nacogdoches, Texas, on January 15, 1948, to Frank and Mildred Austin. Nacogdoches was a small, sleepy town in the eastern part of the state and claimed to be the oldest town in Texas. With a new mouth to feed and little in the way of job opportunities for a young black man, Frank made the decision to move his family. Texas was still very much a part of what was termed the "Jim Crow South" in the years following WWII, and many black families were moving farther west, hoping for a better life.

Leaving the security of a large and extended family in Nacogdoches, the Austins packed their meager belongings, and praying the old car would make the hot and dusty trip, drove some 1,200 miles to Arizona. They settled in Phoenix, which was a bustling city of over one hundred thousand people. A housing boom was underway, and there seemed to be ample opportunity for work.

By the time Oscar started school at Booker T. Washington Elementary in 1955, the traditionally black school had been desegregated for two years, primarily with Hispanic children. In most every other way, Phoenix, which was 80 percent white, 15 percent Mexican, and 5 percent black, remained racially divided. A "colored" man did not go anywhere north of Van Buren Street unless he was pushing a lawnmower or had on some type of uniform. Nearly 100 percent of the black population lived south of Van Buren in the worst housing area in the city.

Restaurants outside of the "colored" and Mexican areas served only whites, and most had signs in their windows indicating nonwhites were not welcome. The lone exceptions were the bus and train station restaurants, where black families could go and dine out. They could shop in the drug stores and department stores, such as Woolworth's Five & Dime, but their lunch counters were closed to them, and if a black person dared to sit there, he would be ignored. Public restrooms were also segregated with separate facilities for "whites" and "colored." The public swimming pools were closed to nonwhites every day but Monday, after which the pools were drained, scrubbed, and refilled for the white families to use during the coming week.

Oscar's little brother, Eddie Ray, was born in 1958, and money got even tighter. His parents continuously struggled to make ends meet financially. His father could never seem to find long-term employment, and the strain on their marriage began to take its toll.

Oscar moved on to Phoenix-Union High School in 1963 and worked whatever odd jobs he could find to help augment the family finances, but there was never enough money. Frank eventually moved out, leaving Mildred to fend for herself and the two boys.

One of his classmates said, "His family was going through a divorce; mine had gone through a divorce, so as kids we were just working a lot to help out our families. Oscar was throwing papers and working at a laundry. I was working at a grocery store just trying to make a dollar."

After graduating from high school in the spring of 1967, Oscar went to work fulltime in the laundry at the Uniform Supply Warehouse, but he wanted more of a future than Phoenix had to offer. He had watched his father struggle for as long as he could remember. He was eighteen years old. He did not want to contend with poverty and debt his entire life.

Part 2

The war in Vietnam was going full tilt with additional American forces being shipped there every few weeks. Oscar could not afford college, and without a college deferment, it was only a matter of time before he was drafted. Older friends had already been called up and were now in Vietnam, or soon would be. Considering the few options he had, Oscar talked to his mother and made the decision to enlist in the Marines. The Corps would provide him with some security and a steady income, which would allow him to help his mother and little brother.

Mildred hated to see Oscar go, but maybe the military was a way to break the cycle of poverty for him. If he liked the Marines and could make a career of it, he could rise above the financial quagmire the family had been trapped in for generations. Oscar was such a good boy. He deserved better.

Oscar enlisted in Phoenix on April 22, 1968, and the months that followed flew by in a flash. He completed recruit training with the 3rd Recruit Training Battalion at Marine Corps Recruit Depot San Diego in July. The training was tough, but Oscar had never had a problem with discipline. He was quiet and easy going, so he had little problem with the drill instructors. He respected what they were trying to do and did everything he was asked to do. He was too likeable for the DIs to hassle him for long.

Austin graduated from individual combat training in August and basic infantry training with Weapons Company, Basic Infantry Training Battalion, 2nd Infantry Training Regiment at Camp Pendleton, in September. Promoted to Private 1st Class on October 1, Austin was assigned to Company E, 2nd Battalion 7th Marines, and shipped out for Vietnam later that month.

The 2nd Battalion 7th Marines had been fighting in Vietnam since 1965, and Austin soon found himself in the middle of major fighting in Quảng Nam Province, south of Đà Nẵng. His MOS was 0341—Marine Corps Mortarman, but he was assigned to serve as an assistant M60 machine gunner, a tough and very dangerous job. Machine guns were one of the deadliest weapons in the Marine arsenal; therefore, it was always top priority for the enemy to take them out as quickly as possible.

Emphasis had been placed on counter-guerilla operations, and literally thousands of patrols and missions had been ordered. The tempo of combat increased in November with Operation DARING ENDEAVOR, twenty miles south of Đà Nẵng, followed by Operation MEADE RIVER.

There had been heavy NVA infiltration into the area, and a major attack on Đà Nẵng was expected. Đà Nẵng was the site of the northernmost major airbase for American forces in Vietnam and was located just eighty-five miles south of the DMZ, the demilitarized zone that separated the two Vietnams. The proximity to the north and its high military value meant it was subject to frequent attacks from both North Vietnamese Army and Việt Cộng forces.

Operation MEADE RIVER was a bloody affair. The operation was a "County Fair" mission, utilizing a cordon technique during which the Marines mission shifted from defense to offense. Platoons or companies cordoned off an area and searched and cleared inward, literally foot by foot. The Việt Công had infested hamlets west and south of the vital Da Nang airstrip, and they had to be rooted out. The first major contact of Operation Meade River was made on November 20 by the 2/7 Marines. While the troops were moving eastward and attempting to close in, they encountered a sizable enemy force in well-fortified positions in the bend of a small river in an area known as the "Horseshoe" A large-scale enemy force had been caught in the cordon.

On November 22, Echo Company, Oscar's unit, tried to maneuver its way across the river into the Horseshoe, but the volume of enemy fire was too heavy, and the Marines had to move back to their previous position. The 11th Marine artillery carried out precision destruction missions against the enemy positions during the remainder of the 22nd, and on the 23rd, the objective area was secured. The Horseshoe contained a multi-bunkered complex of fighting holes and trench lines that had been a battalion defensive position. Many of the bunkers had been constructed by civilians and enemy soldiers using ties removed from under the tracks of the Vietnam North-South Railroad.

After the Horseshoe was secured, the 2/7 was ordered to provide security for the engineers who were lifted in to blow the numerous bunkers and level the fortified positions. Many bodies were found in the bunkers in addition to large stocks of equipment and field gear and thousands of rounds of ammunition. Also uncovered were many sacks of lime and lime sprayers used by the enemy to sanitize and hasten the decomposition of dead bodies.

Nearly five hundred Marines were killed or wounded during the operation, but over a thousand enemy troops were killed or captured, along with seventy members of the VC leadership for the region. Major caches of enemy food, and medical supplies were also seized, and the attack on Đà Nẵng was averted.

Part 3

Oscar spent most of his free time in the Đà Nẵng area. His best friends were nineteen-year-old Lance Corporal Douglas Payne and Corporal John Chu, their squad leader. Oscar had never known a white man before joining the Corps. He had worked for a few, had encounters with a few, but he had never actually known one and had certainly never had one for a friend until he met Doug Payne.

Chu was of Asian descent, so the three made an interesting ethnic combination. Payne and Chu were both Southern Californians, and their social backgrounds were totally foreign to Oscar. Chu was from Woodland Hills, an affluent community in the San Fernando Valley, and Payne was from Spring Valley, just east of San Diego. What had brought them together was their mutual love for the Vietnamese children and their joint efforts to help a local Catholic orphanage.

"Oscar was a very low-key person," Chu said with a smile. "Physically he wasn't a big guy, but he was outgoing, even after a hard day of hiking." Oscar was just a great guy to be around.

Austin's unit did not see much action over Christmas week. He and his compatriots put up a Christmas tree for the children in the orphanage. They wrapped gifts in bright paper for each of the youngsters, which were delivered by a red-clad and white-whiskered Oscar. He arrived on Christmas morning in a decorated jeep with his huge red bag of toys, and the kids squealed with delight. Oscar and Doug cavorted and roughhoused with them for most of the day. The Marines supplied candy for the kids, and the nuns caring for them provided pitchers of tart lemonade.

It was a warm and sunny day—a good day—but Oscar really missed his mother and little brother. There was never much money for Christmas presents at home, but "Mama" had him and Eddie at South Phoenix Baptist Church for candlelight services on Christmas Eve and again Christmas day. They did not need money to celebrate Christmas; all they needed was family and lots of love.

On January 15, Oscar's buddies took him to one of the local watering holes for a surprise birthday party. He was celebrating his twenty-first birthday, so it was considered a major event. Oscar was officially and legally "a man." The more his friends had to drink, the funnier they seemed to think that was. Of course, everything eventually became hilarious. Oscar, who was not a drinker, simply sat and watched most of the evening with a bemused look on his face. He had received a letter from "Mama" that day, wishing him "happy birthday" and thanking him for money he had sent her in a Christmas card. He felt happier and more content than he had most of the days of his life.

Part 4

For the next month, Austin's company participated in routine patrols and day-to-day counter-guerilla operations. The Marines did not encounter large numbers of the enemy, although there was little doubt the usual NVA infiltration was taking place.

Early on the morning of February 23, Echo Company was in the field some 6.5 miles west of Đà Nẵng. The unit was part of the security cordon surrounding the city and its bases. John Chu's squad was manning an observation post, and his Marines were dug into fighting holes along a low ridge. Oscar Austin, serving in his usual capacity as ammunition man and assistant machine gunner was dug in with Lance Corporal Joe Ramsey and his M60. Doug Payne was some twenty yards down the slope in another fighting hole.

It had rained off and on during the night, and the heavy air was almost cool as the day dawned. It was Sunday morning. Wisps of ground fog were beginning to lift as a slight breeze stirred the tall grass to the rear of their position, and hundreds of birds in nearby trees were singing and squawking. There was a small stream nearby, and Oscar could hear frogs croaking loudly. He liked hearing the natural sounds. He had rarely heard such sounds while growing up in the shantytown south of Van Buren Street in Phoenix. These foreign sounds symbolized freedom to him, and he looked forward to the new life he anticipated for himself and his family when he returned to the World in November. He would then have two years stateside to decide if he wanted to re-enlist and remain in the Corps.

Suddenly the morning stillness was shattered by a loud explosion, and that was followed by a barrage of even louder explosions as the entire area was besieged by a flood of hand grenades, satchel charges, and heavy small arms fire. A fierce ground attack had been launched by a large NVA force that had quietly infiltrated the area during the night. The North Vietnamese hoped to overwhelm the American positions with the element of surprise and the massive onslaught of grenades. The Marines began to return fire into the trees and brush surrounding the ridge, but saw very little to shoot at. The enemy was well concealed in the dense undergrowth.

As Austin fed ammo into his partner's M60 machine gun, he saw from the corner of his eye, a grenade explode, and Doug Payne was blown out of his fighting hole. Oscar could see some movement, but the youngster was obviously injured, probably unconscious, and was lying in a very vulnerable position. The grenade had landed near Payne and detonated before he could get away.

"I was forced to the ground in a state somewhere between consciousness and total blackout. I had head wounds, and I couldn't hear a thing, but I could still see to a point," Payne said later, recalling the incident.

Austin saw his buddy in trouble and, exposing himself to the barrage of enemy fire sweeping the area, jumped out of the comparative safety of his fighting hole and sprinted toward his friend. Grabbing him by the shoulders, Austin quickly dragged him into a nearby sandbagged bunker and began to tend to his wounds.

Then another grenade landed close to Payne on the other side of the bunker. Without hesitation, Austin threw himself across the bunker, placing his body between the grenade and Payne.

There was a deafening roar as the grenade exploded, and Austin was seriously wounded.

"After the grenade exploded, his abdomen was a bloody mess," Payne said.

Dragging himself to his feet, bleeding heavily and in great pain, Austin moved back to Payne, checking his wounds and attempting to move him deeper into the bunker where he would be better protected.

At that moment, a North Vietnamese soldier appeared at the top of the bunker and aimed his weapon at Payne. Realizing there was no way he could reach the attacker, Oscar jumped and sprawled across Doug Payne's body, taking the bullets meant for his friend.

"I started yelling for a corpsman," Payne said, "but I couldn't tell if anyone could hear me, because I couldn't hear."

When the corpsman arrived, it was evident nothing could be done for Austin, so Payne was placed under better cover.

The entire squad had witnessed Oscar's heroic acts, which had lasted only a few short minutes, and fought even harder to beat off the NVA attack. The company counterattacked and the enemy troops melted into the misty countryside. The fog had moved back in and drizzle began to fall as Chu and his squad stepped out of their fighting holes. One by one, the Marines surrounded the body of Oscar Austin, but no one spoke. They had no words.

Doug Payne was fully conscious and being tended to by a Navy corpsman. Fighting back tears, he struggled to understand why Oscar had chosen to die for him. "I will always be haunted by doubt," he said, "that my life was worth the sacrifice of his."

Part 5

In Phoenix, Mildred and Eddie Ray Austin were broken-hearted. Oscar had become Mildred's rock, the one she could always depend on, and Eddie idolized his older brother. As she struggled to grasp the reality of his death, Mildred made the decision to move back to Texas—back to the security of her family. There was nothing keeping her in Phoenix. It was time to return home to Nacogdoches.

When Douglas Payne returned to the States at the end of his tour a few months later, he was unprepared for the welcome he received. He walked into the terminal in Los Angeles wearing his Marine dress blues and was immediately besieged by antiwar protesters, spitting on him and calling him "baby killer." He caught a bus from LA to San Diego to visit his sister before going on home. He called her house from the bus terminal, but there was no answer.

She was not home. Unwilling to face more ridicule from his fellow countrymen, he remained within the secure confines of the phone booth until he was finally able to contact her—six hours later.

On April 20, 1970, Mildred and Eddie Austin were quietly ushered into the White House in Washington, DC, and in a special ceremony, a citation was read:

"The President of the United States of America, in the name of Congress, takes pride in presenting the Medal of Honor to Private 1st Class Oscar Palmer Austin, United States Marine Corps, for conspicuous gallantry and intrepidity at the risk of his life above and beyond the call of duty."

Epilogue

Honor and Sacrifice

Twenty-eight years later, on November 7, 1998, Mildred Austin was the "matron of honor" for the launch of the USS *Oscar Austin*, a state-of-the-art Aegis Guided Missile destroyer. It was a proud day for Mrs. Austin as she watched the ceremonies and listened to the high-ranking dignitaries as they honored her son. Five weeks later, she passed away in Nacogdoches—December 14, 1998.

On August 19, 2000, the ship was commissioned in ceremonies at its homeport in Norfolk, Virginia. A crowd of over two thousand people attended the event, including a couple of special guests: Oscar's Marine buddies, Doug Payne (a retired Navy lieutenant) and John Chu.

"It is a bittersweet trip for me," Payne said. "I am so proud they finally got around to honoring my friend, and I am so saddened... that it is in death that he will be honored. He gave his life for me. It is a debt I can never repay in this life. Our association and our deep friendship were all too brief. John and I tried to find some of the others, so they could come too, but most of them are with Oscar now, or just could not bring themselves to face such an emotional event. Oscar was a Marine through and through, but he was a loyal and loving friend above that.

"The first time I met any of Oscar's family I was feeling guilty," Payne recalls. "Oh yeah, and I could see where his family would feel that I wasn't worth him giving his life for me."

"Rest assured I still remember the kids at the orphanage. We never knew for sure, but they probably joined Oscar in death that same day, thanks to the VC," Payne said wistfully.

Unbeknownst to John Chu and his squad on the ridge that foggy morning in 1969, elements of the Việt Cộng and North Vietnamese Army had launched a second major Tet offensive against US and South Vietnamese forces. More than 110 targets throughout Vietnam were struck that morning. The 2nd NVA Division supported by Việt Cộng Sappers initiated the offensive in and around Đà Nẵng. NVA and VC units had infiltrated the area during the night and supported the main attack that was launched from south of the city at daybreak.

After fighting off the initial NVA attack, Echo Company had been ordered back to help defend the city and its bases, as soon as weather permitted. The enemy forces had launched a mortar and rocket attack on the fuel and ammunition storage facilities, and some areas of the city were in flames.

The Navy corpsmen had taken Doug Payne to a field hospital on the outskirts of the city to have him checked out, despite his protests. From that vantage point, he could see the area where the orphanage was located. It appeared, through the misty drizzle, to be one of the hardest hit locations with occasional explosions and billowing black smoke. He begged the doctors to let him go check out the orphanage, but they were too busy with a steady influx of wounded to talk to him. It was two days later before he was able to make the trip to the orphanage, and he found only a burned out shell of a building. He never determined if any of the children or nuns survived the attack.

"I think we gave them some joy in the little time we had with them," Payne said. "No one would listen when I tried to get help to save them, but God, I tried. I hope that counts for something."

As part of the commissioning ceremony for the *Oscar Austin*, the "spirit" of Pfc. Austin was piped aboard the ship, and the sailors among her crew believe it will reside aboard the DDG-79, watching over them and protecting them in the years ahead.

The *Oscar Austin* was the twenty-ninth of fifty-one Arleigh Burke Class destroyers authorized by Congress. The high-tech Aegis Guided Missile destroyer was first deployed in 2002 in the opening strikes of Operation IRAQI FREEDOM. The ship's motto is "Honor and Sacrifice."

As Doug Payne goes about his daily life, he takes Oscar with him.

"To this day I think he's always been with me," says Payne. "It's just amazing that someone cared enough to do what he did. He expected no less of me, of course, and I would have done the same for him. That's the way it was in Vietnam."

During Payne's days as a teacher, he often toured prisons and spoke to inmates, telling them stories of his days in Vietnam.

"I used to spend a lot of time talking to gangbangers and inmates, and they'd tell me about their friends who'd gotten them in trouble. They'd always use the excuse, well, he's my friend. But soon I'd have those tough convicts in tears as I told them my story.

"I'd tell them about Vietnam," Payne says. "I'd tell them about a friend of mine named Oscar."

A smile or a tear has not nationality;
Joy and sorrow speak alike to all nations,
And they, above all the confusion of tongues,
Proclaim the brotherhood of man.

"Composite Nation"
—Frederick Douglass

In addition to the USS *Oscar Austin*, memorials were erected in Texas and Arizona. Austin Hall, the Enlisted Club at Marine Base Quantico, Virginia, was named in his honor, and a section of Texas State Highway 21 was named the Oscar P. Austin Highway.

11

Joseph Andrew Matejov

Killed on Paper

Joseph Matejov

For some families patriotism is ingrained, a tradition, a way of life. A prime example was the Matejov family. Following the end of World War I, the Austro-Hungarian Empire collapsed. Joe Matejov's grandfather, Frank, had attained high military rank at a young age in an army that would soon be disbanded. The Czechoslovak First Republic emerged from the chaos, but jobs were few, and inflation was rampant. Wanting to start a family and seeking a better future, Frank Matejov and his wife, Veronica, immigrated to the United States. They settled in a Czech neighborhood on the East Side of New York City. That is where their son Stephen was born on New Year's Day 1925.

Frank and Veronica saved enough money to purchase a neighborhood bar, and Stephen, Joe Matejov's father, was reared within that insular Czech community. English was rarely spoken at home; therefore, young Stephen started public school with a thick "foreign" accent, which belied his US birth.

Highly intelligent and driven to succeed, Stephen graduated from Immaculata High School in Manhattan with honors. The year was 1942, and the war in Europe and the Pacific was raging. Feeling the pull of the family's military tradition, the young man wanted to attend the US Military Academy at West Point, but he was only seventeen years old. Not wanting to lose his academic edge, he attended Fordham University for a year, and then applied for appointment to the Academy. With high school medals for mathematics and science and letters in several sports, Matejov received his appointment quickly and was not required to take an entrance examination.

On July 1, 1943, Steve Matejov entered West Point, and his life changed forever. Life as a plebe was intentionally difficult for everyone, but for Matejov, it was a living hell. As the war in Europe intensified and the number of American casualties climbed, xenophobia reared its ugly head. Matejov's thick Czech accent and limited cultural experience made him the target of those upperclassmen who were determined to break his spirit and see the "kraut" wash out. The young man suffered extreme physical and mental abuse during "Beast Barracks," the two-month "introduction" to the Academy, and that was followed by nine months of plebe hazing and harassment.

Meals were particularly trying because plebes were required to sit at a brace during meals. They had to sit on the front half of their chairs with their backs absolutely straight and their chins tucked in making it very difficult to eat. Harassment during mealtime was frowned on by the administration, but it occurred nevertheless. Cadet officers, who were assigned to monitor such behavior, walked by staring straight ahead. What they did not see, they could not report. And all of it was exacerbated by the unexpected death of Steve Matejov's father midway through that first terrible year. He was determined, however, not to let the bullies win and survived by sheer grit and good humor. He needed to show his mother he could succeed and graduate with his commission.

He immersed himself in the academics, especially the sciences where he excelled. He even found time to help other plebes, including his roommate. In 1946, Matejov graduated as a 2nd lieutenant in the Coast Artillery Corps, US Army.

Matejov completed the Basic Artillery Courses at Fort Sill, Oklahoma, and Fort Bliss, Texas, and paratroop training in 1947. He was assigned to an artillery battalion in Korea and after a year moved to Japan to serve as a battery officer with the 865th AAA Battalion. He married Mary Stacher in Alameda, California, on July 24, 1948. Mary was a former USO hostess with a yen for adventure and travel. She had camped in the California wilderness, shot Class 6 rapids, and loved to see a handsome man in uniform. Steve returned to Japan with his new bride, and in 1950 they welcomed their first child, a daughter named Anne.

When the Korean War broke out, Matejov's unit was deployed to Korea and Mary returned to California. Their first son, Stephen Jr. was born there in 1951. Steve's battery was attached to the 17th Infantry as it fought north to the Yalu. On November 17, 1950, elements of the 17th Infantry routed North Korean forces at Sogu-ri, and Steve earned a Silver Star for "gallantry in action against an armed enemy."

The summer of 1951 saw Steve and Mary return to Fort Sill, Oklahoma. He attended the Artillery Advanced Course, and they welcomed their second son, Joseph Andrew, on 2 February 1952. From there Steve was stationed in Pennsylvania and then moved on to Germany in 1953. After being assigned to two more artillery units, Steven Matejov's military career took a major shift in direction when he was assigned as operations officer with the 532nd Military Intelligence Battalion. The 532nd MIB was part of an integrated three-sided team composed of US armored cavalry, West German border police, and US Army military intelligence (which provided liaison between the first two). The team screened refugees who entered the US Zone and patrolled along the communist border to "observe" East German and Czechoslovak border security installations. The foreign language capability of the MI units included Russian, German, Czech, French, Polish, Hungarian, Bulgarian, and Rumanian. The units gathered most of their positive intelligence information about Eastern Bloc countries through almost daily liaison with the West German border police and the interrogation of refugees who managed to survive as they made their way across the border. Steven Matejov was finally making use of his Czech language skills.

The Matejov's first five children were born on military bases in Japan, California, Oklahoma, Pennsylvania, and Germany. In 1956, the family returned to the US and settled down in Steve's home state. He was stationed at Ft. Totten, New York, until his retirement from active duty in 1961.

Part 2

Joe Matejov was four years old when his family moved back to the States in 1956. The boy had never lived in one place much longer than a year. His little brother, John, had been born near Pittsburgh, Pennsylvania, and his sister, Kate, in Germany. He would see the arrival of five more brothers and sisters in New York State over the next few years.

Of his nine siblings, Joe was closest to his brother, John. "He was a year older," John said. "We were best friends, but we also competed, both physically and academically, whenever we had the chance.

"He always had me physically," John continued. "He could outrun me, and he would tackle me all the time in games of football. But I always seemed to have the upper hand, just marginally, in academics. I remember our retailing class in high school. I sat in front of him, so when we got our tests back, I always got one or two points above him. I got to see his scores because he sat behind me, and I passed the tests back over my head. It made him so angry. One day he didn't show up for class, and the teacher informed me he had dropped the class. He hadn't bothered to tell me."

The Vietnam War began, and Mary Matejov supported the war effort. She picketed the concerts of Joan Baez and other anti-war activists with Joseph, John, and the other children firmly in tow. The boys thought it was great fun and thoroughly enjoyed the outings. They did not understand what was going on, but the entire family was brought up to believe in God, country, and the US military. That had been the family mantra their entire life.

In his teens, Joe discovered girls, and more importantly, girls discovered him. Strikingly handsome, athletic and popular, the young man enjoyed a busy social life. His older brother, Steven Jr. delighted in teasing him.

"Joe was a womanizer," Steven said with a laugh. "All he had to do was stop running. The girls were always after him. He would stand in front of the mirror combing his hair until it was just right. Every hair had to be in place. His clothes always had to be perfect, too. He was worse than any of my sisters," he continued, shaking his head with a smile.

"Joe and I shared many rites of passage growing up," John said. "I can't begin to tell you all the mischief we got into. Most of the time we didn't get caught."

"Joe and John were always going out together," Steven said, laughing. "They would sneak out of the house at night. A friend would climb onto the roof, knock on their bedroom window, and they would take off with him.

"Joe was a daredevil," Steven continued. "He and John would swing from branch to branch in a tree down near our church, St. Raphael's. They'd pretend to be hurt when they finally landed on the ground. Then, when there were enough people around, they'd jump up, run off, and have a big laugh over it."

After graduating from East Meadow High School in the spring of 1970, Joe became the second of the Matejov children to enter the military. Steve Jr. was already in the Navy.

"Joe and a friend had planned to join the Marines together, but the friend backed out, so Joe enlisted in the Air Force," John said. "I enlisted in the Marine Corps to prove to myself I could do something physically Joe had chosen not to do."

Part 3

Joe shipped out for hot and steamy San Antonio, Texas, in July 1970. During basic training at Lackland Air Force Base young Matejov was subjected to an intensive battery of tests. He was never told what he was being tested for, but after graduating from basic, he was informed he had been selected for Air Force Security Service. He would never know what it was like to be in the "real" Air Force after he left Lackland.

Security Service airmen were meticulously culled from tens of thousands of Air Force recruits and comprised the top half of the top one percent of enlistees. USAFSS was a tight-knit, top-secret command which operated under the direct authority of the National Security Agency (NSA). Its members had the highest security clearances issued by the US Government (TOP SECRET CRYPTOLOGIC—"Code Word") and were tasked with monitoring, collecting and interpreting ELINT—the electronic military communications of "countries of interest." The intelligence which USAFSS operatives collected was often analyzed in the field. The results were then transmitted directly to NSA for further analysis and distributed to other intelligence recipients who had "the need to know."

Joe Matejov departed San Antonio early on a Friday morning in late September. The newly-minted "airman" was en route to Keesler Air Force Base in Biloxi, Mississippi, where he would undergo 292/Morse Code Intercept training, better known as "Ditty Bop School." Arriving late that evening, he was assigned a bunk in the transient barracks and was free to do whatever he wanted for the weekend—no directions, no restrictions, and no sergeants telling him what he could and could not do. After two months of basic training, it was like being sprung from prison. Changing into civilian clothes, he went to the airmen's club, drank a few 3.2 beers, and met some of the other newly arrived airmen. The base was within walking distance of the beach, so he divided his time between beach and bar all weekend—not a bad way to start his tour.

On Monday he was directed to the 3478th School Squadron. His class was not starting for three weeks, so he was assigned to the Personnel Awating Training Flight, which really sucked. He and his fellow PATs had to report to formations three times a day, at which time they were assigned whatever lousy details the First Sergeant could come up with to keep them busy and out of trouble. Joe spent a week on KP before being saved by the bell. School started, and he began to learn Morse code and basic typing. Fortunately, he knew how to touch type, so that was to his advantage.

Weekends were still free, and Joe spent as much time as possible outside the barracks. The wooden buildings were WWII-era open-bay barracks with no air-conditioning, and the weather along the Gulf Coast remained hot well into the fall months. Some of his buddies had cars, so he had the opportunity to get off base and enjoyed weekend excursions to New Orleans, Gulfport, and Mobile.

Morse school was easy for Matejov, and he finished near the top of his class of dittyboppers. Graduating in the spring of 1971, he headed back to Texas. He would undergo technical training at the only Security Service base on US soil—Goodfellow Air Force Base in San Angelo, Texas.

San Angelo was a great town. The local citizenry was much friendlier toward airmen than the "locals" in Biloxi. With hundreds of USAFSS retirees living in the area, the community took pride in referring to itself unofficially as the "Home of Spies" and enjoyed a warm relationship with Goodfellow and its contingent of several thousand Air Force personnel.

Upon completion of his training, Joe headed home for thirty days leave. His buddies had assignments all over the world:

Karamursel in Turkey; Oona Point on Okinawa; Peshawar Air Base, Pakistan; Darmstadt, Germany; Shemya Air Force Base, Alaska; Shu Lin Kou Air Station on Taiwan; Clark Air Base in the Philippines; and RAF Chicksands, near Bedford, England. When his leave was over, Matejov departed for the 6921st Security Group, Misawa Air Base, Japan.

Joe served at Security Hill in Misawa from 1971 through the spring of 1972. During that time he earned the nickname "Kiwi." According to Mike Kallin who worked with Matejov on Dawg Flight, "Joe had a well-earned reputation for being the sharpest-looking airman in the unit."

Joe's spit-shined boots always looked like mirrors, and some of his fellow airmen created the "Kiwi Award," a "medal" fashioned from a purple "Crown Royal" whiskey bag and the lid from a can of Kiwi shoe polish. There was a big "Purple Jesus" party in the barracks one night, and the medal was presented to Joe "Kiwi" Matejov, the sharpest man in the 6921st SG.

On 12 April 1972, Matejov volunteered for an assignment to Detachment 2, 6994th Security Squadron at Da Nang Air Base, Vietnam. The 6994th air crews flew in unarmed WWII-era EC-47 aircraft. Using top secret electronics surveillance and communications intercept, the unit operated in support of ground combat commanders. Their motto was "Unarmed—Alone—Unafraid."

As a result of their work, many attacks on friendly forces were averted or mitigated, and it has been reported 80 to 90 percent of the B-52 attacks in Vietnam were based all or in part on information collected by the 6994th and Army Security Agency aircrews. The 6994th was one of the most highly decorated squadrons in the history of Air Force Security Service, which is remarkable considering most of their activities held the highest level of security classification, and few people knew about their exploits.

A few months later, Matejov was reassigned to Detachment 3, 6994th Security Squadron at Ubon Royal Thai Air Base, Thailand. He had been promoted to sergeant and was serving as part of an aircrew tracking the movement of communist troops and equipment along the Ho Chi Minh Trail.

By February 1973, Joe Matejov had turned twenty-one. He had been deployed in the war zone for ten months, and his tour was wrapping up. He had nearly one hundred combat missions under his belt, several Air Medals already earned, and a Distinguished Flying Cross in the pipeline. He had been home on leave in November and was ready to get back to the World permanently. He had seen enough of Asia to last him a lifetime.

The Matejovs had been so proud when Joe was accepted into the ranks of the elite "for-your-eyes-only/need-to-know" ranks of Air Force Security Service. Lt. Col. Matejov was familiar with the top-secret unit from his days in military intelligence and knew getting into Security Service was a million-to-one shot. It confirmed to him just how special his son was. Joe cut a dashing figure with a shoulder holster and a penchant for disappearing on hush-hush military-intelligence forays. Steve and Mary were thrilled to see Joe between assignments. He would come jetting into LaGuardia Airport on courier runs with a briefcase of classified material handcuffed to his wrist and catch an air shuttle on to DC and NSA headquarters at Ft. Meade, Maryland.

"The last time I saw Joe at the airport in New York, I had a bad feeling," Mary said. "It was a strange premonition I had never had before. He only had fifty-six days left in the Air Force, but my gut told me he would not complete his tour."

The Vietnam War was declared over on January 27, 1973. Back home, the Matejovs, and the families of thousands of other servicemen and women still serving in Southeast Asia celebrated the war's end with a sense of great relief, but top-secret US spy planes continued to fly. The covert missions, flown over countries Pres. Nixon never talked about, were operated to ensure the communists were keeping their part of the peace agreement that had been struck in Paris.

Anticipating the cease-fire, the Pathet Lao, the communist guerrilla forces in Laos, had attacked government positions in three key Laotian towns. Communist forces in Laos were under the firm control of Hanoi and the North Vietnamese Army, which was keeping them well supplied with Chinese and Russian arms and ammunition.

Joe Matejov

At 11:05 p.m. on February 4, eight days after the official end of the war, Joe Matejov's EC-47Q, call sign "Baron-52," taxied out onto the runway at Ubon Air Base. The Security Service team's mission was to conduct aerial and electronic surveillance to confirm the location of NVA tanks and trucks which Project IGLOO WHITE indicated were moving down the Ho Chi Minh Trail toward Kontum and Pleiku.

The critical but elusive nature of targets along the Ho Chi Minh Trail had prompted the Department of Defense to apply new technology to the interdiction problem. The IGLOO WHITE program employed a network of remote sensors and surveillance systems. The most reliable was the air-delivered seismic intrusion detector (ADSID), which resembled a lawn dart. Dropped from aircraft, the antenna was the only part of the sensor that was visible after it drilled into the ground, and that was camouflaged to resemble the stalks of weeds. An Air Force officer said, "We wire the Ho Chi Minh trail like a drugstore pinball machine, and we plug it in every night."

Those aboard Baron-52 belonged to two distinct units. The flight crew or "frontenders" were from the 361st Tactical Electronic Warfare Squadron based at Nakhon Phanom, but detached to

Ubon, Thailand. They were Capt. George R. Spitz, pilot; Capt. Arthur R. Bollinger, navigator; 1st Lt. Robert E. Bernhardt, co-pilot; and 2nd Lt. Severo J. Primm, III, co-pilot.

The intelligence crew or "backenders" were from Detachment 3, 6994th Security Squadron. They were S. Sgt. Todd Melton, voice system operator; Sgt. Joseph Matejov, airborne mission supervisor and Morse system operator; Sgt. Peter Cressman, Morse system operator; and Sgt. Dale Brandenburg, Bravo maintenance technician.

The aircraft was flying at a lofty ten thousand feet as the airmen monitored the communications of the convoy of North Vietnamese vehicles which were moving south toward the tri-border area joining Laos, Cambodia, and South Vietnam. Security Service flight crews had recently begun flying at the higher altitude to avoid artillery fire; however, parachutes were packed, and each crewmember carried a survival radio preset to an emergency frequency, just in case. The night missions had all taken ground fire. Some had even come back early because of the amount of fire they were taking, but it was still unusual for one of the aircraft to suffer damage.

The flight had left US radar coverage as it moved into Laotian air space, but the airborne command & control center, call sign "Moonbeam ABCCC," was up and circling in the night sky over Laos. The skies over southern Laos were busy that night—another Baron aircraft (Baron-62), "Spectre 20," an AC-130 gunship, three F4 aircraft, and perhaps others were in the air over southern Laos during Baron-52's mission. Baron-52 contacted command & control by radio every twenty minutes with a status update.

At 1:25 a.m. Capt. Spitz reported Baron-52 was encountering AAA antiaircraft fire, but had sustained no damage. At 1:30 a.m., the captain reported in again and said everything was "normal." At 1:40 a.m., Baron-52 reported it had been fired on by radar controlled AAA guns at a location about sixty nautical miles northeast of Attapu (Attapeu). The aircraft was almost directly over the main north-south corridor of the Ho Chi Minh Trail. That was the last contact command & control had with Baron-52. At 2:00 a.m.,

Baron-52 failed to report in. A communications and electronics search began immediately. Moonbeam ABCCC, two ground stations, and other aircraft in the area tried to contact Baron-52 on various frequencies and other radio channels, but to no avail.

Baron-52 had in fact been downed by enemy fire over Saravane (Salavan) Province, Laos, about fifty miles east of the town of Saravane (Salavan). It was approximately twenty miles west of the Lao/South Vietnamese border. An air search & rescue mission was launched over southern Laos at dawn, and four days later, the crash site was found, buried deep in hundred-foot-tall bamboo and triple-canopy jungle.

After Baron-52 was located, an Air Force Special Operations team was dispatched to the crash site. It was just after daybreak, and a US Air Force HH-3E "Jolly Green Giant" helicopter hovered over a steep and rugged Laotian hillside. The pilot could barely see any sign of the wreckage through the mist and broken bamboo below as three Air Force pararescuemen (also known as PJs) and an intelligence expert, Tech. Sgt. Ronald Schofield, were lowered to the ground. The area was extremely hostile, so the men worked quickly. Their chopper had encountered AAA gunfire, and been targeted by a surface-to-air missile as they neared the crash site. Two North Vietnamese Army bases were only a few miles away.

"When we got there two of the PJs set up a perimeter," Schofield said. "The third PJ and I were looking for bodies." Sgt. Schofield was also there to ensure all top-secret Security Service equipment and materials were located and destroyed.

The EC-47 had hit the top of a jungle-covered hill, flipped over on its back and plunged down the steep hillside. Crashing through the dense jungle growth and tall bamboo, both wings had been sheared off. Part of the tail section was atop the hill. The rear of the plane where Matejov and his team had worked was badly damaged due to the fire that had ensued from ruptured fuel tanks after the crash.

The bodies of the flight crew members were visible in their "Nomex" (fire retardant) flight suits in the front of the aircraft, but the team was only able to recover the partial remains of co-pilot

Bernhardt, which had been partially ejected from the wreckage. The pararescuemen had no means of lifting the inverted fuselage or recovering the rest of the frontend crew during their brief forty minutes at the site. They saw no other bodies in or near the crash site. What they found was consistent with the SOP (Standard Operating Procedures), which stated the frontend crew should ride the plane in, if possible, and the enlisted personnel in the back should bail out.

There was no sign of the backend crew in the wreckage. "There should have been some remains of the backenders in the fire, but there wasn't anything," Schofield said later, "there was absolutely nothing."

The search-and-rescue report found no evidence of survivors. However, Schofield remembered a clue in the burnt fuselage that pointed to crewmembers escaping through a rear door. "These aircraft flew with the doors on. If that aircraft had crashed with the door on, there would have been some of it left at the crash site" where the plane had burned, he said. "It was gone. It looked like it had been kicked off."

On February 13, 1973, a. week after the crash, Joe Matejov's wing commander, Col. Francis Humphreys, wrote a letter to Steve and Mary Matejov.

"After careful consideration, I feel there is a possibility one or more crew members could have parachuted to safety," the colonel wrote, "therefore, your son will continue to be carried in a missing status until a final determination can be made."

Over the next week, pressure mounted from the families of the missing men over the MIA status. They wanted progress in finding the airmen. A cable from Air Force command to Humphreys on February 21 said the father of one of the missing men had contacted their office after receiving "your letter about possible survivors." Air Force command wanted the issue resolved as quickly as possible.

The release and return of almost six hundred American prisoners of war by the North Vietnamese was hanging in the balance. Many of the POWs were Air Force pilots, and Air Force command wanted no complications.

A few days later, Humphreys sent a second letter to the Matejovs and other crew families. With no new evidence, the commander had reversed his opinion and listed Matejov and the others as killed in action. "A careful review of all available facts has been made," the colonel said, "there is no reasonable doubt that there were no survivors."

"We did employ a certain amount of conjecture in trying to visualize the events as they took place," Humphreys wrote. "However, we made logical assumptions based on all the available facts and information. The Baron-52 flight was blown out of the air suddenly, leaving no time for escape. The high-tech equipment on the EC-47 and the crew's survival radios were key to this determination. The airmen never made contact again in the moments and days after the crash. The intensive training of all flying personnel makes it improbable that at least one of the crew members would not have instinctively transmitted on one of the many pieces of communication equipment available in case of an emergency, unless all were immediately and completely incapacitated."

The letter was met with enough doubt and frustration from the families that the colonel wrote to them a third time in March. Humphreys denied his decision was premature or lacked sound basis. "I believe the search-and-rescue evidence showed no one could have escaped the crash," he wrote.

The Air Force Report of Casualty on each of the airmen states: "Held to have been MIA from 5 February 73 to 22 February 73, the date of receipt of evidence in HQ USAF that the above named person could not have survived."

Part 4

Within hours of the "Baron-52" downing, analysts in Room 7A119 of the National Security Agency at Fort Meade, Maryland, were on alert. Four NSA listening posts near Laos, other spy planes in the area, and ground-based electronic surveillance sites had all intercepted NVA communications about the crash.

According to declassified NSA reports. North Vietnamese officials, transmitting in code, reported their soldiers were "holding four pilots captive" in the vicinity of the crash. This was soon after the downing. There were also references to "four pirates" being moved north and another message that stated: "The people involved in the south Laotian campaign have shot down one aircraft and captured the pilots." US intelligence analysts said North Vietnamese interchangeably used the terms "pilots" and "pirates" to characterize US fliers of any rank.

Capt. Lionel Blau was serving as operations officer in the 6994th Security Squadron at the time of the Baron-52 crash. He was skeptical of the push for KIA status and pressed Humphreys to look into the intercept. "I went in and simply told the colonel, 'Please do not make a decision until we can get straightened out what this intelligence is about,'" Blau said.

On May 24, 1973, Roger Shields, assistant to the assistant secretary of defense, and Henry Kissinger's point man on the POW/MIA issue for the recently signed Paris Peace Accords, wrote an internal memo that reads, "DIA (Defense Intelligence Agency) feels there is some reason to believe the four may actually have been captured.

"My chief concern is that the KIA determination was wrong. Nobody at the time this decision was made could have said without any question that these men were dead. During the Vietnam War, the military often classified troops as missing in action," Shields continued, "and assumed further effort might bring them back alive, even when the facts indicated otherwise. Troops were rated MIA even when witnesses saw their aircraft go down with an intact canopy, and no rescue beacon was activated. We just saw too many cases where it looked like the chances of survival were not that good but it turned out that people did survive."

Finally, according to Robert Wilhelm, a former security analyst with the 6994th, members of the squadron received a message from a "usually reliable Laotian friendly," who had reported seeing "four, clean-shaven Americans in flight suits," being led through the Laotian jungle by North Vietnamese soldiers one day after the crash. The families of the missing crewmen were not told any of this.

Jerry Mooney, an NSA analyst, was in Room 7A119 at Ft. Meade when Baron-52 was shot down. Mooney was one of several analysts who read the messages. He said the first message was heard after the plane went down and while none of the NVA reports referred specifically to Baron-52, "There was no other plane shot down that day, and the code systems they were using pertained only to that area.

"I personally wrote the message that these men had been captured alive, that they were Americans and had been transported to North Vietnam. In secure phone conversations with the DIA, we were in total agreement that these were the crew members of the EC-47Q.

"The report of the messages was signed off on by the other analysts who were present and sent to the Defense Intelligence Agency and the White House," Mooney concluded.

In the days following the crash, there was a flurry of additional messages with reference to the Baron-52 crash. A 6994th Security Squadron communiqué stated its belief that "crew members could have bailed out and possibly been carried north by the winds." Air Force headquarters in Nakhon Phanom, Thailand, suggested: "There is a chance crew members bailed out and landed safely on the ground. There is no conclusive evidence of death."

For five years there was no doubt for the Matejov family, just grief. From 1973 to 1978 they never questioned what they had been told. They believed the airmen were all dead.

"We believed in God and country, and we believed God and country had taken our son," Steve Matejov said. "We were a military family. We closed ranks and went on with our lives."

The family had a military memorial service at the urging of the Air Force, and the Air Force provided all the rights and courtesies afforded any family that has lost a son or daughter in battle. An official color guard was present at the service.

Mary packed up all of Joe's clothing and gave it away; she burned a calendar he had made with all the family birthdays, because it was too painful to look at. They cried, they prayed, and they cried some more. Gradually the family came to accept Joe's death. Then in August 1978 everything changed.

It was a bright sunny morning. Mary Matejov was sipping her second cup of coffee, reading the morning paper and half-listening to *Good Morning America* on the TV. One of the program hosts was interviewing investigative reporter Jack Anderson. Suddenly Mary was jerked to full awareness when she heard Anderson say US interception of Laotian radio traffic had shown that "four Americans who survived the crash of an EC-47 electronic surveillance plane over Laos on February 5, 1973, were captured by the Pathet Lao, and turned over to the North Vietnamese."

Mary felt her blood run cold, and she nearly dropped her cup of coffee. "My God," she screamed, jumping to her feet. "They are talking about Joe!"

"When Mom heard the report about the possibility of Joe being captured, we began our roller coaster ride," John Matejov said. "It was a shock to us all. And while I cannot answer this question for all my siblings, I can speak for myself. It was incomprehensible."

The communications intercept described by Jack Anderson was a Pathet Lao radio communiqué which reported the capture of four "air pirates" on the same day the EC47Q carrying Joe Matejov was shot down. In Mr. Anderson's opinion, there was no question this information pertained to that specific crew because it was the only aircraft downed during that time frame. No other plane was missing that day. Anderson's information also indicated reconnaissance personnel had forty uninterrupted minutes in which to survey the crash site.

While still on active duty, Lt. Col. Matejov had been an operations officer in US Army military intelligence, and he still had friends in the Pentagon with the security clearances required to read the classified material in his son's file. "I'm going to get answers," he vowed.

The reconnaissance report of the Air Force Special Ops team, which had not been provided to the families during the ensuing five years, showed that three charred bodies, thought to have been the officers because of the seating arrangement, were found strapped in their seats. The partial remains of Lt. Bernhardt, which were found outside the aircraft, were easily recovered. No remains or any other evidence was found of the four additional airmen who had been aboard the aircraft.

No identification was brought out from the crash site, and no attempt was made to recover the three other bodies from the downed aircraft. It is assumed the Air Force reconnaissance team, operating at the behest of Air Force Security Service, was primarily interested in destroying any classified equipment or materials that remained aboard the EC47Q.

Through his contacts, Matejov learned about the intercepts and other classified information the Air Force had never told the family.

"Dad was able to get to the heart of the new found information," John Matejov said. It did not, however, provide him with an answer as to why his son was still listed as killed in action. It just brought forth a flood of new questions, and he came to believe the United States government did not want to admit to the world that it was dispatching spy planes to Laos when the war was over. Also, he told his wife, Baron-52 was shot down right before the North Vietnamese were about to release 591 POWs. He believed the government did not want to endanger the release by asking Vietnam for four more men. Then, after they had sacrificed the four young airmen, the government authorities began the process of covering their own asses, and that had continued. No one in the upper echelons of the government was willing to open up the Pandora's Box that would result if the truth was revealed, and they would do about anything to ensure that did not happen.

Part 5

Angry with the government to which he had dedicated most of his life and for which he had risked his own life, and convinced it was withholding vital facts and information about his son, Steve

Matejov grew more and more withdrawn. His life ended tragically in 1984, when he fell off the roof of the family home while doing routine repairs. He died a broken man, filled with bitterness and disappointment over the manner in which his son's case had been handled and convinced that Joe could still be alive.

Despite what they were telling the families of the missing airmen, US officials were still secretly requesting information about the Baron-52 crew into the 1980s according to documents Mary Matejov received through various sources.

In the fall of 1990, Sen. Charles E. Grassley (R-IA) complained on the Senate floor that despite DoD assurances, he and his colleagues were still being denied full access to classified files.

Grassley noted that Ann Mills Griffiths, the salaried head of the government-approved National League of Families, had a full security clearance. Griffiths had written the Defense Department in August arguing that members of Congress should be denied similar access.

Grassley wanted to know what had compelled such an unreasonable attitude toward a legitimate Senate investigation of documents that did not affect national security.

Grassley noted that Griffiths's security clearance enabled her to review the very documents she has so strenuously trying to deny members of Congress. This had given her authority to state to League members and to Congress that the secret intelligence showed no evidence American citizens were left behind in Indochina.

After this latest public protest, permission was granted for Senate staff investigators to examine the relevant intelligence files, but only with Grassley present.

Despite his senatorial duties, Grassley spent long periods of time searching through the files for over two weeks. His findings indicated that a secret war had been waged against those Americans who served in Southeast Asia and against those family members, like the Matejovs, who refused to abandon their servicemen," but ultimately Grassley's efforts were for naught.

In February 1991, Col. Millard A. Peck, a highly decorated hero of the Vietnam War, resigned as head of the Defense Intelligence Agency's Special Office for POW-MIA Affairs. A few days later, his letter of resignation was leaked to the press. Here are selected portions of his letter:

> My initial acceptance of this posting was based upon two motives: first, I had heard that the job was highly contentious and extremely frustrating, that no one would volunteer for it because of its complex political nature. This, of course, made it appear challenging. Secondly, since the end of the Vietnam War, I had heard the persistent rumors of American Servicemen having been abandoned in Indochina, and that the government was conducting a 'cover-up' so as not to be embarrassed. I was curious about this and thought that serving as the Chief of POW-MIA would be an opportunity to satisfy my own interest and help clear the government's name...
>
> From what I have witnessed, it appears that any soldier left in Vietnam, even inadvertently, was, in fact, abandoned years ago, and that the farce that is being played is no more than political legerdemain done with 'smoke and mirrors,' to stall the issue until it dies a natural death...
>
> Although greatly saddened by the role ascribed to the Defense Intelligence Agency, I feel, at least, that I am dealing with honest men and women who are generally powerless to make the system work. My appeal and attempt to amend this role perhaps never had a chance. We all were subject to control. I particularly salute the personnel in the POW-MIA Office

for their long suffering, which I regrettably was
unable to change. I feel that the Agency and the
Office are being used as the 'fall guys' or 'pat-
sies' to cover the tracks of others.

Col. Peck's letter stirred up a hornet's nest on Capitol Hill
and as always, the denunciations were swift. Defense Secretary
Dick Cheney said a few weeks later there was "no foundation to
support" Peck's charges and that "no further action is required."
But that was just the first salvo.

When members of Congress asked the Defense Department
about Peck's allegations, Assistant Defense Secretary Duane P.
Andrews assigned an aide, Ronald J. Knecht, to conduct a full
inquiry.

According to Knecht's report, Col. Peck's charges were
"self-serving nonsense" and came from a man who "was incompetent and had already been told he was being fired when he resigned."

Knecht concluded: Peck "had no evidence for his accusations and made no real attempt to obtain any." He "did not understand that his assignment was the impartial sifting of intelligence
reports—he had his own agenda, to organize rescue missions for
the POWs he believed [were] still captive in Vietnam."

The Pentagon investigated Peck's allegations and declared them
groundless. Officials also confirmed they had planned to fire him.
Lt. Gen. Harry E. Soyster, the DIA director, said Peck was "poorly
suited for this position—a case of a good officer in the wrong job."

In May 1991, Col. Peck was called to testify before the House
Foreign Affairs Subcommittee on Asian and Pacific Affairs.
Chaired by Rep. Stephen Solarz (D-NY), the subcommittee's
panel members were frustrated at Peck's unwillingness to provide
details in public. The colonel insisted on meeting with panel members in a closed session.

A 1991 *Wall Street Journal/NBC News* poll showed that almost
70 percent of the US public believed Americans were still being
held against their will in Indochina, and over 50 percent believed
their government was doing little or nothing to rescue them.

Pres. George Bush's July 1992 address to the National League of Families of American Prisoners and Missing in Southeast Asia disintegrated into a shouting match when some in the audience interrupted his remarks chanting, "No more lies! Tell the truth! No more lies! Tell the truth!"

Eight presidents from Johnson through George W. Bush had declared that "the fullest possible accounting" for missing Americans would be "the highest national priority."

In August 1991, Secretary of Defense Dick Cheney made a speech to the National League of Families of American Prisoners and Missing in Southeast Asia. Cheney said "resolving the issue of prisoners of war and missing in action is, and will continue to be, a matter of highest national priority."

The release of much-publicized photographs purporting to show missing servicemen alive in Southeast Asia focused renewed attention on the MIA/POW issue on Capitol Hill and across the country, and the Senate voted to establish its own committee to investigate.

The Republican staff of the Senate Foreign Relations Committee issued a 117-page report charging that the government had rejected or covered up information on American prisoners left in Southeast Asia after the war.

On August 2, 1991, the United States Senate approved a resolution introduced by Sen. Robert Smith (R-NH) providing for the creation of a Select Committee on POW/MIA Affairs to serve during the remainder of the 102nd Congress.

Vietnam veterans serving in the Senate at the time were expected to serve on the committee, and they did, reluctantly. It was seen as a thankless and time-consuming task that was certain to be controversial. Most did not expect anything of substance to emerge from the committee and saw no upside to it politically. Former POW, Sen. John McCain (R-AZ) said, "It was a no-win situation."

In October 1991, Sen. John Kerry, (D-MA) was appointed chairman, Sen. Smith was named vice-chairman, and ten additional members were appointed to the committee. A resolution providing funding was approved, and the hearings began on November 5, 1991.

The committee's task was to investigate the events, policies, and knowledge that guided US Government POW/MIA-related actions over the previous twenty years.

During the course of eighteen months, the Senate committee interviewed numerous individuals and considered their sworn testimony.

Kerry appointed his legislative assistant and former chief of staff, Francis Zwenig, as chief of staff for the senate committee. Committee members were equally divided between the two parties.

Sen. Kerry worked most closely with former POW Rep. Douglas "Pete" Peterson (D-FL) to authorize funding for the new effort to account for missing American servicemen in Vietnam. As a result the Joint Task Force-Full Accounting was formed by the US Pacific Command in January 1992. In order to gain acceptance of the new plan, Sen. Kerry also coordinated his efforts with Sen. McCain.

In implementing Kerry and Peterson's plan, Zwenig worked with Virginia Foote, the President of the US/Vietnam Trade Council, Allen "Gunner" Kent, former Commander-in-Chief of the Veterans of Foreign Wars, and Kenneth Steadman, at that time the Director of National Security of the VFW.

Many on both sides of the aisle contended the government itself was largely to blame for the problems it was facing on the POW-MIA issue. At a minimum, Washington was guilty of hypocrisy, hyper-secrecy and insensitivity to the legitimate concerns of families and others who wanted to know more about the fate of those missing.

Sen. McCain, who was respected by both sides of the issue, expressed concerns about how the government was handling the issue. "I have talked to many, many family members who clearly have had big problems," he said. "The Pentagon is overprotective of many of its sources of information and the information that it has," McCain said. He promised to sponsor a "truth bill" that would open up decades-old files on the POW-MIA issue, but

National security adviser Brent Scowcroft had reservations about opening the old records stating that it would "raise more problems than it'd solve."

"At one time in the past, the Pentagon allowed fairly wide access to the records," Scowcroft continued. "What happened as a result is that family members started getting letters from unscrupulous people who had some of the data and who were preying on those people."

The Pentagon claimed to have traced a recently released photograph—one in which three families have publicly claimed to recognize missing relatives—to what it described as "a ring of Cambodian opportunists led by a well-known and admitted fabricator of POW-MIA information."

Dr. Roger Shields, the DoD point man on POWs, was questioned under oath if there were intercepts or other sources of intelligence that showed some of the Baron-52 crew had in fact been captured. At that time, National League of Families attorney Dermot Foley asked in exasperation, "For your protection, over my protest, this information is declined because of the possibility that it is classified. Is that right?" Shields answered, "Right, I do not want to go to jail."

On September 22, 1992, former secretary of state Henry Kissinger appeared before the committee to rebut charges that he and Pres. Nixon had abandoned American captives at the end of the Vietnam War.

"That allegation is a flat-out lie," Kissinger blustered. "What has happened to this country that a congressional committee could be asked to inquire whether any American official of whatever administration would fail to move heaven and earth to fight for the release of American POWs and for an accounting of the missing? Can anyone seriously believe that any honorable public official would neglect America's servicemen, and especially those who had suffered so much for their country, or, even worse, arrange for a conspiracy to obscure the fate of the prisoners left behind?"

Kissinger was ferocious in his denials and accused committee chairman Kerry of "unforgivable libel." He went on to charge

Kerry and other antiwar activists with having tied his hands as he negotiated the release of American captives in Paris.

"I didn't ask for this job," Kerry replied. "I'm here because twenty years later this question still confounds America."

During the course of the hearings, a Defense Intelligence Agency analyst testified the radio intercept was not related to Matejov or the Baron-52 case.

"Remember this name," John Matejov said. "Robert Destatte. Destatte was a senior analyst for the Defense Intelligence Agency's Special POW-MIA Office. Practically all the spin in the controversy about this case came from him, directly or indirectly."

"Destatte testified under oath that the Laos intercept was received forty-four minutes after Baron-52 crashed. That was one of the primary reasons the four 'air pirates' mentioned in the intercept could not have been related to Joe's plane. He said forty-four minutes was simply too short a period for four men to be captured, rounded up, and a message sent to higher HQ.

"Using this specific bit of information, I was convinced by him that all of the men had died." Matejov continued. "It wasn't until I received a copy of a message pertaining to his testimony stating that his 'forty-four minutes' was actually 'five and a half hours,' that I knew the truth. That's quite a different story isn't it? Four men can easily be captured, rounded up, and any number of messages sent off to higher HQ within this new timeframe. Mr. Destatte was then asked by the Senators present at the hearing "who the four 'air pirates' could be if they were not members of the Baron-52 crew?" Destatte replied there had been several ARVN helicopters shot down near the time of Joe's shoot-down, and the four 'pirates' could have been any number of crewmen from the helicopters.

"I sent an inquiry as to the times and dates of Destattes' ARVN helicopter shoot-downs, and the reply amazed me. The closest date to the date of Joe's crash was ten days before. Destatte then went on to explain that his message was simply misinterpreted by the analyst in question, and had the message been sent through proper channels, his 'musings' would not have been wrongfully blown out of proportion. I have the document in which he later 'corrected' many things he said while under oath."

Jerry Mooney, long retired and living in Montana testified before the committee and repeated his story and analysis of the "four pirates" intercepts. But the committee also heard from Pentagon officials who still maintained that no one aboard could have survived.

Robert Destatte continued to refute Mooney's analysis. He blamed Mooney for putting his own "spin" on things through "unwarranted and arbitrary personal speculation."

The committee concluded "there is no firm evidence that links the Baron-52 crew to the single enemy report upon which Mooney apparently based his analysis."

Charles Trowbridge of DIA testified, "We can find no live-sighting reports or hearsay reports acquired in 1973 which were ever correlated to the unaccounted for crewmembers of the EC-47Q."

So why were the intercepts and reports of sightings ignored? Why were the men declared KIA despite contrary evidence? The key here is that no one correlated the live-sighting reports to the EC-47 crew because the DoD had decided after the repatriation of the POWs in 1973, no one was being held back by the communists. Therefore, anything to the contrary had to be debunked, using any logic that looked "reasonable," not necessarily plausible—only reasonable. Therefore, despite the findings of the men on the ground that the escape door of the EC-47 had been kicked off; despite no bodies found in the back end of the plane; regardless of the radio intercepts made of the capture and live-sighting reports on the ground; in spite of all alternative suggestions and plausible theories; and irrespective of the confutation of Robert Destatte's testimony—the men were declared dead.

In his sworn deposition for the Senate Select Committee, Sgt. Ronald Schofield testified the plane's rear door was missing. "It was nagging in my mind," said Schofield in his deposition. "The parachute door was missing. Those men got out of the plane alive. I knew it from that day."

His silence had eaten at him, but like all Security Service veterans, he believed he had a duty not to reveal secret information. Apparently, though, Schofield decided the right thing to do was to speak out. He did not think the backenders' bodies burned up in the crash because he recognized the bodies of the frontenders. "They were wearing Nomex suits," he testified. That meant that if there were other bodies there, they should have been recognizable too, because the Nomex had done its job preserving the bodies.

Schofield testified he believed the men kicked out the door and bailed out before the plane crashed. "I think some of them got out," Schofield testified. "That parachute door should have been there, and it wasn't."

In October 1992, Sen. Kerry forwarded his recommendation to the Lao Government that the planned crash site investigation for Baron-52 take place as scheduled. In November 1992, a survey team arrived at the crash site. During its preliminary examination of the area, a team member "looked down and found, laying in plain sight and totally exposed to the elements, a military dog tag in pristine condition with Joe Matejov's name on it."

Since the Baron-52 crew was supposed to be flying "sanitized"—wearing no dog tags, no insignias or rank on their flight suits, and no personal identification—this find was both miraculous and extremely suspicious. It is always possible some of the men were wearing dog tags, but it is highly unlikely any item lost in 1973 under the cover of triple canopy jungle would be found lying on the ground in plain sight twenty years later.

The American excavation team recovered twenty-three bone fragments and half a tooth, a pre-molar reportedly belonging to Peter Cressman. Interestingly, the commander of the Central Identification Laboratory-Hawaii (CIL-HI) publicly stated that the bone fragments "cannot be proven conclusively to be human." Requests from the families for DNA testing of these bone fragments to establish identity were denied.

Joe on leave, November 1972

In a visit home three months before he disappeared, Joe Matejov had told his mother the missions he was going on were so politically sensitive no one was allowed to wear any identifying tags or insignia on their uniforms—no name tags, no dog tags, no IDs.

"So why are there suddenly dog tags there," Mary Matejov asked, "if not other than to convince me?

"Well, I am not convinced!" she said sternly. "I believe today, as I have for almost twenty years, that Joe parachuted from that plane with possibly three other airmen and was captured. I will not accept what they say without positive proof anymore.

"At first Steve and I believed what the Pentagon said. He believed so much in that honor system they taught at West Point—honor, duty, country. But now I believe that all I am hearing are excuses.

"There are men alive out there. I have no doubt about that," Mary Matejov continued, "and one of them is Sgt. Joseph Matejov, who would be forty-one this year."

The Senate Committee concluded its investigation, issuing a final report on January 13, 1993, a week before Bill Clinton's inauguration. The committee had spent eighteen months traveling the globe and holding hearings on Baron-52 and other possible POWs from the Vietnam War. The group concluded there was no evidence the US had left anyone behind.

The hearings had been contentious. Sen. Smith was considered to be a controversial figure on the committee because he did not automatically accept what government officials said under oath as fact. Roger Shields and Robert Destatte viewed him as a zealot and responded to his questioning negatively.

Smith and his committee staff were viewed as "true believers who like the MIA/POW families were ready to assume a cover-up," said Frances Zwenig, the staff director of the committee and a Democrat. "You want to believe your loved one wasn't killed," she said. "Not my brother's teeth," she added, presumably referencing the Cressman family in a somewhat callous comment.

As the committee moved toward adjournment, it became increasingly apparent that, rather than accounting for missing American servicemen, its primary goal was to remove the POW/MIA issue from the path of normalizing relations between the US and Vietnam. That would help clear the way for lucrative trade deals and millions of dollars in profits for those individuals and businesses positioned to take advantage of the change in status.

Members of the Committee pledged to continue to monitor the issue, but in reality only Sen. Bob Smith had kept his promise to the MIA family members and veterans. He was the only one who made any real effort to find the truth. That was what made him "controversial."

He had sponsored the legislation that brought about creation of the Senate Select Committee. He was its vice chairman and had signed the final report that said, "There is at this time, no compelling evidence that proves any American remains alive in captivity in Southeast Asia," but he was never fully convinced of that.

A few months later the senator returned to Vietnam. Following his visit, he held a news conference announcing there was now "very compelling" evidence of live prisoners. "I can't go into more detail," he said, "but after the conversations I had with the Vietnamese, I can say again, it's compelling evidence."

The senator wrote a letter to Attorney Gen. Janet Reno accusing ten officials of crimes aimed at covering up the government's "botched" efforts to find the truth. The letter angered Senators Kerry and McCain. Both said Smith's charges "recklessly endangered reputations."

Smith contended that the overall investigative effort had been a total fiasco. "When you have got the whole damn United States government and several communist governments against you, it's hard," he said.

"I am not a conspiratorialist," he continued, but "if you don't raise hell on this issue, be aggressive and really push people, you don't get any answers."

In his letter the senator listed "potential" federal criminal violations in four areas: "false testimony and statements," mail fraud, destruction of classified documents, and improper classification procedures. He requested a Justice Department investigation.

Kerry said, "It's very unfortunate to publicly drag people into something by accusation, rather than simply to have an investigation quietly to determine whether something was worthy of putting their careers in that vise."

McCain said, "In my dealings with these people, it's clear that mistakes may have been made in a very complex set of issues. But at no time was there any indication they were giving anything but their most dedicated efforts. I frankly don't feel it's appropriate to publicly make these charges without public substantiation."

Justice Department officials met with Sen. Smith and examined his accusations, exploring whether the charges, if proved true, would actually constitute a crime.

Kerry said Smith had written to him explaining his charges involving "false testimony and statements" allegedly made to senators or the select committee. "Speaking as a lawyer," he said, "I would have a hard time making a case of perjury. You might make a case of sloppiness of diction or memory."

"In retrospect, I probably shouldn't have [released the letter]," Smith said, "but I did so because I was angry to find on my trip to Vietnam, confirmation of the existence of prisons that the DIA had said did not exist."

Smith also insisted he had no intention of making a continuing campaign out of his accusations. "If the Justice Department comes back and says there isn't anything, so be it," he said. "It's over." Attorney Gen. Reno turned down Smith's request for an investigation.

In January 1996, Mary Matejov wrote an eloquent letter to Cong. Bob Dornan (R-CA). "I do not dispute a burial for the three men we know died on this flight," she said. "Captains Spitz and Bollinger and Lt. Primm deserve this honor. They kept that aircraft in the air long enough to give the backenders: Joe, Pete Cressman, Todd Melton and Dale Brandenburg, time to jettison the electronics equipment and bail out. However, in honoring these men, the government should not be allowed to ignore the reams of intelligence data which prove my son, along with Sergeants Cressman, Melton and Brandenburg, were captured."

"Thankfully the officers' families have the peace of mind of knowing where their loved ones now lie," Mary continued. "For us, only questions remain."

Twenty-plus years after the plane crashed, twenty-three bone fragments, half a tooth and a pristine dog tag found resting on top of the ground were all the DoD needed to claim all crewmembers from Baron-52 were dead. A group burial was staged to take place at Arlington National Cemetery on March 27, 1996.

It was a cool sunny morning as four white draft horses pulled a caisson bearing a single flag-draped coffin. A bugler played "Taps," and seven white-gloved men in Air Force blue uniforms fired three volleys as three C-130 turboprop aircraft flew overhead in salute.

The Matejovs and Cressmans had tried to forestall the group funeral. They did not want their sons' names on the headstone, but the names of the four backenders were chiseled in anyway. The government wanted the entire matter finalized once and for all. Some of Lt. Primm's family members were angry with the

Matejovs and Cressmans for delaying the ceremony, but Primm's father said, "I can understand the families' feelings."

The families of the missing airmen ultimately made the decision to attend the service, not to say goodbye to their own men, but out of respect for those they knew had died. Members of Peter Cressman's family wore yellow armbands. Pat Cressman, Pete's brother, said, "It was a beautiful funeral. The only thing missing was the corpse."

"There's no question in my mind that Joe and three others were 'buried' under very questionable circumstances," John Matejov said. "I wish someone would tell me how they can do what they did here when the bone fragments were not even proven to be human.

"Those boys were killed on paper!" Mary Matejov stated firmly. "They were not killed in action—they were killed on paper at the peace talks. I blame the leadership from the military all the way up to the president. It doesn't matter if they are Republican or Democrat. They call MIAs the highest national priority, but it is lip-service and nothing more."

Part 6

Mary Matejov and Evelyn Cressman, Pete Cressman's mother, went to see Roger Shields. They said Shields told them their sons' names had initially been placed on the US list of POWs to be returned in 1973 (those for whom the US insisted on an accounting based on its own intelligence that they were alive). The mothers said Shields told them the names had then been crossed off the list. Shields wanted them to know he had not made that decision.

Soon after Steve's death, Mary left New York and moved to Hampton, Virginia, where the two had planned to retire. She and Steve had fought tirelessly for the government not to abandon Joe, and she carried on with numerous newspaper and magazine interviews, as well as radio and television. She traveled across the country, speaking on MIA/POW issues and became well-known among groups championing US servicemen reported missing in action during the Vietnam War. She immersed herself in her mission and was rarely home more than a few days at a time.

On 30 May 1997, the 301st Intelligence Squadron dedicated the Matejov Community Center at Misawa Air Base, Japan, to the memory of Sgt. Joseph Matejov. What made the Memorial Day ceremony extraordinary was the attendance of Mary Matejov and Steven Jr. Mary spoke briefly and unveiled the plaque that would adorn the entrance to the building.

In 1998, Mary suffered a heart attack while telling the story of Baron-52 during a public appearance and had to slow her activities. In her early seventies, she was "feeling old" after decades of fighting the federal bureaucracy she believed had kept her from finding her son.

"The next generation of servicemen should not have to wonder if they'll answer the call to defend their country only to be abandoned," Mary said. "We must stop this tragedy and never allow it to happen again. The government is trying to wait me out until I die," she continued with a wan smile, "but I hope I irritate the hell out of them for the rest of my life."

Mary (Stacher) Matejov passed away peacefully on Sunday, August 15, 2010, following a stroke. She was eighty-five years old. She was laid to rest next to Steve at West Point Cemetery, West Point, New York. In lieu of flowers, the family requested donations to the National League of Families of POWs and MIAs.

Billy Hendon's 2007 *New York Times* bestseller, *An Enormous Crime*, co-written with Elizabeth Stewart, argued American soldiers were abandoned in Southeast Asia following the end of the Vietnam War. *Publishers Weekly* reviewed the book and stated: "controversial former North Carolina congressman Hendon and attorney Stewart make the case that the US knowingly left hundreds of POWs in Vietnam and Laos in 1973, and that every presidential administration since then has covered it up." *Kirkus Reviews* called it "a sprawling indictment of eight US Administrations."

Just one day prior to the release of Hendon's book, The Raleigh *News & Observer* ran a story about a passage in Douglas Brinkley's book, *The Reagan Diaries*. Brinkley wrote: "After being briefed by then–Vice Pres. George H. W. Bush," Pres. Reagan had written that Hendon was "off his rocker" with allegations about Americans still being held in Vietnam. Reagan is also quoted as saying, "The lady who heads the MIA-POW family organization (presumably Ann Mills Griffiths) gave further evidence that Cong. Bill Hendon is absolutely wrong in his wild charges that our government has info about the POWs and is covering it up."

Although out of the public eye in later years, Billy Hendon remained an active voice on POW/MIA issues. He passed away in Forest City, North Carolina, in June 2018.

A variety of weapons have been used over the years against those who have sought to prove American POWs were and are still being held in Southeast Asia. Disinformation against dissenters has been one of the weapons of choice. For example, former Defense Intelligence Agency Director Gen. Eugene Tighe assembled an expert team to examine intelligence on missing Americans. After his task force agreed unanimously that Americans were being held in Indochina, Tighe was publicly denounced by his former colleagues, and his report was classified. Like Gen. Tighe, Cong. Hendon, Sen. Bob Smith, and Col. Peck, those who failed to support the official government position were immediately met with public scorn and humiliation. They were portrayed as "controversial," "out of sync," "incompetent," or worse.

Delay has been an equally potent weapon. As the years have passed, many of those presumed to be in captivity have most certainly died, and many of the family members searching for answers have also died or given up in disgust. The living evidence, if it ever existed, has disappeared amid the heat, rot, and tropical growth of Southeast Asia and the American public has a short memory. Meanwhile, evidence files have been retired, weeded, and sanitized, or remain classified and buried in routine intelligence procedures and regulations. It all works out in the end if there are those who might seek to obfuscate the facts and hide the truth.

John Matejov wrote a letter to Pres. Obama on Veterans Day 2013. After watching him lay a wreath at the Tomb of the Unknowns, John thought maybe a personal appeal to the president might have some impact. He received no response.

With the help of a masterful team of "pro bono" attorneys and strong support from congressional representatives from Wyoming, the Matejov family was finally able to schedule a formal hearing with the Defense POW/MIA Accounting Agency (DPAA) and the Department of the Air Force. The hearing was scheduled for February 2016, and the legal team would present their evidence in the hopes of changing Sgt. Joseph Matejov's classification from KIA to MIA.

In January 2016, shortly before the presentation was scheduled to take place, Matejov's lead attorney asked John if he had searched for pertinent documents at the Texas Tech Vietnam Center and Archive in Lubbock, Texas. Texas Tech houses the largest collection of Vietnam War documents, photos, and oral histories in the world. Matejov had not researched the TTVC archives, so the attorneys undertook the job and their search resulted in what became known as the "Tourison documents."

On February 5, 2016, the Matejovs made their formal presentation to the DPAA, the Department of Defense, and the Air Force. It was the forty-third anniversary of the shoot-down of Baron-52. The family had spent two decades questioning and searching for answers to simple questions that remained unanswered. All nine of the Matejov siblings and other family members gathered in a conference room in Arlington, Virginia. No members of the Matejov party were permitted to take cell phones, cameras, or other recording devices to the hearing. The family's premise was that Joseph Matejov's status had been changed prematurely from MIA to KIA—that the change in status lacked evidentiary support, was contrary to Air Force regulations, and was the product of political and policy imperatives. One of the more glaring omissions was the fact that the Air Force commander responsible for Sgt. Matejov's original reclassification from MIA to KIA was not aware of NVA communications intercepted a few hours after the shoot down, which referred to four captured prisoners or "air pirates." After the status of the four backend crewmen was changed from MIA to KIA, their names were removed from the POW/MIA lists, everyone stopped looking for them, and the investigation into their disappearance ceased.

The goal was to finally convince the agencies and the Air Force to relist Sgt. Matejov as MIA. That change would allow a reopening of the official investigation into his disappearance and could lead to a new accounting of his remains.

The Matejov team introduced a former Vietnam War pilot, retired Air Force Col. Ralph Wetterhahn, as its technical expert on crash analysis and communication protocols during the war. Col. Wetterhahn had been trained in crash investigations and provided much of the crash site analysis that appeared in the presentation. The later portion of the presentation focused on his analysis of the crash and evidence that some of the backend crew could have survived the crash.

The family and its legal staff concluded the presentation secure in the fact they had done all they could do. Believing justice would finally be served, little emphasis was placed on the newly-discovered "Tourison documents" during the presentation, but the documents were included as part of the complete presentation package which was submitted to the DPAA. The family was assured all the material would be analyzed. According to the documents, the DIA's own records indicated the four airmen might have remained alive years after the crash occurred. What more evidence could the agencies possibly need?

On 19 August 2016, John Matejov was informed the decision on Sgt. Matejov's case was still pending final review by the Secretary of the Air Force. Family members were given no reason for the delay, but they continued to wait and hope.

On November 8, John Matejov received the official resolution phone call from the office of the Secretary of the Air Force. Lt. Gen. Gina Grosso, the Deputy Chief of Staff for Manpower, Personnel and Services, had a panel of six other officers assembled in the conference room to witness the phone conversation.

"I have determined there is no basis to re-examine or disturb the original 1973 KIA determination," the General said.

Matejov was stunned and immediately interrupted Grosso. He asked for an explanation how this was possible considering the Tourison documents, which were submitted as part of Sgt. Matejov's case, clearly showed the Defense Intelligence Agency recorded that four of the eight crewmen were "captured."

Gen. Grosso could not offer an immediate explanation, but assured Matejov the documents had been analyzed, and he would receive an explanation, along with the written analysis accomplished by DPAA. The written analysis arrived a week later, but there was no mention of the Tourison documents. It was as if they had never existed.

The written analysis simply stated the Defense POW-MIA Accounting Agency Department and the US Air Force had reviewed and weighed all the evidence for eight months and ultimately decided they would not reopen the case, period!

"It's a sad day all around," John Matejov said, "for all who wear the uniform, past, present and future. In my view, this is nothing more than a silly chess game between the Defense Department and the POW/MIA families. At least our family got a chance to present our case, but to no avail. Our fight will continue."

After the 2016 hearing and its outcome, the Tourison documents became the centerpiece of the Matejov case. The documents comprised a series of memos from Sedgwick Tourison to Frances Zwenig during the Senate Select Committee hearings in 1991 and 1992. Sedgwick D. Tourison Jr., a former senior analyst with the Defense Intelligence Agency's Special Office for POW-MIA Affairs was one of thirty-one "non-partisan" staff members hired by the Senate Select Committee to "examine tens of thousands of documents, interview hundreds of sources, depose nearly two hundred witnesses, prepare for public hearings, and provide the advocacy on both sides of the POW/MIA issue that [had] been lacking in other examinations of this matter." Frances Zwenig was the staff director of the committee.

Highlights of the Tourison memos include the following:

- The Baron-52 crewmen "were reported as having been killed by the [USAF] three weeks after their loss, in the absence of any compelling evidence of death and in a manner inconsistent with normal casualty investigation procedures."

- "The reporting to the [DoD] that the EC-47Q aircraft personnel were 'Dead' and not 'Unaccounted for' effectively removed these eight individuals from any serious consideration for recovery. The simple fact that the [USAF] had reported them as having died, removed them from all lists of 'Unaccounted for' and would reasonably have moved them into a category of 'died' which had the effect of making them invisible to those US intelligence personnel, who had the mission of actively collecting information on the fate of those 'Unaccounted for' or who had died without their remains being recovered.'"

- "Furthermore, US military intelligence resources in Laos and Thailand which could have been employed to help determine the fate of such personnel may have been actively prevented from doing so by the CIA station in Vientiane, Laos. In short, US intelligence resources were available in the area to help learn about the fate of the EC-47Q personnel but were not used or authorized.

- "18 servicemen listed in DIA's own internal documents with a casualty code of having died in captivity. DIA responded that the code (KK) has been used for the last nineteen years to indicate died in captivity. However, in early 1973 it was used briefly to signify died while missing." SSC Staff Comment: "DIA's response is reasonably explained by both the casualty files and other archival documents. However, DIA's own declassified documents indicate an analytical judgment through at least 1979 that the crew of Baron-52 may have survived into captivity. The four in this case are not in DIA's list of eighty-three possible live POW candidates and further explanation is required."

On April 27, 2017, Matejov received the following response to a FOIA request he had sent to DIA:

"This is an interim response to your February 9, 2017, Freedom of information Act (FOIA) request for any and all correspondence or communication sent to or received from the Defense POW-MIA Accounting Agency, and Secretary of the Air Force pertaining to the Tourison documents and their relevance to POW case # 1983 (Baron-52) during the period 5 February 2016 through 9 February 2017. We received your request on February 14, 2017, and assigned it case # FOIA-0201-2017. We will be unable to respond to your request within the twenty-day statutory time period due to unusual circumstances. These unusual circumstances could be: (a) the need to search for and collect records from a facility geographically separated from this office: (b) the potential volume of records responsive to your request,: (c) the need for consultation with one or more other agencies which may have substantial interest in either the determination or the subject matter of the records. For these reasons, your request has been placed in the queue and will be worked on in the order the request was received. Our current administrative workload is in excess of 1,139 requests."

The Matejov family asked the Congressional Representatives from Wyoming to intervene on behalf of the family and ask all the direct questions still not answered.

"We have complied with all guidelines dictated to us by the government," John Matejov said. "We have provided the Tourison documents, which are "new and compelling evidence," but that evidence has been completely ignored.

On March 20, 2018, a letter was sent from the Wyoming Congressional Delegation to the Secretary of the Air Force. The delegation "respectfully" asked for a comprehensive review and reconsideration of the Matejov family's request to change the casualty status of Sgt. Joseph Matejov from KIA to MIA. The letter reiterated the forty-year history of the Baron-52 case and the family's quest to change Sgt. Matejov's status. It stated their belief additional evidence presented to the Air Force in 2016 was not evaluated in reaching its conclusion.

The delegation also requested the Air Force coordinate its effort with other agencies "to ensure all available evidence relevant to this case, including intelligence reports generated or maintained by agencies outside the DoD, is thoroughly and impartially evaluated, specifically the Tourison Documents." It concluded by asking the Air Force to provide an analysis of how its review of Sgt. Matejov's status complied with relevant statutory and regulatory requirements by April 15, 2018. The letter was signed by Senators Michael B. Enzi, John Barrasso, Jeff Merkley, and Ron Wyden, and Representatives Liz Cheney and Suzanne Bonamici.

Some two months later, the following response was received by Sen. Enzi: "While evidence obtained over the years and credible statements from individuals with knowledge, not of the crash or site, but of their understanding of common practices, has been presented, none have discredited the original determination made by the commander with firsthand and immediate eyewitness accounts of the scene.

"On several occasions, evidence was presented to the Secretary with the same result; no new or compelling evidence has surfaced that was not already considered in this case. In our thorough analysis and consideration of every piece of information and evidence presented, there is nothing substantial to drive a recommended status change by the Department of Defense or a determination of change by the Air Force. Therefore, the determination of the commander in 1973 that all members of the EC-47Q crash perished on February 5, 1973, remains the definitive decision.

"As always, if any further information concerning Sgt. Matejov becomes known to the Air Force, we will expeditiously share it with the family."

The crucial line in the response from the Secretary of the Air Force states they have thoroughly analyzed and considered "every piece of information and evidence presented," yet John Matajov's response from the DIA FOIA Request Center states DIA has had no correspondence or communication with the DPAA or the Air Force pertaining to the Tourison Documents—documents that state DIA records indicate four of the Baron-52 crewmen were captured. There would seem to be a disconnect somewhere.

In August 2018, with the impending return of the Korean War remains from North Korea, Rear Adm. Jon Kreitz, Deputy Director of Operations, DPAA, addressed the audience at the Korea/Cold War Annual Government briefing. Printed above his slide presentation was the official government slogan: "Fulfilling Our Nation's Promise."

"If I were lost, I would look forward to someone bringing me home to my family," Admi. Kreitz said solemnly. "Everyone matters to us at DPAA."

"As an aside," Matejov concluded, "Donald Trump's youngest son's name is 'Baron.' Could that be one of those potential 'moon and stars' alignment things? Stay tuned," he said. "More news at 11."

Out of fear
We disappear
As bullets pierce
Our holy flesh
Out of fear
We fight for freedom
Until we find
There is none left
It is too late
When lines are crossed
It is too late
When lives are lost
Forever gone
But not forgotten
As pain remains
In all of us

"Disappearance"
Gints Bija

12

Patrick Michael Corcoran

One of "The '74"

Patrick Corcoran

Born and raised in the 9300 block of Jackson Street, Pat Corcoran was a good-looking, Irish-American boy from the Torresdale neighborhood of northeast Philadelphia. Thomas Corcoran, his father, was a butcher in a local grocery, and like most of the neighborhood youngsters in those days, Pat was taught early in life the value of a dollar. The oldest of three children, he began delivering papers when he was eleven years old and big enough to tote a paper bag. After getting his driver's license, he moved on to the big time: the more lucrative and socially rewarding job of delivering pizzas. Life was good in Philly in the sixties, especially if a guy was cute and had a few dollars in his pocket. To the neighbors, Pat was simply "the good, hard-working Corcoran kid from down the street."

Like most of his buddies, Patrick grew up in Catholic parochial schools. He was a proud member of the Crusaders football and baseball teams at Father Judge High School and graduated in June 1968, at the height of the war in Vietnam. Not seriously interested in college, Pat began to consider his options and discussed them with his best friend, his dad. Dozens of Philly boys had already come home from Vietnam in boxes—thirty-two had died in May 1968 alone. The newspapers were filled with their death notices every week and the draft was hanging over the young man's head. He was thinking about enlisting in the Navy, but he wanted his dad's blessing.

"I thought he would go in and get it over with," Tom Corcoran said. "I talked to him. I thought it was a good idea. I was in the Navy. You learn a lot. You grow up."

In August 1968, Patrick Corcoran joined the Navy. After completing recruit training at NTC San Diego, he was assigned to the USS *Frank E. Evans* (DD 754). The destroyer had been docked at the Long Beach Naval Shipyard since May 1968 for an overhaul. At the end of February 1969, the *Evans* departed for a ten-day shakedown cruise along the California coast, and Pat had his first experience with sea sickness. A week or so later, on March, 19, the *Evans* sailed for Pearl Harbor en route to the western Pacific and military operations off the coast of Vietnam.

Pat was assigned a bunk in the forward section (bow) of the ship. It consisted of a piece of canvas laced between a framework of metal pipe with a two-inch-thick mattress, and it was reasonably comfortable. The racks were stacked three high, and taking the word of more seasoned sailors, Pat acquired two adjustable straps with clips on the ends to strap himself in during rough seas. It was better than hitting the deck on his head in the middle of the night. He had a personal locker under the bottom rack that was about thirty inches square and ten inches deep, and that was "home." He kept all his uniforms, shaving gear, books, and personal possessions stowed safely in his locker.

Pat thought Pearl Harbor was paradise. The ship's crew was mustered out on deck one morning to watch WWII-era Japanese Zeros diving at a mockup of the 1940s Pacific fleet. It was like going back in time to December 7, 1941. The sailors were told later they were filming the epic movie *Tora, Tora, Tora*. If only his dad were there to watch it with him. That would have made it perfect.

After fueling and provisioning, the ship departed Hawaii on the next leg of her journey to Yokosuka, Japan. The *Evans* arrived there on April 26, 1969, and joined the aircraft carrier USS *Kearsarge* (CV 33) as part of the Carrier Anti-Submarine Task Group that would be operating in the Gulf of Tonkin. The task force put to sea four days later, en route to Subic Bay in the Philippines where the ships would refuel and resupply before deploying to Vietnam. As a seaman apprentice, Patrick was kept busy painting, chipping paint, painting, sweeping, painting, swabbing, and painting. It never seemed to end.

During the times in port, there was liberty, and young Corcoran had an opportunity to leave the ship. He had celebrated his nineteenth birthday somewhere between Hawaii and Japan, and liked to have a good time ashore. With some 270 men in the crew, the *Evans* was like a small town, and after weeks at sea, Pat knew most of the men on board. He had become friends with Kelly Jo Sage, another young seaman apprentice. Kelly would turn nineteen a few weeks after Pat, and they would celebrate together. Kelly was from a little town in Nebraska, and Pat was amazed to learn he had two older brothers on board the *Evans* with him. He never dreamed brothers could serve together.

Gary, Kelly Jo, and Gregory Sage

In early May the *Evans* cast off and headed for Vietnam and the "gun line." She would be firing her five-inch guns in support of US ground operations there. The sailors were usually at battle stations when the guns were being fired. They were extremely loud, and the ship would shake from bow to stern with each shot. Pat and Kelly Jo might be on board a ship out in the Gulf of Tonkin, but as they helped haul hundreds of fifty-pound shells to fire in support of the Marines on shore, the two boys finally felt like they were in the war.

During their free time on board, there was not a lot to do. The youngsters would lie in the sun on the fantail, enjoy the ocean breeze, and read or just talk. On the surface, the two young men seemed about as different as they could be; one was from the crowded streets and ethnic neighborhoods of metropolitan Philly and the other from a farm on the vast prairies of northern Nebraska. Put quite simply, they were both good kids and recognized that goodness in each other. They soon became close friends.

One afternoon, after finishing the day's duty on the firing line, the *Evans* was anchored just off the coast of South Vietnam. Suddenly, there were large splashes in the water nearby, followed by loud, echoing reports along the shoreline. Alarms were sounded; the crew was called to battle stations, and the ship prepared to return fire. It was quickly determined the US Army was engaged in target practice with their own artillery and were over-shooting their target. After a certain amount of jawing between the Navy and the Army, the situation was resolved. The sailors returned to sunning on the fantail, although they maintained a somewhat leery eye on the shoreline from that day forward.

After two weeks on the gun line, the *Evans* along with the other destroyers in her task force was ordered back to Subic Bay for Operation SEA SPIRIT. She joined forces with some forty ships from other SEATO countries and headed toward Thailand. The *Evans* was assigned to the Australian carrier HMAS *Melbourne* for the exercise and accompanied her south as part of her security screen.

Late on the evening of June 2, Pat Corcoran and Kelly Sage were enjoying the evening air on the fantail. The ship was gliding effortlessly through the glassy waters of the South China Sea, and many of the sailors were up on deck. The moon was full, and the sky was perfectly clear. They could see the Southern Cross sparkling just above the horizon. After two weeks in the hellish heat and humidity of Vietnam, this night was pure joy. The *Evans* would dock in Thailand in a few days, and the young men were excited about the prospect of some well-earned liberty ashore.

Kelly's brothers, Gary and Greg spotted the two boys and stopped to talk. Gary was the oldest, a boatswains mate second class and a seasoned sailor. Greg was a radar man. He had married his high school sweetheart and had a little boy of his own back in Nebraska. The three brothers were the first family group allowed to serve together on a US warship since WWII, and they were proud of it. About 9:45 p.m., the group began to move toward their respective quarters. Pat and Kelly had watch at 4:00 a.m. the next day and needed to get some rest. All four bunked forward in the bow of the ship, so they walked together most of the way, laughing and talking as they made their way below decks.

Patrick undressed and climbed up into his rack. Pulling the sheet under his chin, he thought about home. He needed to write, but it was difficult when he had no news. The ship's photographer had recently taken individual photographs of everyone on board for the ship's book. He had made sure his hair was combed so he could send copies of the photo home. Maybe he would wait and write when he had the picture. Rolling onto his side, he took a long, deep breath and closed his eyes. He could hear snoring all around him. There were thirty other men in his compartment. The mid-watch would be shaking him awake before dawn, so he needed to get to sleep. It had been a good evening.

Part 2

Nineteen-year-old Joe Mulitsch was a fireman on the *Evans*. He was working the mid-watch that night having come on duty at midnight. "I had just completed work on my log sheet, when I decided to go up to the upper level," Mulitsch said. "It was some-time after 3:10 a.m. I grabbed the ladder with one foot on the bottom rung. All at once the ship rose up and the lights went out. Water began rushing in from everywhere. I was swept up in the darkness, under the water with whatever last breath I had taken. My mind was working with so many thoughts simultaneously. I was looking for the hole where the ladder went up and onto the upper level. I was looking for an air pocket where I could get more breath, all the while thinking of what my family would think about me being gone; about my girlfriend; and wondering what had happened."

Mulitsch finally escaped and began helping other survivors get up and out onto the deck. "As I looked aft I could see the motor whaleboat hanging in two pieces from its davits," he said. "I thought maybe a plane had crashed into us. I stepped back and then turned forward. To my total amazement the forward part of the ship was gone."

The *Melbourne* had signaled the *Evans*, one of five Allied destroyers on its inner screen, to prepare to take up the position of plane guard, one thousand yards behind the carrier. It was the fifth time that night the *Evans* had carried out that maneuver. The sea was dead calm, the water moonlit. As an extra precaution, the *Melbourne* had her navigation lights turned to their full brightness. Procedures had been clearly established for the smaller vessel to turn away from the carrier before falling into a position well behind it. However, the American destroyer had turned the wrong way and directly into the huge carrier's path. The *Melbourne* hit the ship with such force that one of the *Evans'* lookouts was thrown into the air and landed on the *Melbourne*'s flight deck, seriously injuring him. The *Evans* rolled onto its side and broke in half.

The bow half of the ship rose up on end and seemed to pause as if in some ghastly ballet. With sea water streaming down its sides, the side-ways numbers "754" glowed eerily on its prow, reflected in the brilliant lights of the *Melbourne*. Then the *Evans'* bow plunged beneath the dark waves, taking most of the men who had been sleeping in the lower decks with her to the bottom—a depth of 1,100 fathoms (1.25 miles). Patrick Corcoran, Kelly Jo, Greg, and Gary Sage; and sixty-nine of their shipmates were gone forever in less than three minutes.

The collision had occurred at 3:15 a.m., and the scene was chaotic; however, the Australian crewmen seemed to be everywhere. Aussie aircrews who had been preparing to launch aircraft shut down the engines and rushed to assist the American sailors. Some dangled fire hoses over the aircraft carrier's side as makeshift lifelines, while others secured the stern of the *Evans* alongside the *Melbourne* with mooring cables. *Melbourne* officers dropped cargo nets over the side and scrambled down to assist American sailors in the water. Many of the survivors were badly injured, and Australian sailors dived off the carrier into the water to assist them. Four Aussie officers later went through the aft section of the *Evans* to personally make sure no one was left on board.

Thirty-eight of the 111 men in the bow section of the *Evans* had been able to escape or were thrown into the water before it sank. Within a half-hour of the collision, all those men had been rescued in the darkness and taken aboard the *Melbourne*. Aussie helicopters were called upon for maximum effort. Overhead, their crews were stunned by both the macabre scene and the event itself. They had flooded the area with searchlights, and the sea was cluttered with fields of floating papers and debris. Brightly colored life rafts, rescue boats and more wreckage had dispersed in an ever-widening circle as the search continued for survivors. And beyond it all was the incredible sight of half a ship, tethered to the side of the huge Australian carrier like some sort of wounded animal. As men of the sea, that image was almost more than the Aussie crewmen could bear.

The helicopters flew all day on June 3, landing only to refuel, and then returning to the search area. The events of that morning and the ensuing hours were like some surreal dream. The last of the 198 sailors saved from the sea was Chief Petty Officer Larry Massey. He had clung to floating debris, semiconscious, and drifted away from the crash area before he realized what was happening. He could see the lights and hear the choppers for a while, but no one could hear or see him in the darkness, and he continued to drift away. He had given up all hope when he was rescued late in the day. The Aussie helicopter pilot said, "Hang on, mate, I think I see someone swimming for the Philippines," and they winched Massey on board.

The surreal dream continued to play out on board the *Melbourne*. The carrier's captain ordered its band on deck to play American tunes and help calm the survivors; the beer vault was opened and cans of Fosters beer were passed out to the US crewmen. Most of the *Evans* 272-man crew had been sleeping when the collision occurred, so many of the survivors were wearing only shorts; some were naked. The Australian sailors began giving them the clothing off their backs. Some went below and brought up their entire "kit," handing out items of civilian clothing and uniforms until the clothing stores were opened.

After his miraculous escape from the engine room, young Joe Mulitsch had been ushered onto the fantail. There were endless musters and roll calls as the *Evans* officers attempted to determine how many were missing and who they were. Mulitsch had suffered cuts on his elbow and near one eye; he was wet, but basically in good shape. The rest of the engine room watch had not fared as well. As the boilers and pipes had ruptured, many had suffered critical burns from the 950-degree steam. Joe was one of the lucky ones. Everyone he had eaten dinner with that evening had gone down with the bow of the ship.

Blankets were passed out, and the most seriously injured were provided emergency treatment by Aussie medics. A call was made for blood donors to fall in, and Aussie sailors lined up to give blood. Medical staff and medical supplies were flown in from other ships in the fleet, and the steady stream of seriously injured and burned survivors were taken care of as quickly as possible. Many of those not physically hurt were suffering from shock and also in need of care.

The USS *Kearsarge* arrived in the area, and its crewmen crowded the upper decks to get a glimpse of the tragic scene. "It was unreal," said Dennis Kennedy, one of the sailors aboard the *Kearsarge*. "The Evans had been sliced in two like someone had used a giant knife. I could see the different decks; I could see where the laundry had been, and there was a washing machine perched on the edge of the sheared-off deck. It was a sight I will always remember."

The Aussies began lifting the Americans off the carrier and transferring them to the *Kearsarge*, and as the US sailors were departing, the Australians heard something they did not expect and would never forget. The survivors of the *Frank E. Evans* stood on the quarterdeck and gave them three cheers.

"We had just cut their ship in half," one of the Aussie sailors said with tears in his eyes, "and here these Jacks were giving us cheers." The end of the *Evans* was the beginning of a lasting bond between the crews of the two ships. A memorial service was held on the *Melbourne*'s flight deck late that afternoon. The service was simple and emotional for many of the Australian carrier's crewmen.

Two days later, two men in US Navy uniforms knocked on the door of the neatly trimmed house on Jackson Street in Torresdale, Pennsylvania, and broke Thomas Corcoran's heart. They told him his son, Patrick M. Corcoran, had been killed and lost at sea, and part of Tom Corcoran died too.

On a farm near Niobrara, Nebraska, Eunice Sage turned on the *CBS Evening News* and heard Walter Cronkite solemnly announce the USS *Frank Evans* had been cut in half in the South China Sea. He said "The three Sage brothers of Nebraska are believed missing," and she fainted. The family had not been notified. As she regained her senses, she heard crying coming from a bedroom where their six-year-old son, Douglas, was supposed to be napping. The boy was saying, "Oh my brothers, my brothers, my brothers, my brothers."

The family was in agony until the official word was delivered a short time later. It was true. None of the three brothers had survived. With tears streaming down his weathered face, Ernie Sage put his head in his hands and repeated over and over: "I've lost all my boys. I've lost all my boys."

Gregory Sage's widow called a close girlfriend whose husband also served on the USS *Evans*. "My husband is dead," Linda Sage told her tearfully.

"So is mine," her girlfriend cried.

The disaster made front-page headlines, but only for a day or two. The papers were filled with other war news. There were some 540,000 US troops in Vietnam, that summer. Man would walk on the moon in the following month, and a half-million people would wallow in the mud of Woodstock a month after that. The American public, led by the US media, were quick to forget and move on with their lives.

A military memorial service was held at Long Beach Naval Station, the home base of the USS *Evans*, during the week following the collision. It was attended by thirty-four of the grief-stricken families, who were each presented with a folded US flag. There was also an Australian delegation headed by the Australian Naval attaché and the Australian Consul General from Washington, DC. The group also included six active-duty Aussie Navymen. The memorial was held at Gull Park, and at its conclusion, base Marines fired three rifle volleys—then "Taps" echoed westward across the Pacific where seventy-three of the seventy-four US sailors still rest at the bottom of the South China Sea.

In Niobrara, Nebraska, the lives of the Sage family changed forever. "I think we were all numb," Linda Sage said. The news was especially devastating for this young mother of Greg's thirteen-month-old son, Gregory Jr. "I don't think we really knew anything that was going on," she said. "It was just such a stress. Flags were at half-staff all around town. We were just all zombies."

A memorial service was held for the Sage brothers at the school gymnasium in Niobrara. All three boys had graduated from there and played sports in the gym. The Navy's Blue Jackets Choir sang, and over a thousand people attended the service.

In Torresdale, a mass was celebrated for Pat Corcoran at St. Katherine of Siena Church on June 13. The seemingly endless summer of 1969 passed in mourning on Jackson Street. Kind neighbors took up donations and built a memorial in the local park, but the family never stopped grieving. Their son never came home; there was no closure.

"It was really hard," Linda Sage said. "I think if there had been a body I could have accepted it. Every time I would see a sailor, I'd break down. I would look and see if it was Greg. Maybe he's really alive! Maybe he didn't die, maybe he's got amnesia, and he got onto another ship, and they picked him up. Or he's on a desert island, and he's waiting for me there. That was probably the thought of not just me. I think all the widows had that hope and dream that we would find them someday on a deserted island."

Little Doug Sage just thought his brothers were lost. When a story about Vietnam came on, he stopped what he was doing and sat glued to the TV, hoping for news that they were coming home.

Part 3

In 1982, Thomas Corcoran was crushed to discover Patrick's name was not inscribed on the Vietnam Veterans Memorial Wall in Washington, DC. When he inquired, he was informed that according to the Defense Department's criteria, those servicemen who lost their lives outside the Vietnam-Laos-Cambodia combat zone are ineligible for inclusion on the national monument. Since the USS *Frank E. Evans* was operating outside that zone when the *Melbourne* collision occurred, those men who had died on board the ship could not be included on the Wall.

The DoD's arbitrary combat zone designation ignores the fact that the Seventh Fleet's ships steamed in and out of the "combat zone" almost weekly. It also made those US sailors going into or returning from harm's way ineligible for the memorial, unless they happened to be in what the Defense Department designated as exactly the right spot when they lost their lives.

"This broke Ernie's heart," said Linda Sage. "And he went to his grave feeling extremely sad that his children were not considered casualties of the war. That was also Eunice's dream.

"Eunice took comfort in meeting survivors from the disaster and treating them as if they were her own family," Linda continued. "The first time she met one of the young men, and he looked at her with his face just dropping clear down to his toes, and he said, 'I am so sorry your boys are dead and I'm still alive.' She looked and she pointed her finger at him and said, 'I don't ever want to hear you say that again. I am so glad you are alive, and you are here for a reason,'" Linda recalled. "Eunice felt that way about every one of the survivors because they're the ones that have kept the memory, the hopes and the dreams of her boys alive."

Five years later, in October 1987, Thomas Corcoran attended the dedication of the Philadelphia Vietnam Veterans Memorial. Hundreds of people crowded the sidewalks near Penn's Landing searching for the names of their sons or brothers, husbands or fathers carved into the memorial's stone walls. Corcoran's eyes searched the monument, but Patrick's name was not there, and he departed in tears. While creating the memorial, Philadelphia's volunteers had relied on Defense Department casualty lists to find local men killed in Southeast Asia. However, those lists did not include the seventy-four sailors who had died on the USS *Frank E. Evans*.

This time, Tom Corcoran decided to fight. Directors of the Philadelphia Vietnam Veterans Memorial were going to hear petitions for additions to the memorial. Most were from relatives of men who were native Philadelphians, but who were listed as living outside the city at the time of their deaths. Corcoran contacted the directors and arranged to present his case.

"My argument was Patrick was on the destroyer," Tom Corcoran said. "And they had just left Da Nang. The ship had shelled Da Nang for three days, and as they left Da Nang they joined this naval exercise, and that's when his ship was hit. It may not have been in the combat area, but he was coming from combat." After Corcoran's personal appeal, the Memorial directors began to consider the case.

"We felt the boy would have never been in that part of the world in the first place if it wasn't for being on that destroyer," said Robert J. Connolly, president of the Philadelphia Vietnam Veterans Memorial Society, who supported Patrick's case.

The directors of the Philadelphia monument had originally adhered to the DoD criteria regarding the combat zone, but Corcoran's case was unusual, and his death no less grim than one sustained in the heat of battle. Patrick and his shipmates had fought in the war—why should they be just a footnote to it?

One year later, almost twenty years after that terrible summer of 1969, Tom Corcoran stood before the Philadelphia memorial and ran his fingers over his son's name, now carved in the cold, gray granite. As Michael Ruane of the *Philadelphia Inquirer* reported: The elder Corcoran "stood motionless before the Penn's Landing monument that now bore his son's name—a solitary figure with a wooden cane reflected in the polished permanence of the stone. He pulled a white handkerchief from a back pocket and wiped his eyes, then stretched out his right hand and caressed the letters with his fingers, as one would stroke a child."

"It's beautiful," Tom Corcoran said, "beautiful." His story made the front-page of the major Philly newspaper, and there was a poignant photograph of him standing alone in front of the memorial, wiping his eyes and leaning on his cane.

Earnest Sage died in 1996; Thomas Corcoran died in 2006, and Eunice Sage in 2010, but their fight continues. The names of "The 74" are still not inscribed on the Vietnam Veterans Memorial in Washington, DC, and the members of the USS *Frank E. Evans* (DD 754) Association continue their efforts to change that. The association is composed primarily of the survivors of the *Evans*'s last crew, family members, and now their descendants. They made a promise forty-five years ago never to forget their fallen shipmates, and they intend to keep it. "Lest We Forget" is not just a catch phrase for the group. They have petitioned the government for years; letters have been written; bills have been introduced in Congress. The secretary of the Navy has supported their effort; however, the Defense Department continues to deny them the justice and the recognition they believe their shipmates deserve.

On some level, the entire crew of the USS *Frank E. Evans* is still together. Seventy-four men died in the collision; seventy-three of them went down with the ship; other shipmates have gone on to their final reward in the forty-five years since, but the survivors keep the memories of all of them alive. As Paul Sherbo wrote in *Unsinkable Sailors*: "They're together as a crew and in a sense, they sail on together forever."

The men of the *Evans* are still a fighting crew, and their war is not over.

> They love the sea,
> Men who ride on it
> And know they will die
> Under the salt of it
> Let only the young come,
> Says the sea.
> Let them kiss my face
> And hear me.
> I am the last word
> And I tell
> Where storms and stars come from.
>
> "Young Sea"
> —Carl Sandburg

Author's Note

The onboard scenes and dialog in this story are fictional and were created for dramatic effect. I hope this chapter will serve as a tribute to "The 74," spread their story to an ever-widening audience, and support the mission of the USS *Frank E. Evans* (DD 754) Association in its quest for the national recognition these young American sailors deserve (GBB).

13

Vernon Leroy Downs Jr.

Duke

Vernon "Duke" Downs Jr.

Vernon Downs was a pilot for Transcontinental & Western Airlines (TWA) prior to WWII. When war was declared, he enlisted in the US Army Air Corps, received his officer's commission, and was soon on his way to the European Theater of Operations. After the liberation of Paris in August 1944, Maj. Downs was assigned to a post there and met the love of his life, Paulette Simone Paquet and her daughter, Viviane.

Vernon and Paulette were married in 1946, and their first child, a boy, was born in June 1948. They were still living in Paris. The boy was the son Vernon Downs had always dreamed of. He would not hear of naming him anything other than "Vernon Leroy Downs Jr.," so they struggled with what to call him. There was already another "Leroy" in the family, and "Junior" was not a popular choice. After much discussion, they settled on "Duke." Duke Downs had a certain "je ne sais quoi," as Paulette would say.

After Duke's birth, Maj. Downs resigned his commission, brought his family home to the US and resumed his job at TWA, which had changed its name to Trans World Airlines. Blue-eyed, with a shock of sandy hair that bleached out white in the summer sun, Duke was a delight from the day he was born. Paulette tried not to dote or be overly protective, but she hated to see him hurt. She would apply the mercurochrome and Band-Aids to his skinned knees and cut fingers (iodine burned too much), and then she would slip into the bathroom and cry. She knew if he were seriously hurt, she could never deal with it. Duke, the gentle ruffian, always held his mother's heart in the palm of his hand.

Civilian life was short-lived with the outbreak of the Korean War in June 1950. Maj. Downs was reactivated into the new US Air Force, and he moved his family to Hawaii. A second son, Denis, was born in Honolulu in 1952. Remaining in the Air force after the Korean armistice, Downs and his family traveled the world. A third son, George was born in 1954, followed by Anthony, born in Morocco in 1957, and finally Phillip in 1959.

The Major retired in 1965 and accepted a position with NASA at the Marshall Space Flight Center in Huntsville, Alabama. He was assigned to work on projects associated with the Apollo Program. The Downs family could finally settle down in a permanent home deep in the heart of Dixie. Paulette's daughter Viviane, who was twenty-three, had finished college and was out on her own.

Duke was a rising high school junior when his family moved to Alabama. He was a good athlete and made friends easily, like most "military brats," but he had become more quiet and introspective as he grew older. The sixties were turbulent years in the US, and the young man was troubled by the turmoil he saw around him. Governor Wallace had stood in the doorway at the University of Alabama in 1963, daring National Guard troops to remove him and admit the first black students. The following September, Wallace had tried to block integration of Alabama's public schools.

As a military dependent, Duke had attended Department of Defense Dependent Schools his entire school life. He had been around black people and had black friends for as long as he could remember. His mother, Paulette, had just become an American citizen in 1951 and could not comprehend the Jim Crow South or the codified system of racial apartheid still prevalent in Alabama. She had taught Duke the Golden Rule: be kind to all people, and they would treat him the same way in return, but now he was not so sure.

The bitterness and hatred the teenager saw on the stark, black and white TV news and in the local newspapers affected him deeply. Segregation was a fact of life in Alabama, and the young man struggled to deal with it. The Selma-to-Montgomery marches in 1965, including "Bloody Sunday" on March 7, the beating and tear-gassing of marchers by Alabama state troopers, and the murders of two pastors involved in the protests left him confused and disheartened.

Duke was also troubled by the war in Vietnam. He knew if he opted not to go to college, he would be thrown into the draft pool, and that held little appeal for him. Huntsville had been a military town for many years. As home to the Redstone Arsenal, the US Army Missile Command, and NASA, the military population had grown dramatically throughout the early sixties. As his high school years drew to a close, he would have to make a decision. He could discuss it with his father, who was always ready to listen, but not his mother. Paulette left the room when the topic came up.

After graduation, Duke Downs enlisted in the Marine Corps. He had just turned eighteen on June 15, 1966. His dad understood and supported him; his mother never would. He left for boot camp at MCRD Parris Island, South Carolina, in July and quickly discovered why they called it "Hell Island."

When he arrived, Duke saw civilians of every size, shape, color, and background. The men were mixed together in units called platoons and were herded en masse for physicals, immunizations, showers, shaves, haircuts, issues of new green uniforms, and then crammed into hot squad bays with steel bunk beds for eighty-six recruits. The recruits ran from one processing point to another while being verbally assaulted every step of the way. All individual identity was gone. The indoctrination was designed to tear the recruits down mentally to their basic, raw material, and then transform them into blank slates ready for the rebuilding process. The remaining seven weeks of training would mold and shape them into Marines ready for graduation. Duke was in excellent physical condition, and with his strong, quiet manner, he made it through with little problem.

His next step was combat training. He wrote home as often as he could. His dad was not much for writing letters, but he knew both parents yearned to hear from him. He continued to train and gain experience over the next year. By July 1967, Downs had risen to the rank of lance corporal, and he shipped out for South Vietnam. He was assigned to H&S Company of the 3rd Battalion, 9th Marines as rifleman, radioman, and squad leader, and was promoted to corporal in October. The 3/9th manned both Cà Lu Combat Operating Base and the Rockpile in western Quảng Trị Province. Duke Downs was based at Cà Lu. It was located at the terminus of Route 9, a rugged dirt trail that had once extended from Cam Lộ to Khe Sanh and on to Lang Vei, near the Laotian border. The area was in the northern-most region of South Vietnam and was extremely dangerous.

For Cpl. Downs, the first six months in-country had been a routine of patrols and search & destroy missions. The action intensified with the start of the Tet Offensive in 1968, as thousands of NVA regular infantry poured across the DMZ. On Valentine's Day, Kilo Company 3/9 was sent out on a mission to destroy an NVA mortar position about two kilometers due east of the base. The enemy position had been shelling Cà Lu almost daily. During the afternoon, the company located the NVA emplacement on a steep ridgeline under triple canopy jungle. During the ensuing fight, the company's platoons became separated, and the NVA killed about ten of the lead element Marines. Subsequently the command section took heavy hits from a supporting NVA position on the next ridgeline eastward. The company commander, Capt. Al Ward, was mortally wounded; Lt. William Reese, the executive officer, and Hospital Corpsman 2nd Class Larry Goss, the chief corpsman, were killed along with others in the command group. Most of the remaining elements of Kilo Co. straggled back into Cà Lu during the evening; however, Third Platoon was still separated and was left out in enemy territory with a newly arrived 2nd lieutenant.

Later that night, the missing platoon was located, but it was engaged in an intense firefight and had taken numerous casualties. Around midnight, Capt. Bill Conger, the S-3 (operations officer), volunteered to be inserted into the platoon's position as the "relief commander"; Cpl. Downs volunteered to go with him as his radio operator. A CH-46 picked them up at Cà Lu and headed west. The besieged unit was under heavy mortar attack as the new commander and his radio op approached the area in the darkness. Downs could see mortar rounds exploding and streams of bright green tracers splitting the night air. The chopper slowly descended, and then circled the area.

Part 2

Around 2:00 a.m., Conger and Downs were lowered in a sling through the floor hatch of the Chinook under extremely heavy enemy fire. The helicopter hovered overhead as the barrage continued. The crew chief followed them down and assisted in the sling evacuation of both dead and wounded Marines. Capt. Conger immediately organized the remaining Marines into better defensive positions; the chopper pilot maintained his hovering position until casualties were lifted up to the ship. When the sky was not lit up by mortars, the night was totally black.

Downs had been trained as a radio operator, but had served only as a rifleman and squad leader since arriving in-country. He had no experience as an RTO in the field. Now he began calling in effective mortar and artillery fire on the enemy positions. He accurately directed supporting arms fire and had an immediate impact on the platoon's defenses.

At dawn, the Marines prepared to assault the entrenched enemy. The NVA force occupied the crest of a steep ridge, which was covered with brush and thick jungle. Positioned directly back of the commander, Downs acted both as the RTO and a rifleman, continuously exposing himself to enemy fire as the platoon launched its assault up the steep slope. Capt. Conger was wounded in the initial moments of the attack, but Downs moved on without him. The lieutenant and most of the remaining platoon leaders fell, one by one, but Downs continued to push ahead fearlessly. Moving among the men, the young corporal shouted words of encouragement and urged them on. Firing his weapon as he ran, he pushed his fellow Marines up the hill and maintained the momentum of the attack until they reached the top.

Largely due to Downs' leadership, the Marines seized the ridge and inflicted heavy casualties on the retreating NVA force. As the platoon consolidated its position, Downs was clearly in charge and seemed to be everywhere at once. He sent squads to recover the dead and wounded and rendered medical aid to many of the two dozen casualties himself. He passed out ammunition, directed the clearing of a medevac landing zone, and then radioed for emergency medevac and ammunition resupply. The time was 1:00 p.m. on February 15—six hours since the attack began.

Settling down to wait on the choppers, Duke dropped to the ground and leaned back against a large boulder. The weather had been cool and rainy, but the humidity was about 90 percent. Removing his helmet, he could feel the beads of sweat slowly make their way down the side of his face and neck, soaking into his collar. He was covered in a layer of red dirt. He could almost hear his mother's voice as she called to him from the screen door on the back of their house. She would laugh softly, wrinkle up her nose and tell him to "get in the house and wash that dirty face, tout de suite!" A smile flickered across his lips as he pulled a crumpled pack of Luckies out of his blouse pocket and fished out a cigarette. Man, he missed home—especially his mom.

Finding his Zippo in a side pocket, Duke lit the soggy cigarette, and sucked the smoke deep into his lungs. Snapping the lighter closed, he flipped it over in his hand and looked at its silvery surface. A buddy had given it to him a few weeks back when he finished his tour and rotated back to the World. Engraved on one side were the words: "WHEN THIS MARINE DIES HE WILL GO TO HEAVEN BECAUSE HE'S SPENT HIS TIME IN HELL." The other side had a small globe and anchor. He slipped the lighter securely into his pocket, laid his head back against the cool stone, and closed his eyes. Relaxing for the first time in over twelve hours, he realized he was very tired.

Looking across the strip of red mud and rocks they had fought so hard to claim, he saw Capt. Conger and the other wounded men lying on their poncho liners. He hoped the choppers arrived soon. Some of the Marines were in bad shape. They needed more than the first aid they could provide in the field. The captain was seriously hurt, but he would survive, and Downs was relieved to know that. Conger was a good man. He was probably no more than five or six years older than Duke, but he reminded him of his dad; and that was a good thing.

About 1:20, Downs heard the sound of choppers approaching and got to his feet. As the birds appeared over a nearby ridge, intense enemy ground fire opened up on them, and the mission was quickly aborted. HQ contacted Downs on the radio and informed him India Co. had already been dispatched to reinforce them and should reach their position by 4:00 p.m.

After India Co. arrived, another medevac helicopter attempted to land, but was hit with ground fire and three of its crewmen were wounded. With little hope of getting medevac choppers on the ground and no desire to spend the night in the field, the Marines loaded up their wounded and began the cross-country trek back to the combat base. The dead were left behind. They would be recovered the next day.

The lead elements of India Co. reached a rutted stretch of Route 9 about 7:00 p.m. and almost immediately encountered enemy artillery fire. The remaining India platoons and the survivors of the Kilo Third Platoon, led by Cpl. Downs, continued to move in along the road, carrying the wounded that were unable to walk. Lt. Col. Gorton Cook, the 3/9th battalion commander, left Cà Lu with a security force from Lima Company and additional Navy corpsmen and met the Marine units. With their escort, all units were safely within the fortifications of the combat base by midnight, and the most seriously wounded were loaded on CH-46 helicopters for medevac to hospitals.

A few days later, after a quick return from his medevac to the rear, Capt. Bill Conger, the "relief commander," completed and submitted the requisite paperwork and statements recommending Cpl. Downs for the Silver Star for "for conspicuous gallantry and intrepidity in action." Capt. Conger stated that without Downs' courage and leadership the unit would never have accomplished its mission against the NVA force on Valentine's Ridge. Duke Downs had returned to his regular position in Headquarters Company with no idea he was being recommended for one of his nation's highest awards for valor in combat.

Part 3

A month later, Downs was sent to the Rockpile for a four-week tour of duty. It was a jagged piece of rock shaped like Gibraltar that rose 750 feet in the air and was located seven miles south of the DMZ. It was strategically important because it held commanding views of five major valleys, all of which were NVA infiltration routes from North Vietnam.

The Rockpile was relatively safe. It was considered to be the ideal duty for a Marine "short-timer." He could put in his last few weeks there and feel reasonably sure he would get back to the States in one piece. It would take an enemy force five hours to climb it if they were unopposed, and they would arrive at the top, cut, bruised and exhausted. They would also have to climb the Rock in single-file, making it difficult to mount an effective attack.

The top of the Rockpile was forty feet long, by seventeen feet at its widest point, and life there was normally quiet and uncomplicated. The radio operators received and relayed messages from one unit to another twenty-four hours a day. There was a 105mm artillery crew; a team of artillery forward observers with powerful binoculars; and a Marine sniper team based there. The snipers were said to have hit VC in the head from as far away as 1,500 meters with their telescopic sights, so the enemy usually kept their distance. The 1st Radio Battalion, the Marine Corps' signals intelligence unit, also maintained a four-man team for direction-finding and communications intercept. There was not much room left to spread out, so most of the men stayed in their tents out of the strong wind, which blew constantly. They only emerged to work, stretch their legs, or go to the small "mess hall" tent where they could have a warm beer and eat their c-rations.

Duke Downs was working the day shift in the commo tent. He had been on the Rock for about a week and was enjoying the solitude. He had time to read and had written a couple of letters home. He thought he might try and extend his time up there. He liked the lack of red mud, and he could certainly save money. His $65 a month combat pay did not go far, but if he could save enough and combine it with the GI Bill, he might try college when he got out. His dad would probably help him, and it would please his mother.

Duke's shift ended at 3:00 p.m. He picked up his jacket and walked out of the tent, pausing for a moment to breathe in the fresh air and watch swallows swoop in to the mud nests they had built under the rocky cliffs. It was a beautiful sunny day. Then he headed for the mess tent. He was going to grab a beer and finish reading the book he had in his pocket. He was reading *The Confessions of Nat Turner*, about a slave revolt in Virginia before the Civil War, and it was hard for him to put it down. "I might decide to pursue a history degree," he thought with a wry smile.

As Duke reached the tent and started to enter, he heard a roar, combined with an evil whining sound. He turned to look up at the sky, and there were several violent explosions.

The journal of the 3/9th Marines for 23 March 1968 reads: "1506 hours—The ROCKPILE (982545) received 'incoming' 122mm rockets from 934532 and 944531. The rounds landed in the messhall area and the 105mm artillery battery area. The 105mm ammo bunker exploded. Casualties were one (1) KIA, two (2) WIA serious, and six (6) WIA minor."

Cpl. Vernon L. Downs Jr. the hero of Valentine's Ridge, was the lone fatality in the rocket attack on the Rockpile. Several weeks later, Capt. Bill Conger discovered his recommendation for Downs' medal had not been acted upon, so he resubmitted it, and it was forwarded to the Commandant of the Marine Corps for approval.

Duke Downs was buried with full military honors at Woodlawn Memorial Park and Mausoleum in Orlando, Florida in April 1968. On July 17, in a solemn ceremony, Maj. And Mrs. Vernon L. Downs Sr. listened as the citation was read detailing the events of Valentine's Day 1968, when by his courage and leadership, Vernon Leroy Downs Jr. had salvaged and accomplished a mission that otherwise could have resulted in failure and the loss of numerous Marine lives. Vernon and Paulette were then presented with their son's Silver Star and Purple Heart. Duke Downs was nineteen years old.

The young dead soldiers do not speak.
Nevertheless they are heard in the still houses.
Who has not heard them?
They have a silence that speaks for them at night
And when the clock counts.
They say: We were young. We have died.
Remember us.

"The Young Dead Soldiers Do Not Speak"
—Archibald MacLeish

14

Michael James Hatfield

One of "God's Lunatics"

Michael "Mike" Hatfield

If there was ever an archetypal "All-American Boy," it had to be Michael Hatfield. He was athletic, handsome, popular, and considered by most of his peers to be "one of the nicest guys you could ever meet." He was the only son of the chief of police in Grayling, a small town in northern Michigan. And to make the story almost perfect, in 1968, he had married Janet, the high school sweetheart he had been in love with since elementary school.

Mike's father, "Bum" Hatfield, had been a US Army sergeant and tank commander during World War II and had been wounded in January 1945. The Hatfields had always stepped forward to serve when their country called, and Mike was no exception. He discussed it with Janet and his dad and decided he would apply for the US Army Warrant Officer program and become a helicopter pilot.

Enlisting at the end of 1968, Michael went through Army basic training and then on to Ft. Wolters, Texas, for primary helicopter training. He was assigned to Class 69-37b3, and they began with a four-week indoctrination course. The WOCs (warrant officer cadets) lived in barracks and were subjected to rigorous military discipline, in addition to daily flying time and academics. They marched in formation wherever they went and were frequently on the receiving end of "constructive" remarks from their training officers.

For someone who had spent his entire life in northern Michigan, Mineral Wells, Texas, was another world. Over 70 percent of Crawford County, Michigan, is state or federal land and covered with dense forest. With the AuSable and Manistee Rivers, along with numerous lakes, Mike and his sister, Marcie, had grown up in a wilderness paradise. They had spent the cool summers fishing, boating and swimming. In Mineral Wells, the average temperature for the month of July 1969 was one hundred degrees, with little or no rain. The WOCs were scheduled to fly mornings one week and afternoons the next; however, there were many afternoons when temperatures topped 105 degrees. Training was halted because they could not get the helicopters off the ground with both student and instructor on board.

Basic flight training consisted of learning to hover, takeoff, and land a helicopter. That was followed by learning to land and take off from a confined area, land on a pinnacle, and execute cross-country navigation. The academic portion of the training included: aircraft maintenance, aerodynamics, flight safety, navigation, weather, and radio. The courses were challenging, and the wash-out rate was 20 to 40 percent, but with mandatory evening study hall, Hatfield had little problem.

After completing the basic course, Hatfield moved to Ft. Rucker, Alabama, for advanced training and learned to fly the UH-1 Huey, the Army's workhorse in Vietnam. Academic studies continued with courses in military and aviation tactics and pre-flight techniques. This was the most challenging program he had ever been involved in, and he looked forward to each day. Time flew by, and he graduated in mid-December, receiving his wings and the rank of warrant officer 1.

Northern Michigan in December was a winter wonderland, and Michael enjoyed spending Christmas with his entire family. He and Janet had never really had a honeymoon, however, so they spent hours together, just the two of them. They took long walks in the snow, enjoyed romantic dinners, and talked about starting a family. He dreaded the thought of leaving her for a year, but they had known from the beginning—Vietnam loomed at the end of his training.

Early on January 18, the Hatfields and Janet drove Michael to the new Cherry County Airport in Traverse City for his long trip west. He told everyone "goodbye," gave Janet one last kiss and a tight hug around the neck, and then hurried out to board his North Central flight to Chicago. Struggling to control his emotions, Mike settled into his seat, fastened his seatbelt, and stared out across the frozen tarmac. The plane was filled with passengers, but he had never felt so alone in his life.

Warrant Officer Hatfield arrived in South Vietnam on January 20 and was assigned to the 190th Assault Helicopter Company "Spartans," based in Bình Tuy Province. He arrived early in the morning and was shown around the company area. He was escorted to the flight line to see the helicopters; there he met some of the maintenance and hangar guys and a couple of off-duty crewmen. He had an opportunity to look around and was assigned to guard duty on the flight-line that afternoon to help familiarize him with the helicopters. He would work the first guard shift that evening so he could get off at midnight and get some sleep before the crews took off the next day. He was scheduled to fly his first mission then, and he would fly for the next month straight without a break.

Hatfield was assigned to fly as copilot on Huey "slicks," and in spite of all his training, he felt "pretty lost" the first few days. It seemed like most of the other crewmen were "short-timers" and due to DEROS back to the States within a few weeks. The last thing they wanted to contend with was an "FNG" (newbie) warrant. The Spartan crews were hauling troops, supplies, and ammunition all day every day, and on occasion, the "AC" (aircraft commander) would allow Mike to fly the aircraft. He knew how dangerous the job was, but it blew his mind that he was actually there. He thrived on the adrenaline rush.

It did not take long for Mike's personality to win over everyone around him, and he became buddies with Jonathon Logan. Jonathon was only nineteen years old but was an accomplished pilot and already an aircraft commander. He had been in Vietnam for several months and lived in the hootch next to Michael. They would sit around in the evenings, have a few beers, and BS about home.

The second week of March, Mike came running to Jonathon's quarters, pounding on his door and calling his name. When Logan opened the door, Michael was standing there with tears in his eyes and pushed his way inside. Ordering Jonathon to sit down, he began to read the letter he had just received from Janet. She was pregnant. He was going to be a father. He was so excited and so happy. Jonathon jumped up and gave him a hug, and the two young men ran out the door looking for someone else to tell. Mike Hatfield was going to be a daddy!

The days that followed were routine with troop insertions and supply drops. Logan often requested Hatfield as his co-pilot, and Mike was on top of the world. He wrote to Janet or his mom nearly every day and would tell them about the guys he flew with and the day-to-day stuff they were involved in. He avoided recounting the near misses; the rounds coming up through the floor of the Huey as they descended with a load of ammo or pinging off their plexiglass canopy as they prepared to off-load a squad of six infantrymen on a combat assault mission. They had lost a door gunner a few days before, but none of those details reached Janet or his mother, Ilene. They were already worried enough. He chose not to add to their concerns.

Part 2

On March 22, 1970, the 190th AHC was operating in support of Charlie Company, 4/12th Infantry, as part of an air assault in a mountainous area west of Tanh Linh. There were ten Spartan slicks making single-ship insertions of Charlie Company grunts onto a rocky ledge surrounded by dense jungle. The LZ, nicknamed "The Rock," was only large enough for one ship at a time to move in and hover as the troops jumped off and ran for cover.

Jonathon Logan's Huey, call sign "Spartan 17," was the sixth or seventh helicopter in line to descend over the LZ. Mike Hatfield was his pilot. As the Huey moved forward, Hatfield glanced back over his shoulder at the anxious faces of the young infantrymen behind him. He had the utmost respect for these eighteen-, nineteen-, and twenty-year-old soldiers with their M16s. They were the cream of American youth and deserved more respect than they were getting Stateside these days. Nodding his head at them, he flashed a reassuring smile. As Jonathon edged the Huey in, Mike saw the rock ledge below them.

The chopper had reached the point when it stopped flying and began hovering; the rear crewmen were preparing to discharge the load of Charlie Company troops, along with their weapons and gear. Everything seemed routine, and then a powerful explosion ripped through the ship. The helicopter jerked violently in midair and seemed to disintegrate as it fell to the ground in a mass of smoke and flames.

Warrant Officer David Bailey was the aircraft commander of the helicopter directly behind Logan's Huey. "If I close my eyes I can still see the rocket hitting the aircraft as it came to a hover in the landing zone," Bailey said.

Inside the Huey was total chaos. A rocket-propelled grenade had struck the port side of the ship back of Logan's seat. The explosion had separated the main rotor and tail boom from the body of the helicopter, causing the ship to crash onto the rocky ledge and had sprayed shards of deadly shrapnel throughout the ship. Shrapnel had gone through Logan's left thigh and right calf, and he was bleeding profusely. He turned to look at Hatfield, but all he could see was the blood. Mike's chin was resting on his chest, and there was so much blood.

The Huey was ablaze; they were taking small arms fire from the surrounding jungle, and the noise was horrendous. Several other Hueys were circling overhead, their door gunners looking for targets hidden in the jungle growth below. Nearly all the crewmen and infantrymen in the back of Logan's ship were injured. They were yelling above the roar, struggling to get out of the broken ship, and assisting the more seriously wounded. Logan shook his head to clear it. He managed to unfasten his shoulder harness and lap belt and turned again to Hatfield.

The ship was filling with acrid smoke as Jonathon fought franticly with Mike's shoulder harness. The buckle was jammed, covered in gore, and would not budge. There was no way he could free him. It was apparent from the terrible wounds to Michael's head and face, and the quantity of blood-loss, that he had died instantly; however, Logan's only thought in those desperate moments was to get his friend out of the burning aircraft. Holding his breath in the dense smoke, with tears streaming down his face, Jonathon made one last futile attempt to unfasten the harness. Then, as the heat became unbearable, he squeezed his buddy's shoulder in one final gesture and pushed himself out of the Huey. Falling hard onto the ground, he crawled into the cover of nearby boulders and pulled the .38 Colt out of his holster.

"While still taking fire, I tried to get Michael out of the copilot seat," Logan said, "but I could not move him. Door gunner Jerry Skinner was off-loading his M60 machinegun and hundreds of rounds of ammo, even with most of his left knee blown away. We got the troops off the aircraft and lay between some rocks while it burned."

Logan and the other crash survivors were pinned down on the ground for about ninety minutes before a medevac helicopter could land to rescue them. During that time, Charlie Company troops that had been off-loaded earlier came to their rescue, counter-attacking and fighting off soldiers from the North Vietnamese 33rd Battalion that had launched the attack on Spartan 17.

Logan and seven other troops from the Huey were medevaced to the 93rd Evacuation hospital at Long Bình where they were treated for their wounds. The next day, March 23, Logan was awarded the Purple Heart on his twentieth birthday. He would be hospitalized for nearly two months.

In Grayling, Michigan, the news of Michael's death was devastating. The following days were a nightmare for Janet, Bum, Ilene, and the rest of the Hatfield family. As always, a host of friends from community and church stepped forward to surround and support them in their grief. Michael was buried with full military honors, and a few months later, the family was invited to a ceremony where they were presented with his medals: The Distinguished Flying Cross, for heroism in aerial flight; the Bronze Star for valor; the Air Medal with five Oak Leaf Clusters; the Army Commendation Medal; and the Purple Heart. Michael Hatfield had been in Vietnam for exactly nine weeks and was twenty-one years old.

The one bright spot for Janet was the knowledge that a part of Michael was growing inside of her. Seven months later, she was blessed with the birth of a beautiful daughter, and the baby was named for her father: Michelle.

David Bailey, who had witnessed the attack on Logan's helicopter said, "I'll always remember Mike's cheerful outlook on life, and I'll never forget his excitement over finding out about the baby he and his wife were expecting. Everyone who knew him lost a terrific friend that horrible afternoon."

For Jonathon Logan, Michael's best friend, it was much more personal. "Mike and I shared many good times while he was in-country," he said. "I can think of no one, before or since, who has made such an impression on me. He was a genuinely nice guy and I think of him often."

In later years, Logan made a long-delayed pilgrimage from his home in California to Michael's grave in northern Michigan. "There are a few things in this life that make no sense, and his loss is certainly one," Jonathon said. "Tomorrow, I will travel to Grayling, Michigan, to visit Michael and tell him of my son—named Michael."

Author and Vietnam veteran Joe Galloway paid tribute to the Huey flight crews at The Wall in 2000 and said, "Is there anyone here today who does not thrill to the sound of those Huey blades? That familiar whop-whop-whop is the soundtrack of our war, the lullaby of our younger days.

"I love you guys as only an Infantryman can love you. No matter how bad things were, if we called you came, down through the green tracers and other visible signs of a real bad day, off to a bad start. To us you seemed beyond brave and fearless—that you would come to us in the middle of battle in those flimsy thin-skinned crates—and in the storm of fire you would sit up there behind that plexiglass seeming so patient and so calm and so vulnerable—waiting for the off-loading and the on-loading. We thought you were God's own lunatics—and we loved you.

"We honor the memory and sacrifice of 2,209 helicopter pilots and 2,704 crewmen who died while doing their duty in Vietnam from May 30, 1961 to May 15, 1975."

Larrie Goldsmith, another of Mike Hatfield's pilot buddies probably said it best: "While reaching for the stars Mike, you found heaven. Rest in peace; you have not been forgotten."

> Though my soul may set in darkness,
> It will rise in perfect light;
> I have loved the stars too truly,
> To be fearful of the night.
>
> "The Old Astronomer"
> —Sarah Williams

15

James Milton Warr

The Kid from Atascosa County

James "Jimmy" Warr

It has been said Texas is a wonderful place to be rich and a terrible place to be poor. Atascosa County was a tough place to grow up poor in the 1950s. There were over 1,200 square miles of thorny cactus, mesquite, live oak, and tall grass waving in the hot Texas wind and a lot more scrawny cattle, armadillos, and rattlesnakes than people.

Life started out rough for young Jimmy Buford, and it just seemed to get tougher. He was born in June 1948, and his brother, David came along a year later. His parents divorced in 1950; his father, Robert Warr, enlisted in the Army and went off to fight in Korea. Jimmy did not remember him.

His mother, Bonnie Faye, remarried a year later—she had to provide for her two sons—and the family moved to Houston. Jimmy's stepfather, RC Buford, was a hard man—some even used the word "tyrannical" when it came to his dealings with his wife and stepsons. Work and money were difficult to come by in South Texas, especially if a man tended to be a bit lazy and not overly intelligent. Buford changed jobs frequently and took out his frustrations on those who were nearest and most vulnerable.

Jimmy grew up feeling responsible for his mother and younger brother. The boy was fearless and often stepped in to take blows meant for David and his mother, but neither of the boys were big enough or strong enough to stop the mental and physical abuse they were regularly subjected to.

When Jimmy was five, a little sister was born. The family had moved to San Antonio. Buford had taken a job at Kelly Air Force Base as an aircraft electrician, but that did not last. He decided he wanted to try his hand at farming, so he moved the family to a fifty-acre hardscrabble farm near LaCoste in Medina County. They were there about a year. There were other places and other jobs—more debt and more poverty. Nothing was permanent or regular or steady, except the abuse. For Jimmy and David, that never stopped. When Bonnie tried to intervene, she felt RC's fists too.

Another sister came along when Jimmy was seven and a brother when he was nine. The three children fathered by RC were named Ramona, Rebecca, and Reginald and all had the initials RC, at Buford's insistence, to stroke his ego. He was always quick to remind the two older boys (and anyone else within earshot) that they were not his. They were "just two extra mouths to feed." He refused to allow them to use their real last name, demanding they use the name "Buford" but making it clear he had no intention of adopting them. It was all part of the cruel mind games he liked to play.

Buford was gone frequently, moving from job to job. Life was easier when he was not around, but he never seemed to bring home any money, and the family lived in extreme poverty. For Bonnie, it was a constant challenge to put food on the table for herself and the five children. She often went hungry. When he was old enough, Jimmy found work in the cotton fields and on local ranches to help supplement the family income, but many of the jobs were seasonal and the pay was low. The family was living on a small ramshackle farm in Atascosa County, near Pleasanton, Texas.

At the end of his junior year at Pleasanton High School, Jimmy began to think about joining the Army. It looked like the only way out of the dark hole he had been trapped in his entire life. David was sixteen and growing taller every day. He was big enough to take care of himself, and with a regular paycheck coming in, Jimmy would be able to send his mother money each month. He and one of his classmates, Danny May, talked about enlisting on the "buddy system." The recruiter guaranteed they would go through basic training, job training, and their first assignment together.

Jimmy came striding into the back yard. Bonnie loved the fine young man she saw before her. He took off his sweat-stained hat and settled to the ground as she brought him a dipper of cold water from the well. He had been her strong right hand since he was a child. She could not have survived without him. As they sat in the shade of a large Mimosa tree behind the house and discussed his future, she reached out and touched his smooth, tanned cheek. A gust of wind rustled his sandy hair as he ducked his head away and grinned at her. He had grown into a man when she wasn't looking.

As he talked about enlisting and getting out on his own, Bonnie saw an excitement in her son's face and a light in his blue eyes she had not seen since he was a little boy. Jimmy would make something of himself, if she allowed him to. She had to have the courage to let him go. There was no future for him in Atascosa County—only pain, abuse, and poverty.

The war in Vietnam was building up. It seemed like more boys were being shipped over there every month, and more were coming back dead too. When she turned on the radio, all she heard was news about the war. Jimmy tried to reassure her he would be okay. The Army would teach him a trade and he might even make a career of it.

That summer, RC announced the family was moving to Comfort, Texas, northeast of San Antonio—about eighty-five miles away. Bonnie Faye had not told RC about her conversations with Jimmy. He and Jimmy did not speak at all, and this was between her and her son. Wishing to complete high school with his senior class, Jimmy talked Bonnie into allowing him to stay with a family in Pleasanton for his final year. He also had a steady girlfriend he was not eager to leave. The girl's father did not approve of their relationship; the Bufords were not exactly "high society," but the two teenagers managed to get together in spite of her dad.

Jimmy turned eighteen in June 1966, and in October, he and Danny May enlisted. From that day on, the young man would call himself "James Warr." He took the battery of Army entrance exams, and the tests confirmed what Bonnie already knew: Jimmy was highly intelligent and a natural leader. And she was not surprised he scored highest in mechanical comprehension and automotive skills. He and his buddies were always tinkering with old cars, and he kept her old car running most of the time. Mechanics seemed like a natural field for him to move into, and it would provide him with a future career. A basic training class was starting at Ft. Polk, Louisiana, in a couple of days; the recruiter would have James and Danny on a bus from San Antonio to Leesville, Louisiana, the next day.

Bonnie picked up the two young men the following morning and took them to the bus station in San Antonio. With tears in her eyes, she kissed Jimmy's cheek and reached up to hug his neck. Then she placed a wadded five-dollar bill in his hand, squeezed it shut between her hands and told him to "Do good." He protested, but she pushed his hand away. "You might need a sandwich," she said softly. Then she got into her old car and drove away. It was a lonely drive to Comfort, but she was sure Jimmy had made the right decision. He was finally going to be free from his stepfather's cruelty and moving forward with his life.

From day one of basic training, James Warr found a home in the Army. He had three good meals a day, more new clothing than he had owned his entire life, and a secure feeling he had never known before. As long as he did what he was told, he had little problem with the drill instructors; he was too likeable for anyone to give him a hard time for long. He missed David and his mom. Danny May was usually around, but David had always been his best friend. If he could have brought his little brother with him, everything would have been perfect.

After basic training, James was assigned to the aviation maintenance school at Ft. Rucker, Alabama. He received aircraft ground handling (MOS 67A10), SE/SR helicopter mechanic (MOS 67M20 for the OH-13 and 23), and SE/SR/T helicopter mechanic training (MOS 67N20 for the UH-1). He was also promoted to private-E2 and received a small raise in pay. He finished school and was assigned to a new helicopter company being formed at Killeen Base, Texas.

James took a Greyhound bus overnight from Dothan, Alabama, to San Antonio. He arrived about noon the next day and called his mother. He had a couple of days travel time and the weekend, but he could not stay in Comfort. RC was working out of town, as usual, but he might turn up any time. The last thing he wanted or needed was a confrontation with his stepfather.

James had arranged to bunk with a friend in Pleasanton and wanted to see his mother and David. Putting the oldest daughter in charge of the two younger children, Bonnie climbed into the old car and headed to a nearby ranch where David was working. If she hurried, they could make it to the bus station in an hour.

Traffic in downtown San Antonio was heavy. Bonnie and David found a parking spot near the bus depot on St. Mary's Street and made their way into the crowded terminal. San Antonio was a major military center with Ft. Sam Houston and Lackland Air Force Base, so the large waiting room was packed with uniformed men, and most were much taller than Bonnie. David finally spotted his brother; James was sitting alone, staring out a window and smoking a cigarette. Taking his mother's hand, David pushed his way through the throng of newly-arrived and departing passengers.

When Bonnie saw James, she was overwhelmed. She had been so excited at the prospect of seeing him. He had been away for several months—she knew he would look and be different, but she had not expected such a transformation. Jimmy was simply beautiful. Immaculately groomed in his Army greens, he stood up, flashed that crooked grin she loved, and held out his arms. With tears streaming down her face, Bonnie ran the last few steps and into her son's arms. David was caught up in the moment, too, and struggled to control his own emotions as he grabbed his brother around the neck and shook his hand. It was going to be a good visit.

Jimmy had sent his mother money every month since enlisting, and he had saved additional money for himself. As they loaded his duffle bag into the car, he told his mother to find a gas station. He would fill up the gas tank, and then they were going to find a place to eat lunch. Neither Bonnie nor David had ever eaten in a restaurant, so they would grab a bite before heading to Atascosa County, "Jimmy's treat!" He might be only eighteen, but he was providing for himself, helping his family, and he was a man with a future.

Part 2

When it was time for Jimmy to leave on Sunday, Bonnie and David drove him to catch the bus for Killeen. Killeen Base was located across from Fort Hood, Texas, and was a three-hour drive northwest of San Antonio. The Army had begun forming the new helicopter unit in October 1966, and was transferring in officers, large numbers of newly trained warrant officer pilots, career NCOs, and a huge crew of new enlisted men who had just completed aviation maintenance training at Fort Rucker and Fort Eustis, Virginia. The Army was increasing its aviation assets in Vietnam, and the 240th Assault Helicopter Company would be its newest addition.

James Warr was assigned to the 619th Transportation Detachment which would provide direct support maintenance for the 240th AHC. The unit's aircraft were assigned by the

Department of the Army, and it would be receiving Bell UH-1H "Hueys" for use as its "slicks" and UH-1C gunships.

Killeen Base was not the most exciting place to live and work—it was in a dry county and there was not much to do, other than train and sleep. The base was some sort of top-secret weapons storage facility with electrified fences and guard dogs patrolling it. Camp scuttlebutt said it had something to do with "nukes." The upside to being stationed there was saving money. The men spent most of their off-duty time playing cards, reading, listening to music, and working out.

The unit had been given six months to draw equipment and train for its deployment to Vietnam. A lot of training went on during the period, particularly weapons training for the gun platoon and slick platoon crew chiefs who would serve as one of the door gunners on the Hueys. Since the aircraft were new, it was difficult to find things that needed fixing, but the maintenance NCOs found ways of ensuring all the mechanics were well-trained before they arrived in the war zone.

A group of officers and twenty-five enlisted maintenance-types left the first week of April with the new choppers for Sharp Army Depot, California. From there the helicopters and men would be transported across the Pacific on the USS *Core*. Another advance party was already at Camp Bearcat, east of Saigon. It had begun preparations for the arrival of the main party by air, and the aircraft and equipment by ship at Vũng Tàu. The 240th AHC would be operating in support of the 9th Infantry Division, known as "The Old Reliables."

Warr's maintenance unit was ready to go and would deploy to Vietnam on April 20, 1967. He had a couple of weeks until he had to report and was permitted to take seven days leave, so he caught the bus back to San Antonio. He had made arrangements to stay with the same friend he had bunked with before and called Bonnie to let her know. He wanted to spend as much time with her and David as possible, and they would meet in San Antonio. RC was away, and that was fine with Bonnie. She would arrange for the younger kids to see Jimmy, but for today, it would be just the three of them.

James had gone shopping at the Post Exchange and looked sharp as he got off the bus in new clothes and a pair of new western boots. He had gained several pounds of muscle and appeared fit and healthy. It was wonderful to see him so happy, and Bonnie hid the cold fear that gripped her heart when she thought about him going off to war. Forcing a wide smile, she waved at him. She would not allow her concerns to dampen the enjoyment of spending these few days with him. She gave him a kiss and stood aside as the brothers embraced. David had turned seventeen and was as tall as Jimmy, although more slender. She was proud of her two handsome boys.

As they drove toward Pleasanton, James could not remember seeing Atascosa County so beautiful. The bluebonnets and Indian paintbrush were in full bloom in early April and covered the low hills and valleys as far as he could see. Bonnie stopped the car along a country road, and the two young men piled out. Taking off at a run, they raced through the field of flowers to a live oak on a low hillock some fifty yards away, yelling and laughing. Turning to face her, arm in arm, they waved at her as they argued over who had won the race. As tears welled in her eyes, Bonnie struggled to capture this special moment. This was a picture of her two sons she would carry with her the rest of her life.

The days flew by. James saw his mother nearly every day and spent hours with David. The two even camped and fished a couple of nights along the Atascosa River, something they had not done in years. They had to keep an eye out for the occasional gator but otherwise had a great time, talking until the early morning hours. James felt a need to cram in as much time as possible with his brother. He had confided to Eddie, the friend he was staying with, that he did not think he would make it back from Vietnam alive. Eddie told him not to go with those thoughts in his head, but they were still there.

The next morning, Bonnie picked up her boys at Eddie's home. David had spent the night, and it did not appear any of the three had slept much. Tossing his bag in the back seat of the car, Jimmy climbed in, followed by David. Laying his head over on his mother's shoulder, the young man was soon sound asleep, and David was snoring softly next to him. Arriving at the bus depot in San Antonio with an hour to spare, the boys had time to get coffee and donuts before the bus started boarding. They made small talk, but there was not much left to say. Each one knew what the other two were thinking and feeling, and it was just too difficult for Jimmy to talk around that damned lump in his throat. Bonnie mumbled something about him taking care of himself; David looked stricken and could not speak. Jimmy gave each of them a final hug and boarded the bus just as the doors were closed.

One week later, James Warr found himself in a different world. His company had boarded a C-130 turboprop the day before, and the plane had hopped from Ft. Hood to San Diego, Hawaii, Wake Island, Guam, and the Philippines, en route to Biên Hòa Airbase in Vietnam. Upon stepping out of the aircraft, Warr was hit with a stifling blast of heat and humidity that was unlike anything he had ever experienced. "Man this sucks, amigo" he said to himself, shaking his head. "Reckon we ain't in Texas anymore."

After a briefing, some lengthy in-processing, the issuing of weapons, ammo, helmets, flak jackets, and web gear, the men were loaded onto a convoy of two-and-a-half-ton trucks for the ride to Bearcat, the 9th Infantry Division's base camp.

The road was narrow and filled with pedestrians, bicycles, and numerous scooters that sputtered about carrying either two American GIs or five Vietnamese. They rode through small villages and past scores of children playing alongside the road. The newly-arrived soldiers stood in the truck-beds with their fingers on the triggers of their weapons, watching the sea of humanity surrounding their vehicles with wary eyes. Anyone could toss a grenade into a truck, but most of the locals ignored them. Warr noted a jet dropping bombs on a distant target, but otherwise the ride was made without incident.

Bearcat was a flurry of activity. Buildings were going up in every part of the sprawling base, and a cloud of red dust hung over the camp. Oil was sprayed on the dirt roads to reduce the dust, and Warr's nose was assaulted by the various odors. There was the smell of the oil and the fuel of the choppers, combined with clouds of putrid-smelling black smoke billowing up behind the latrines where soldiers on "shit detail" were burning the contents. "Wow! What a shit hole," he thought. "Maybe South Texas wasn't so bad after all."

The noise level during the day was constant with the hammering and sawing of the construction crews, the frenzied traffic of jeeps and trucks, the clanking of tanks and personnel carriers, and the continuous "whop, whop, whop" of helicopters taking off and landing. Occasionally, jets swept low outside the perimeter adding to the noise. Things quieted down a bit at night, making the sound of a nervous machine gunner opening up at shadows outside the perimeter all the more nerve shattering. Loud booms frequently punctuated the stillness when artillerymen sent harassing and interdictory (H&I) fire into distant parts of the jungle to disrupt an enemy who preferred moving about in the darkness.

The first few weeks at Camp Bearcat were extremely busy. The maintenance crew was charged with getting the helicopters inspected and ready to fly as quickly as possible. There were also seventy huge CONEX containers packed full of spare Huey parts, building materials, and a variety of additional equipment that had to be unpacked, catalogued and stored. Danny May was in the same unit, but the two men stayed so busy they rarely saw each other. James fell onto his cot totally exhausted at the end of each day.

As the aircrews began to fly missions with the 9th Infantry, the maintenance crews became even busier and more important to the operation. The Vietnamese climate required constant maintenance to keep the Hueys flying, and if a chopper was caught in a firefight, a whole new set of problems arose, including patching up bullet holes. To the infantrymen and other units in the field, the helicopter was literally their lifeline. The "Greyhound" platoons were the Huey slicks that transported the infantrymen into the hot landing zones, and the grunts knew that the Hounds would never hesitate to pick them up when they called for an extraction.

The "Mad Dog" platoons were the 240th gunships that provided rockets and machine gun fire from the air. Circling overhead, they supplied cover for the Greyhounds as they unloaded troops, and when the troops on the ground encountered enemy resistance, the Dogs with their miniguns and door gunners were there to back them up. In return, the men of the 240th AHC knew if their helicopters malfunctioned or were shot down, the grunts of the 9th ID would do whatever it took to get the aircrews out. The 240th AHC's maintenance platoon, called the Kennel Keepers, kept the Greyhounds and Mad Dogs in the air in order to support the 9th ID and carry out their joint missions. Working together, they comprised a remarkable team.

As the months passed, James continued to receive promotions and more responsibility. No one put in more hours or worked harder, and by the end of the year, he had attained the rank of sergeant. The maintenance and support personnel were considered to be "non-flying" members of the AHC team, but just about everybody flew, at least well enough to get back to base or on the ground if the pilots were unable to continue. It was called "self-preservation." And when the flights were over, maintenance began, day or night. After a helicopter came back to base, no matter how damaged it was, maintenance fixed it—they were outraged the pilots had allowed their aircraft to be hit by enemy fire, but they fixed it, and maintenance flew it to test it out. The crew chiefs had to make sure the aircraft was not going to kill the crew that flew in it. The mechanics, technical inspectors, and sheet metal workers all flew, and nobody died or was injured from mechanical failure. Under the conditions they worked in, that was remarkable. And somehow the men in maintenance also managed to dig wells, pour sidewalks and repair roofs, build showers and latrines, and fix refrigerators and air conditioners, too. They rarely took any time off.

The more James watched the aircrews fly off on their missions, the more he yearned to go with them. He had the opportunity to apply for a crew chief's position, and he got the job. He had just turned nineteen, but there was no doubt in anyone's mind: Jimmy Warr was the best man for the job. In Vietnam, age was not a factor. If you had the skills and the respect of your peers, you got the job.

Beyond maintenance skills, there was no training for a crew chief, other than additional weapons training on the M60 machine gun. Jimmy listened to the more senior crew chiefs; he learned the job on the job; and he learned quickly. Lives depended on it. He was finally flying almost daily, and he would not trade places with those that stayed behind for anything.

Jimmy had made many friends among the crews he worked with daily, and upon his promotion, he was taken under the wing of Sgt. Paul LaChance, one of the more flamboyant senior crew chiefs. "Frenchy" LaChance was a character and was the line chief for the Mad Dog gunship platoon. As line chief, he was responsible for all of the crew chiefs, plus he flew as crew chief on his own ship, Mad Dog 156. Frenchy's primary claim to fame was the dubious honor of attracting VC bullets like moths to a flame but he always seemed to come out on top. His maintenance buddies kept patching the bullet holes in his ship. In his spare time, he played drums for the 240th Rock & Roll Quartet.

Part 3

New crew chiefs in the 240th were assigned an aircraft for which they were responsible. It was their "baby," and they lived with it constantly. The crew chief oversaw all of the maintenance, performing most of it himself. He normally stayed on the flight line after a mission to clean up his ship and pull one of the various required inspections of the aircraft. By the time the inspection was complete, he had already missed supper and knew he would be getting up before daylight for the next day's mission, so it was not unusual for him to eat c-rats and sleep with his bird. Many crew chiefs would rather miss food, a day off, or anything short of their DEROS back to the World, than not be with their Huey when it flew. They would fly with any pilot to be with "their" ship, and it was not unusual for a crew chief to extend beyond his normal twelve-month tour to stay with his ship and make sure any new pilots were experienced and going to bring it back in one piece. The depth of this relationship between man and machine was truly unique.

Jimmy Warr was assigned Mad Dog Gunship 705 and it was love at first sight. He washed and waxed his Huey, kept her in immaculate condition inside and out and in perfect flying order. He dared anyone to mistreat her, regardless of rank. "Don't mess with Texas" definitely applied to Jimmy and his Huey. The Mad Dogs operated in two-aircraft fire teams: the lead gunship and the number two gunship or wingman that served as backup. An infantryman served as the door gunner on the right side of the aircraft, and the crew chief, with his M60 machine gun, served as gunner on the left. Frenchy LaChance often flew as wingman with Jimmy Warr. He appreciated his enthusiasm and wanted to do whatever he could to help him reach his full potential. He had never met anyone with so much desire to excel. This young Texan was special.

Operation CORONADO was a series of operations conducted in the waterways of the Mekong Delta south of Saigon. It was an attempt to dismantle Việt Cộng forces and infrastructure in an area that had been a communist stronghold since before the overthrow of the French. The operations began in June 1967 and extended into the summer of 1968. The 240th AHC's primary area of operation during CORONADO was the Rung Sat (Rừng Sác) Special Zone. Known as "a special kind of hell," the zone was located southeast of Saigon, extending to the South China Sea, and covered thousands of acres of mangrove swamps, streams, double-canopy jungle, and salt marsh. Charlie knew the Rừng Sác like his own rice paddy and utilized the thick foliage to efficiently conceal his bunkers and installations. Within the heart of this huge morass, the Việt Cộng were so secure they had constructed hospitals, supply dumps, munitions factories, and areas for R&R. The myriad system of waterways served as resupply routes for their troops and supplies, as well as access points to attack government freighters hauling war supplies to Saigon. The 240th flew in support of units of the US Army Mobile Riverine Force, Navy Riverine Force, Navy SEALs, and US Marines in their ongoing effort to gain control of the area. The Rung Sat was a challenge like no other in which the 240th fought.

With the launching of the Tet Offensive on January 31, 1968, all major cities in the Mekong Delta came under fierce attack; communist forces threatened all government and Allied control in the area. Operating day and night, the 240th AHC supported the Allied response as they hammered the Việt Cộng. With the 3/47th and 3/60th Infantry, the 9th ID, and the Navy's River Assault Squadron 9, they moved rapidly to conduct offensive operations and wrest the initiative away from the VC.

The pace of enemy activity remained heavy for weeks and so did the American response. A long transit on short notice, with the promise of a hard battle on arrival, was the order of the day. The middle of February saw some of the fiercest fighting of the river war during the defense of Cần Thơ, Cái Răng, and Bình Thủy. The battles fought in late February along the Cần Thơ River became part of the heritage of the 240th AHC and the brave grunts and sailors they supported.

On March 7, 1968, Operation CORONADO XII was launched east of Mỹ Tho, aimed at locating and destroying the 261st Việt Cộng Main Force Battalion. Two 9th ID Mobile Riverine Force battalions were deployed, and contact was made the following day by troops of the 4th Bn, 47th Infantry, about five miles northeast of Mỹ Tho. The fighting was heavy and continued throughout the night with Greyhound slicks transporting in infantry reinforcements under the covering fire of their Mad Dog brothers.

On March 8, the 240th Greyhounds continued to insert fresh 9th ID troops and extract the dead and wounded. Mad Dog Gunship 705 was operating in support of the operation with Capt. Charles "Charlie" Jilcott serving as the aircraft commander. Warrant Officer 1 Guy Eisenhart was the copilot. Jimmy Warr had a new infantryman, Jake Klein, serving as his door gunner, and he was in the crew chief's seat with his M60. Unlike the Greyhounds, the M60s used by the Mad Dog crew chiefs were not mounted; they were suspended by a strap from the top of the open door. This gave the gunner more leeway with the weapon when engaging the enemy. In addition, the ship was armed with two miniguns, one on each side, and fourteen rockets.

Jimmy Warr and his Huey

Warr's mind wandered back over the months he had been in Vietnam. It was hard to believe he had only forty-three days left in-country. Because he was a "short-timer," he was not required to fly more combat missions, but he was not ready to turn over his responsibilities or his Huey to someone else, and he had not made a final decision about extending his tour. It was going to be hard to leave these guys and his Huey, but he knew he was going to remain in the Army. He might see if he could get into warrant officer school and become a pilot.

The air was hot and sticky. Jimmy could feel the sweat on his forehead begin to seep into the corners of his eyes. It continuously made its way down the sides of his face soaking into the towel tucked in around the collar of his jungle fatigues. "Gawd, what a miserable f——k'n place to be."

"Man I'd sure like to have a dipper full of cold water from that old well back home," he thought to himself. At least he had the breeze coming in the open doorway of the Huey. Pushing up the tinted visor on his flight helmet, he swiped his hand across his face to clear his eyes and scanned the area for any sign of the VC. He saw nothing, but they were experts at camouflage.

With miniguns and rockets at the ready, Gunship 705 approached the landing zone. The gunship's job was to ensure the enemy was either dug in deep or dead when the slicks landed with their load of troops. Warr stared out across the alien terrain. It was similar to most of the eastern Delta—flat with large areas of marshy swamp bordered by dense jungle and traversed by muddy creeks. A scraggly palm stuck up here and there searching for sunlight.

"It sure don't look much like Atascosa County," he chuckled to himself. "Not a Gawddamned long-horned steer anywhere in sight," he drawled softly to himself, "I ain't never seen so much muck and shit in my life."

It was hard to find areas solid enough to land troops. They had encountered no enemy ground fire as they flew low and slow across the LZ, but that meant nothing. Trouble could pop up in a heartbeat. Jimmy always found air assaults exciting and sometimes a little scary. Everyone went to Vietnam knowing they could be placed in harm's way, but he had the utmost confidence in his Huey and in the crew he was flying with. Charlie Jilcott always had a positive word and an easy smile, and Jimmy knew him to be a cool and competent pilot. It was unlikely they would encounter anything Jilcott couldn't handle.

As they crossed over a patch of nippa palm, a .51 caliber machine gun opened up on them. Warr leaned out with his M60 and viciously raked the stream bank that had produced the enemy fire. Their wingman Warrant Officer 1 Larry "Mac" McKibben and his crew chief Frenchy LaChance were following behind them and also opened fire on the strip of dense vegetation. Capt. Jilcott had begun to climb and turn the Huey back toward the LZ, when suddenly gunfire erupted from several locations; .51 cal rounds struck the main rotor, the side and undercarriage of the Huey, and the ship nosed straight down with flames erupting from the back of the ship. Jilcott had no control of the Huey. It bucked wildly and then crashed headfirst into the jungle bordering the landing area.

Jimmy Warr had no time to think. He and Klein were belted in their seats but were slammed around violently as the aircraft nosed down and crashed. Pieces of the ship, ammo boxes, and anything else not tied down, became deadly missiles. Klein's belt was ripped loose from its moorings, and he was thrown clear of the ship. He landed deep in the undergrowth some distance away and was unconscious. Jilcott and Eisenhart died instantly when the Huey hit the ground. Warr was hanging, suspended by his belt and was semiconscious. He could feel the searing heat from the flames and knew he had to get clear of the ship.

McKibben saw the crash and landed as soon as he could get the Huey down. LaChance hit the ground while the ship was still six feet in the air and sprinted toward the destroyed chopper. Fire from the ruptured fuel tanks had spread rapidly, and he knew he had only seconds if there was a chance of saving anyone still alive inside the burning hulk.

He could see the two pilots completely engulfed in flames, and spotted a figure wearing a flight helmet flailing his arms with his uniform on fire. Braving the flames, LaChance threw himself on top of the man and tried to snuff out the fire, not realizing his own uniform had caught fire from the blazing fuel. The door gunner from McKibben's ship came on the run with a fire extinguisher, spraying Frenchy and the burned crewman, to staunch the flames.

LaChance struggled to catch his breath, still lying atop the injured man. The gunner extended a hand to help him up, and as he rose, Frenchy saw the man's blackened name tag. Staring in stunned disbelief, he read the name "WARR." He had not realized, amid the frenetic rescue attempt, that the man he had tackled was his friend Jimmy Warr.

Warr was in extremely critical condition. He had lost consciousness and was losing blood from several serious wounds. He was badly burned, and barely breathing. One of the Greyhound slicks had also landed, and several crewmen rushed to the scene. It was not often they had to tend to one of their own, and they did so with loving care. Loading Warr on board, medics quickly removed his flight helmet and remnants of his melted nylon flak jacket.

Then they began to strip away the charred remains of his fatigues, dress his wounds and treat him for shock as the chopper lifted off the ground. Rushing him to the nearest field hospital, several of the men waited for word of his condition and were soon advised he would be medevaced to an emergency burn unit at a hospital in Japan. The doctors would do what they could to save him, but it would be a long road back at best.

Frenchy LaChance was also hospitalized with his injuries. He had lost his eyebrows and eyelashes; he had painful burns on his arms and chest and third-degree burns on his legs.

The Mad Dog crews continued to fly their missions with heavy hearts. The deaths of Charlie Jilcott and Guy Eisenhart and the terrible injuries to Jimmy Warr were difficult for the crewmen to deal with. They wanted and needed to believe they were invincible. They were masters at what they did, and combining that with a belief in their individual immortality made it easier for them to do their jobs. However, the loss of their brothers had shaken those beliefs, and if hesitation or doubt crept in, it could have fatal consequences.

Klein, the door gunner was located the following day. He had regained consciousness buried deep in the muck and underbrush and had a broken pelvis. "I woke up and could barely move," Klein said later. "The pain was terrible, and I kept blacking out. One time I came to and heard Charlies all around me. They were jabberin' away, and I knew they'd kill me in a heartbeat if they spotted me. I was so scared, man. I was afraid to breathe. In a few minutes, they moved on."

A squad of 9th Infantry troops found Klein, and he was medevaced out to a field hospital. "We never saw him," Mac McKibben said later. "We thought Klein had died in the crash and fire. I felt terrible. We had no idea he was down there or we'd have picked him up."

Mad Dog crewmen maintained a vigil with Frenchy awaiting word on Jimmy's condition. Two days later, they were informed he had died. His injuries and burns were too extensive for him to survive.

When Danny May heard his buddy had died, he was grief-stricken. "I can't believe it," May said. "This isn't how this was supposed to play out, man."

"We were due to rotate back to Texas in six weeks, six lousy weeks," he continued, with tears in his eyes. "James was gonna stay in the Army and make a career of it. This is just bullshit, man!

"If I re-upped, I could go home when I wanted to," May continued, "so I told my CO I'd extend my tour in Vietnam if I could accompany James' body home, and he approved it. He told me what I had to do—I flew to Japan and picked up James, and we flew home to San Antone together. I was there for his funeral, and then having done what I could for James, I turned my attention to my own life. I married my girlfriend, spent time with my family, and then went back to Vietnam."

Sgt. James Milton Warr was buried with full military honors at Ft. Sam Houston National Cemetery in San Antonio, Texas, on March 20, 1968. Only the immediate family, Danny May and his wife, and a few close friends were in attendance.

Jimmy Warr's decorations included the Army Commendation Medal for "heroism" with one Oak Leaf Cluster and "V" device for Valor, the US Army Air Medal with six Oak Leaf Clusters, and the Purple Heart. He was nineteen years old.

Do not stand at my grave and weep:

"Do not stand at my grave and weep"
I am not there; I do not sleep.
I am a thousand winds that blow,
I am the diamond glints on snow,
I am the sun on ripened grain,
I am the gentle autumn rain.
When you awaken in the morning's hush
I am the swift uplifting rush of quiet birds in circling flight.
I am the soft star-shine at night.
Do not stand at my grave and cry:
I am not there; I did not die.

—Mary Elizabeth Frye

Epilogue: *Texas Nobility*

There is often an ironic side to stories such as that of James Warr. The abject poverty and systematic cruelty he and his brother David were subjected to during their formative years is even more incongruous because of their mother's family history, a legacy the two boys knew nothing about.

James, David, and their mother, Bonnie, nee Rusk, were born in Nacogdoches, forty miles south of Rusk County, Texas. Bonnie was the great-granddaughter of Capt. David Rusk.

David Rusk was a member of Col. Sidney Sherman's Texas Volunteers and fought at the Battle of San Jacinto when Texas won its independence in 1836. In 1837, Rusk became the first appointed sheriff in the new Republic of Texas, when he was named sheriff of Nacogdoches County. He was twenty-three years old. Sheriff Rusk was re-elected to that office four times. He was later appointed a commissioner for the United States and Mexico Boundary Survey, which determined the international border between the US and Mexico.

Rusk's older brother, Maj. Gen. Thomas Jefferson Rusk, was a signer of the Texas Declaration of Independence and was appointed Secretary of War during the Texas Revolution. After the fall of the Alamo and the massacre of Texian forces at Goliad, Texas, Pres. David Burnet sent Thomas Rusk to Gen. Sam Houston with orders to attack the Mexican army. If Houston refused, General Rusk had orders to relieve Houston of his command of the Texian Army and lead the attack himself. Had that happened, the city of Houston might today be named "Rusk, Texas."

Gen. Rusk joined Houston as second in command, and they defeated Santa Ana at San Jacinto. He was later appointed Chief Justice of the Texas Supreme Court. In 1846, he was elected US Senator from the new state of Texas and served as president pro tempore of the United States Senate in 1857.

This is the family line James and David Warr descended from. One must wonder if RC Buford had any idea his wife and stepsons were heirs to one of the Texas Republic's most noble families.

And the tradition continues: Like his brother, David Warr also made his escape to a better life via the US Army. A year after Jimmy's death, he enlisted and served his country for twenty years. His daughter, Capt. Starr-Renee Warr Corbin, served with the US Army in Iraq. Her son was born in 2003. His name is James Warr Corbin.

16

Aldwin Ardean Ellis Jr.

Sparky

Aldwin "Sparky" Ellis Jr.

Aldwin Ellis Jr. was a mama's boy, and he didn't care who knew it. He was born and raised in Portland, Oregon, where his dad, "Stubby," was a furnace operator for Reynolds Metals. Because he hated to be called "Junior," his family called him "JR." A good athlete at Franklin High School, he excelled in any sport he opted to play, and his mother, Gladys, cheered him on at every game. Academics, however, were another story. He had the intelligence; he just was not that interested. He left the academic honors to his older sister, Alonna. With a mischievous twinkle in his blue eyes and a ready smile, JR was satisfied with his athletic laurels and the fringe benefits that went along with his popularity. Hanging out with friends and Linda, his steady girlfriend, always beat studying. He was so good natured and easy-going; no one who knew him could have guessed that beneath that happy-go-lucky exterior beat the heart of a lion.

In the fall of 1966, Ellis became increasingly dissatisfied with school and decided to join the Army. He wanted his parents' blessing; however, he would turn eighteen in December and could go, with or without it. His parents were not enthused with the idea, but his father, a WWII Army veteran, was more understanding. JR's mother wanted him to wait and graduate, but his mind was made up. Promising to get his GED, the young man withdrew at the end of first semester and enlisted. He would be home for Christmas, and then he would leave in January for basic training at Ft. Lewis, Washington.

Two weeks into his training, JR's mother received a letter:

> Sorry I've taken so long to write, but they keep us going from 5:00 in the morning to 11:00 at night. We start the day with PT, and then go full out all day, with more PT along the way. We just got our M14 rifles and are learning to take them apart and put them back together—can't wait 'til we start shooting. I've decided to sign up for paratroops. They say they can only take about three from our company, but I can outdo any guy here, so I think I have a good shot.

A few weeks later, JR Ellis was granted a jump school slot at Fort Benning, Georgia, where he proudly earned his parachutist's wings. Upon finishing his advanced infantry training, his MOS (job description) was listed as 11B1P Infantryman-Parachutist. He went home on leave and then left for a one-year combat tour in South Vietnam.

Ellis stepped onto the tarmac at Biên Hòa airbase on July 21, 1967. Lugging his duffle bag toward the terminal, he got his first taste of Vietnam, and it was not pleasant. It was difficult to breathe. After Oregon, he thought Georgia was miserable, but it was nothing compared to this. The new arrivals were herded onto buses and taken to the 90th Replacement Depot at nearby Long Bình. Settled into open-bay barracks, the new troops spent two days undergoing in-country processing. It involved reams of paperwork and the issuance of individual weapons, clothing, and field gear. For a jump-qualified infantryman, there were only two possible unit assignments: the 173rd Airborne Brigade or the 1st Brigade of the 101st Airborne Division.

The 101st, with its appetite for replacements, quickly grabbed most of the newly arrived paratroopers, and that included JR Ellis. He was going to become a "Screamin' Eagle." Before they were parceled out to the brigade's three line battalions, the "FNGs" (newbies) were subjected to preparatory training. "P-school" was conducted at 1st Brigade's main base camp at Phan Rang, and lasted a week. Experienced cadre taught the classes, passing along hard-learned lessons about the rigors of jungle warfare and enemy tactics. Tough physical training and running exercises were also included to help acclimate and condition the green troopers to the brutal tropical weather.

JR got settled in his permanent accommodations at Phan Rang and wrote his mother another letter:

> I've been in Vietnam over two weeks, and it's miserable here. It doesn't even cool down at night. I went through a week of jungle training in the mountains and am now at my permanent base camp for the 101st. I've been assigned to the Second Platoon, Co. A, 2/502nd PIR (Parachute Infantry Regiment), and we're going out on an operation in a few days. They've made me the radio man for our platoon, so I'm being trained for that, too. They

always give the RTO job to a new guy. I'm big
and strong, so I get the privilege of toting the
radio along with all my other gear. It'll be good
to stop training and go to work. I hope the next
year goes by fast. I hear the same old song
everywhere I go: 'We Gotta Get Out'a This
Place.' It takes on a whole new meaning here. I
can't wait to get home. Tell Linda I'll write her
back soon.

A few days later, Ellis and his platoon boarded helicopters and
headed into the field. Feeling conspicuous in his crisp new jungle
fatigues and unfamiliar with the salty, battle-hardened troopers
in his new outfit, he realized "FNGs" were neither accepted nor
trusted until they had faced combat. As he pondered that situation
and silently wondered how he would react to his first "trial by
fire," he was assigned the unenviable job of being the company
commander's secondary RTO in the headquarters section. He
would be in charge of communication with Brigade HQ. Besides
having to hump a twenty-seven-pound PRC-25 field radio (fondly
referred to as the "prick-25") and extra batteries, along with his
own backpack, the radio antenna was often an irresistible target
for VC snipers or the first enemy RPG round, fired in hopes of
knocking out the unit's command element. A month into his tour,
JR was already carrying a target on his back.

Air-lifted in a matter of minutes, the entire unit was deposited
in a river valley, and the platoons began to spread out, looking for
their designated search & destroy coordinates. They were only a
few miles from the coast, but the targeted area touched upon the
Central Highlands, and the terrain featured steep climbs and rolling hills covered by dense triple-canopy jungle. Daytime temperatures were in the upper nineties and had the humidity to go along
with it. That was topped off by swarms of mosquitoes and every
other kind of biting and stinging insect known to man.

"Oh, to be in Oregon," Ellis thought, "trout fishing in a cold
mountain stream."

Enemy reaction to their arrival was swift. On the first day the platoons had several incidents of light contact resulting in a number of dead VC. It was the first time JR had seen a man shot and killed, and it was not a pleasant experience. The next day, there were several more contacts with additional enemy killed, and this time one of their own troopers was killed and two more wounded. Ellis stuck close to Capt. Arnold, the commander, and began to appreciate the RTO job. It was dangerous, but he saw how important it was. During his athletic career, he had always wanted to be "the go-to guy." Now, he was fulfilling that same role with his company.

On the third morning the troopers hoisted their rucksacks, and the platoon leaders set up the order of march. The company needed to reach a cleared hilltop several miles away by end of day for a supply drop. They were low on ammo and water. Following the point squad, Second Platoon led out, with the command section, including Pvt. Ellis, sandwiched between it and Fourth Platoon. Each trooper was spaced five meters apart to guard against booby traps, and the entire column was strung out over several hundred yards with First and Third Platoons bringing up the rear.

The column followed a narrow trail up a steep incline, and the dense vegetation with its high jungle canopy seemed to swallow them up. The air was hot and thick with the putrid smell of decaying plant life and the ever-present swarms of biting and blood-sucking insects. Terrestrial leeches, alerted by vibrations from those walking below, dropped from overhanging branches onto troopers' necks and arms and had to be constantly swiped away. Vividly colored birds soared, squawking and screeching, as the soldiers invaded their habitat and various kinds of venomous reptiles slithered through the thick undergrowth as the long line of men snaked its way ever deeper into the high jungle. There was an overpowering presence of the enemy all around them, and the men's nerves were on edge as they halted for a break around noon. With guards posted, the soldiers wearily flopped down on the trail and began to break out c-rations.

Within minutes, a forward section of Second Platoon was attacked by an unseen enemy firing from the jungle, and the point squad was pinned down at the head of the column. Capt. Arnold, with his radio operators at his side, directed the counterattack and radioed brigade headquarters at Phan Rang advising them of their situation. Fourth Platoon pushed past the command section on the narrow trail and rushed to assist their brothers in the lead platoon. Ellis was cool and calm amid the chaos, relaying the captain's messages to HQ precisely, and calmly handing him the phone if he requested it. Arnold ordered a squad of Fourth Platoon troopers to splinter off and attack the enemy's flank, but suddenly there was a burst of automatic weapons fire near the command post and violent explosions as grenades were tossed from the trees. Everyone hit the ground as the Fourth Platoon troops opened fire on the jungle around them. And then the VC attack ended as suddenly as it had begun. When the command staff regained their feet, Pvt. Ellis did not move. The youngster was lying face down in the dirt; the radio strapped to his back was in shambles. Quickly checking on his new RTO, Arnold discovered Ellis' uniform was soaked with blood and called for a medic.

Slowly gaining consciousness, the boy had difficulty focusing his eyes and could not hear; he was bleeding from both ears due to the explosive concussion. He had been kneeling when the grenade exploded, and his radio had probably saved his life. He had shrapnel wounds to his right shoulder and minor cuts on his neck, but the PRC-25, strapped on over a flak jacket, had taken the brunt of the blast. An M60 machine gunner and a squad sergeant in Second Platoon had also been wounded during the initial attack. After preliminary medical attention, all three were hoisted out by a hovering medevac helicopter. JR remembered little of the flight back to Phan Rang or the surgery he underwent that night. The next morning, he awoke in a hospital bed, and a general pinned a Purple Heart onto the sling holding his right arm—so much for his first combat mission in Vietnam.

Ellis remained hospitalized for ten days, although he was soon up and around. He was sore, but had too much nervous energy to lie in bed. Alpha Company returned from the field, and several guys from his platoon came to see him, along with his platoon leader, Lt. Anderson, and Capt. Arnold. He had apparently passed muster during his first combat experience. The troopers in Second Platoon now called him "Sparky," an honor dating back generations indicating the men respected his abilities as a radio man. Sparky Ellis was no longer an FNG.

Part 2

By the first week of September, Ellis was back in his own bunk and happy to be out of the hospital. He felt good physically and had been promoted to Private 1st Class. He wrote his mother and girlfriend from the hospital, telling them about his wounding, but left out the more lurid details. He knew the family had received official notification from the·Army and wanted to allay their fears. They worried about him constantly, so he downplayed how easily he might have died that day. He believed strongly that God had saved him.

Called the "Widowmakers," the "2nd O Deuce" (2/502) was one of the storied airborne units to serve in Vietnam and had been part of the 101st Airborne Division throughout WWII and Korea. In September 1967, the 1st Brigade of the 101st was placed under operational control of the Americal Division and was assigned to participate in Operation WHEELER. Its mission was to conduct "search & destroy" operations against enemy forces northwest of Tam Kỳ and neutralize their base camps.

On September 12, the 2/502 air-assaulted into the Quế Sơn Valley, west of Tam Kỳ, in Quảng Ngãi Province. Alpha Company landed in a hot LZ northwest of the battalion command post and encountered small elements of NVA and mines that had been placed in the area. Capt. Arnold, the company commander, was slightly wounded in the face by a mine as his helicopter landed, and it was decided he would be replaced within a few days. It was the captain's second wound, and he was due to DEROS back to the States within a few weeks.

On September 19, Pfc. Ellis stood in formation at a change of command ceremony conducted in a dry rice paddy. Lt. Col. Puckett, the battalion commander, passed the Alpha Company guidon from Capt. Arnold to Capt. Charles Otstott, the new CO, and decorated Arnold with two Silver Stars and two Bronze Stars for heroism. Capt. Arnold then flew off to staff duty for the remainder of his tour.

For the next eight days, Alpha Company patrolled with no enemy contact. The company was in an area of rolling hills dotted with small farms and bamboo hootches, and moving along a well-defined trail that was wide enough for vehicles. The unit was in its usual column of platoons with the command section behind the lead platoon. Sparky Ellis had resumed his duties as the Second Platoon RTO and was operating near Lt. George Anderson, his platoon leader.

Third Platoon troopers had the lead and were moving cautiously, although they had seen nothing in over a week. Late in the afternoon, there was a sharp exchange of gunfire, and the Third Platoon leader reported his unit was pinned down by automatic weapons firing from a large camouflaged bunker. He had also seen soldiers in green fatigues to his front, and the platoon was unable to move.

Capt. Otstott ordered Lt. Anderson to move the Second Platoon south into concealed positions and place fire on the enemy bunker. As the fire fight raged, Fourth Platoon was deployed to the north; however, they were soon pinned down by enemy soldiers with automatic weapons firing from behind a rocky outcropping and could not proceed. Helicopter gunships were called in, but they had no impact on the bunker. The troopers of Second Platoon continued to press their attack from the south; as they came under intense fire from the enemy complex, most of the men were pinned down with minimal cover. The entire company was running low on ammunition, so Otstott called for resupply, and a short time later, Huey slicks landed loaded with water and ammo.

Having stuck close to the lieutenant, Ellis was one of the few troopers in Second Platoon not pinned down by the NVA machine guns, so his squad sergeant ordered him to go after ammunition. Removing his rucksack and PRC-25, Sparky tightened the chinstrap on his helmet, picked up his M14, and set out for the chopper. Moving fast and keeping as low as possible, he managed a broken-field run across a broad, open expanse to the aircraft, attracting only sporadic gunfire. Loading up as much ammunition as he could carry, he knelt behind the aircraft and stared back across at his comrades. It was a long way across the field, and he knew NVA gunners would be waiting for him. He also knew the guys in his platoon were depending on him to make it back across. Their lives could depend on the ammo he was carrying. Saying a short prayer, he began to run back toward his platoon. He had gone only a few yards when a machine gun opened up and began to zero in on him. Hitting the dirt, he burrowed into the soft soil as deeply as he could and paused to catch his breath. Lt. Anderson, the squad sergeant, and several of Ellis's fellow troopers saw him go down and were holding their collective breath as they waited to see if he moved again.

Ellis was lying in a slight depression on the sloping field with his helmet toward the enemy position. The NVA gunner continued to rake the area with rounds but apparently was uncertain whether or not he had hit the American. The edge of Sparky's helmet was dug deep into the red earth, and he did not move. His face was bathed in sweat, and he could feel the dirt in his ear and on the side of his face as it quickly turned to slimy mud. He watched a string of small golden ants with pale green butts make their way single-file across the space in front of his nose, so oblivious to the maiming and killing being perpetrated by the "superior" species above them, and a smile crept across his face. Maybe he should have paid more attention in Mr. Kunzman's biology class. The machine gun had stopped firing. Sparky drew in a long breath, held it for a moment, and then slowly exhaled. Steeling himself for his final race with the enemy gunner, he jumped to his feet and zigzagged his way back to Lt. Anderson, with machine gun rounds kicking up sprays of dirt all around him. Diving in head-first beside the lieutenant and dragging the ammo with him, he rolled onto his back, let out a yell, and broke into a big grin. Sparky Ellis had just scored a touchdown.

Alpha Company was rearmed, but the enemy force could not be dislodged. Artillery was called in as light rain began to fall. At one point someone shouted they were being mortared; the fight continued unabated. Fourth Platoon succeeded in killing the NVA soldiers in the rock outcropping just as darkness fell, and the commander ordered the platoons to move back into a night defensive perimeter. They would medevac the dead and wounded and renew the attack the next morning.

After establishing their defenses and posting guards, Capt. Otstott assembled the platoon leaders in a bunker, and they devised a plan for a deliberate attack on the enemy bunkers at first light the next morning. Fourth Platoon would move to a prominent knoll southwest of the enemy and provide a base of fire. Second and Third Platoons would move via the higher ground to the north and attempt to flank the enemy position. First Platoon would remain in reserve with the command section. The attack would be supported by artillery, beginning at 6:00 a.m., along with gunships and close air support.

After the meeting, Lt. Anderson informed the commander he was going to recommend Pfc. Ellis for a Bronze Star for his actions that afternoon and gave him a brief synopsis of the events. Capt. Otstott told him to submit the paperwork, and he would approve it. Eight weeks in Vietnam, and Sparky had a Purple Heart and a Bronze Star. In a letter to his parents, the young trooper wrote: "I've had a lot of close calls, but God was with me, and there's not anything in hell going to keep me from coming back to the World."

Part 3

At first light on September 29, 1967, troopers of the Fourth Platoon quietly moved into position. They would provide the base of fire for Second and Third Platoons as they assaulted the NVA bunker complex. However, at 6:00 a.m. when the artillery battery was to begin its barrage, nothing happened. Capt. Otstott was advised there would be a delay until around noon, and he was furious. When the assault finally began, the attacking platoons were plagued by sniper fire from spider holes to their rear, so Otstott ordered them to pull back a safe distance and called in more artillery.

Numerous close air support missions were used during the course of the day, including helicopter gunships and aircraft dropping 250 lb. bombs and napalm. A pair of US Air Force F-100s dropped four 750-lb. bombs, nearly wiping out the American troopers, and two Marine aircraft delivered five-inch Zuni rockets, but nothing fazed the NVA, who apparently had an unlimited supply of ammunition. The Alpha platoons tried to advance again late in the day, but without success. Otstott called off the attack and ordered the platoons back to their defensive position. They would try again the next day.

Overnight, it was decided Alpha Company would use the same basic plan of attack they had tried the day before, with minor adjustments. Battalion would reinforce the company with a recon platoon and employ more artillery. Early next morning, the recon platoon air assaulted onto a ridge above the enemy complex and after the artillery barrage ended, attacked downhill in conjunction with Second and Third Platoons. This time, however, they encountered no gun fire.

Second Platoon cautiously advanced toward the enemy position—Lt. Anderson and Sparky Ellis were only a short distance behind their point man; it was eerily quiet. As the men moved forward, they expected all hell to break loose at any moment. Bent low, with every muscle tensed, Ellis grasped his M14 and eased ahead, watching for any sign—straining to hear any sound of the enemy, but there was only the soft crunch of troopers' boots in the rocky soil, the wind in the trees, and the cries of circling birds. If this was an ambush, they were dead. There was nowhere to run.

Reaching a last bit of cover before the seemingly indestructible stronghold, the lieutenant and his radio man knelt down and
surveyed the area. The fortification had been heavily camouflaged
with vegetation and netting and impossible to spot from the air
before the siege. Now, after three days of pounding and napalm,
most of the cover had been destroyed, and what remained was
some sort of edifice built into the side of a rocky hillock. The
structure had thick masonry walls and was reinforced with stacks
of sandbags and huge boulders. This was truly a fortress, but there
was no sign of life. The NVA had withdrawn during the night
and left their citadel deserted. The system of bunkers had been
built around an ancient brick factory, and the NVA had used brick
kilns as nearly impregnable fighting positions. There was a tunnel large enough for two hundred men, and the retreating troops
had left behind much of their equipment, along with two hundred
pounds of marijuana. The commander ordered everything of value
removed over the next two days. Then the complex was destroyed
with explosives, preventing the enemy from using it again.

By the first of October, Alpha Company had moved a mile
southwest to a barren hilltop where they arranged for extraction
of the recon platoon. The hill was covered with grass and large
boulders, and provided excellent visibility over the surrounding
terrain. To the west was a larger hill covered with thick vegetation, and Capt. Otstott suspected it was occupied by NVA forces.
When the UH-1s arrived in the area to pick up the recon troops,
the commander recommended they approach from the east, due
to his concerns about the hill to the west. However, there was a
strong wind from the east, so the choppers swung around to the
west to make their final approach, and fifteen to twenty automatic
weapons opened up on them from the jungle on the western hill.
They could see the green tracers reaching up toward the Hueys,
but there was no serious damage to the ships.

Artillery was called in which blasted the jungle-covered hill
with their 155mm and 105mm batteries for an hour. Close air support followed, and Sparky never tired of watching the gunships
work. He was thrilled as two "fast movers" flew in low, firing their

20mm Gatling guns. They roared in from east to west, devouring the thick foliage on the enemy hill, and showers of golden brass casings rained down on the Alpha Company troopers watching from their vantage point below. It was like the World Series, New Year's Eve, and July 4th all rolled into one as they cheered on the good guys.

The battalion commander decided the enemy force on the hill was too strong for one company to handle, and Alpha would be joined by Bravo and Charlie Companies for a major attack the next day. Alpha spent the night on their smaller hill and then moved out at first light. Charlie was to the south and Bravo, reinforced by elements of the 1st Cavalry Division's 1/9 Cav, was to the north. As Alpha Company began to ascend the enemy hill, Third Platoon was in the lead, followed by Command, Fourth, Second, and First Platoons. The lead platoon soon made contact with the enemy and encountered stiff resistance from automatic weapons and RPGs. Fourth Platoon was ordered right to flank the enemy position but had moved only a short distance before being engaged by the enemy and pinned down. Artillery was called in as close as they dared, and Third Platoon began to move forward employing hand grenades against NVA spider holes.

Late in the afternoon it began to rain. There were about two hours of daylight left when Capt. Otstott was notified battalion command was under attack, and the gunships were being recalled to support its defense. Third Platoon called for a resupply of hand grenades, so Second Platoon was ordered forward to hand over its grenades to Third and reinforce the attack on the enemy. Sparky Ellis relayed the message to Lt. Anderson and stood by as the lieutenant talked briefly to the commander. Ordering his squads forward, the lieutenant and Ellis moved along the narrowing trail and into the dense forest. Heavy rain continued to fall, and water poured from every leaf and twig as the sodden column moved ever deeper into the jungle. Sparky could hear automatic weapons fire and muffled explosions somewhere ahead, but it was difficult to tell how near they were to the action. The thick vegetation damp-ened and diverted the battle sounds. Crossing a rushing stream,

Ellis saw several bodies and destroyed trees where artillery had been called in on an enemy bunker.

Within minutes, the Second Platoon point man reached a field hospital where medics were tending to battle casualties. Anderson went forward to talk to the Third Platoon leader, and Sparky moved back with his own squad as they continued to move into the battle area. Reaching a fork in the trail, Second Platoon encountered a number of Third Platoon's men, and as the two units merged the troopers began handing over their grenades. Suddenly Ellis heard a high-pitched whistle. Yelling "mortars!" he dived off the trail. There was a violent explosion, followed immediately by another whistle and a second loud explosion. And for a brief moment, there was total silence.

As leaves, twigs, and other detritus rained down on the scene, Ellis struggled to regain his feet. Crawling onto the trail, he saw only a dense cloud of bluish-gray smoke. The sharp stink of cordite was thick in the heavy air, and then the groans and cries of the wounded began to rise. Sparky rushed forward to help, and as the smoke cleared, he was met with a scene of complete and total devastation. Broken trees, broken weapons, broken men—the sights, the sounds, the smells were almost more than the eighteen-year-old could process. There was red mud and red blood everywhere—acrid smoke burned his nose and eyes, and tears began to stream down his cheeks. Swiping his face with his hand, he bent down to check on a still form lying on the trail. Rolling the man onto his back, he saw it was Benson, a buddy who slept in the bunk next to his back at their base camp. Benny was one of the troopers who had visited Sparky in the hospital after he was wounded. The soldier's right arm was badly broken, and he was bleeding heavily from shrapnel wounds. Yanking a towel from around his neck, Sparky wrapped it tightly around the mangled arm and applied pressure to staunch the flow of blood. As Ellis moved to check on some of the others, the injured boy opened his eyes—his eyes rolled back, and he began to drool and convulse. Realizing he was going into shock, Ellis removed the young man's helmet, and cradling his head in his lap, calmed him until the seizure passed.

Lt. Anderson came on the run to check on his men. Medics had arrived on the scene and began to triage the wounded. Six troopers had been killed outright, and several of the injured were very critical. Anderson slowly walked amid the carnage, surveying the mayhem that had been his platoon. Kneeling to speak to some of the men, he offered what assistance and encouragement he could. Spying Ellis, who was still sitting in the mud holding his buddy's head and wounded arm, the lieutenant went to him. The young man's uniform was covered in his friend's blood, and Anderson assumed he had been wounded again. Sparky assured him he was okay, but that was little comfort for the officer. Four of the six dead were his boys, and he took the loss of each one personally.

Capt. Otstott ordered the platoon leaders to cease their attack and consolidate their units on the most defensible terrain. The platoons moved to a nearby knoll and formed a tight perimeter in heavy brush. There was a rice paddy north of the knoll, which had been almost dry before the rain started. It would serve as an LZ for the medevac slicks. The casualties were moved to the paddy, and every effort was made to shelter them from the pouring rain. The weather continued to deteriorate, and enemy guns fired on any aircraft that approached the area making medevac nearly impossible. The crew of one of the dustoffs (unarmed medevac choppers) volunteered to come after the most severely injured. Bravo Company had been in heavy fighting a mile northwest of Alpha and had several critically wounded troopers; Alpha had four critical WIAs; and battalion command also had critically injured men to evacuate. As the storm raged, the dustoff flew to Bravo about midnight, picked up some of their wounded, and delivered them to a field hospital at Chu Lai. The pilot was instrument-qualified and had nerves of steel. He returned to Bravo for more critical WIAs and then radioed he was coming on to Alpha and had room for two of their wounded. Troopers lit the LZ with flashlights and the pilot dropped in from the east, taking fire as he landed. The crew loaded Alpha's two most critical and promised to come back for the rest, but when they returned, the weather had worsened and landing was impossible.

The remaining wounded men were laid out on ponchos at the edge of the paddy. Medics tended to them and tried to keep them covered with additional ponchos. Sparky helped Lt. Anderson until their platoon was situated and the troopers had broken out c-rations. Then, he went looking for his injured buddy. Benson's wounds had been dressed, and he appeared to be sleeping as Ellis slipped down onto the muddy sod beside him. Leaning against the paddy dike, he covered Benny's head and shoulders with the tail of his poncho to help shield him from the deluge and tore open the wrapper on a c-rat candy bar. Settling in beside his friend, Sparky tried to relax. It had been one hell of a day. The lieutenant knew where to find him if he needed him, so he laid his head back and closed his eyes. Some of the wounded moaned and called out during the evening, but the cries dissipated as the men fell into exhausted sleep. The captain called in Air Force flare ships to keep the area illuminated all night; the scene was surreal. The storm raged, and the night was pitch-black when the flares burned out, then another flare would explode overhead with brilliant light, combined with sporadic streams of green tracers when guns opened up from the jungle. It was one of the longest nights of Sparky's life. As daylight began to filter through a layer of thick fog, he checked on Benson, who slept peacefully. Rising to his feet, he groaned. He ached in every muscle and joint in his body. Then, he turned to stare at the row of casualties laid out behind him and felt a cold shiver down his spine. The paddy had filled with the torrential rain, and some of the dead and wounded were partially submerged in the muddy, red water.

Part 4

The fog cleared, and dustoffs arrived to collect the rest of Alpha Company's wounded. Medics had worked tirelessly to keep the injured men alive. Two were very critical, and several more were in serious condition—all needed surgeons and clean, dry hospital beds. Blood was seeping through the bandages on

Benson's shattered arm, and he was in extreme pain. A doc came by and gave him a shot of morphine. Sparky talked to Benny and realized the young man had no memory of the mortar attack, so he gave him a brief account. It was good the boy didn't remember some of the stuff Sparky wanted to forget.

The most serious cases were loaded on the choppers first; several were unconscious. Sparky assured Benson he would come to see him when Alpha returned to Phan Rang, and then the wounded were gone. The battalion commander flew in and took some of the dead troopers out in his ship. A resupply slick arrived mid-morning and took the remainder. It had stopped raining, but the sky was dark and overcast, making the day even more somber. Every man in the company knew at least one of the men who had died. Eighteen rucksacks were stacked on the trail, providing mute testimony to the previous day's terrible toll. If possible, they would recover the rucksacks later; if not, the stack would be napalmed, thus preventing the enemy from salvaging them.

Per battalion orders, Alpha Company departed the area mid-morning and linked up with Bravo. Alpha was down to sixty-two men, and Bravo was not much better off. The companies joined up, established a defensive perimeter, and ordered the platoons to settle their troops in and to get some rest. It was apparent Alpha would not return to its previous position soon, so Capt. Otstott called in a napalm strike on the abandoned rucksacks. At noon the next day, a chopper landed carrying breakfast and lunch meals in mermite cans. Alpha took the breakfast meal and Bravo, the lunch. Soon after the Alpha troopers began to eat, they started vomiting, and seventeen became gravely ill. Second Platoon had drawn guard duty that morning and dragged out of their blankets at "oh-dark-30," pissing and moaning. Sparky was on the perimeter with Lt. Anderson when a call came in that medevacs were arriving to pick up food-poisoning victims. Anderson heard no more complaints from his men, and all looked forward to their c-rats when they finished their duty. The sickened men would return in three days, but for now, Alpha's strength was down another 25 percent.

The battalion commander advised Capt. Otstott he had decided to pull Alpha off line to a safe area. The unit would receive replacements and have a few days to assimilate the new troops before returning to the field. The captain opted to take his company back to where the recon platoon had been extracted, and early next morning, the forty-five troopers saddled up to return to the grassy knoll. Retracing their previous route, the unit approached the hill by late afternoon. An hour later, there was an explosion. The company point man had walked into the trip wire of a booby-trapped grenade, seriously wounding him in both legs and critically wounding a platoon sergeant in the chest. A medevac was called, and the docs tried to save the stricken sergeant, but his injury was too severe. He died before the slick arrived to transport him. It was a terrible way to begin a rebuilding period for the beleaguered company.

Fifty replacements arrived the following morning and were turned over to the platoon sergeants. The leaders were ordered to get the new troops into squads, then into defensive fighting positions and out on short patrols in their assigned sectors. They needed to get the new men assimilated as quickly as possible in this relatively benign environment. Sparky Ellis, in his role as the platoon RTO, was out with Lt. Anderson all day. Then, as one of the few experienced troops in the platoon, he worked with the new men in his spare time. The company would return to the line in three days.

The company's defensive sectors consisted of a small knoll on the south assigned to Second Platoon, a taller knoll in the center manned by Third, and a ridge running northeast from the center occupied by First and Fourth Platoons. Sometime after dark, observers on the ridge saw moving lights north of their position. Artillery was called in and the lights disappeared, but Lt. Anderson was uneasy. His gut told him something was about to happen, and his gut was seldom wrong. He had lost some good men in the past week and did not know any of the new troops in his platoon. That was part of his uneasiness. He moved down the southern defensive line, from position to position, making sure his boys were awake and alert. There was no moon, and the night was incredibly dark. On a night like this, anything could happen. Anderson sent out another patrol at midnight. It was Sparky's squad. Of the dozen men, only the squad sergeant, the M60 gunner, the corporal walking point, and Sparky had been in Second Platoon longer than a day. The other eight were all new.

By 1:00 a.m., the squad had gone about a mile, moving in an arc south and east of the south knoll. As the point man made his way through a patch of heavy brush, he collided with an enemy soldier approaching from the opposite direction. With a yelp, the corporal fell back and opened fire, killing the NVA soldier. The troopers hit the ground, and the sky lit up with automatic weapons fire from the front and to their left. They had stumbled blindly into a major enemy force which exploded like a nest of angry hornets. Seeking cover behind rocks, the troopers returned fire at the enemy muzzle flashes.

Ellis was pinned down behind a boulder, and two or three AK-47s had his number. Each time he fired, his boulder was blasted, and chunks of rock rained down on him. Porter, the M60 gunner, was ten yards to his right. Porter was a big, quiet guy from Iowa. He was married and had a little boy. Porter was firing his weapon as fast as he could feed the ammo belts into the gun. Sparky had no idea where the other troopers were, although he heard sporadic fire from behind him, and he had heard someone cry out in pain. He tried to contact platoon, but the radio was dead. Assuming it had taken an AK round, he unbuckled the harness and shrugged it off.

Raising his M14 to fire, another blast of AK-47 fire raked his position, and Ellis felt a jolt to his left shoulder followed by searing pain. Sliding back down behind the rock, he was aware of the cold stone against his hot face; blinking back tears, he waited for the pain to subside, but it did not. It was like a red-hot knife—then he felt pins and needles down his left arm, like hitting his "funny bone," only worse. Dropping his weapon, he reached up to grasp his shoulder with his right hand and felt warm blood soaking through his uniform. The round had struck him at the left arm hole in his flak vest, and he had little use of his left arm. Grabbing his M14, he stuck the muzzle over top of the boulder in the general direction of his attackers and emptied the magazine. "Maybe that'll hold the bastards a bit," he said to himself, loading a fresh mag.

Tugging the green towel from around his neck, Sparky wiped the sweat and tears from his face, and gritting his teeth, forced the wad of cloth in against his wound to help staunch the bleeding. At that moment, he heard Porter cry out. Looking across, he saw the big man slumped behind his M60. Grenades had set fire to brush some distance beyond, and in the flickering light, he saw NVA soldiers crawling through the grass toward Porter's position. Slowly raising his head, Porter looked across at Ellis, and without hesitation, Sparky acted. Surprising the enemy, he abandoned his cover and charged toward Porter. Firing bursts from his M14, several NVA went down, and the youngster was two-thirds of the way across the open space before anyone took aim at him. Then, amid a hail of bullets, he leapt the final ten feet, landing atop Porter. "Another touchdown," he said with a wry smile, then he grabbed the M60 and laid down a barrage of deadly fire into the advancing force.

Ellis continued to fire, but the M60 was nearly out of ammo, and he had only one more magazine for his M14. He had heard no supporting fire from behind him in some time, and enemy fire was increasing. Rounds were also beginning to come in from the right, as the NVA troops moved to surround him.

Feeding in the last belt of ammo, Sparky glanced back at Porter and thought about his little boy in Iowa. A cooling breeze had sprung up, and he turned his face into it, momentarily enjoying the cool freshness of the air on his face. Taking a long, deep breath, he smelled the sweet scent of the grass on the hill. It reminded him of Oregon and home—his mom and dad and Linda. Then he turned and grimly resumed firing at the onslaught of enemy troops.

Part 5

About 2:00 a.m., explosions and automatic weapons fire awakened the Alpha Company command post. It was located down in the saddle between the two knolls. Capt. Otstott and his RTOs moved to a foxhole, and the commander tried to contact his platoon leaders. Green tracers struck the ground around the hole as a trooper came running past from Second Platoon. It was a new sergeant who had just arrived that day. He shouted, "There's a million Cong up there!" and he disappeared into the darkness toward Third Platoon. Moments later, Lt. Anderson reported in. Second Platoon had been overrun. Only a few had managed to fight their way out, and he believed everyone else was dead on the south knoll.

The volume of enemy fire from the south was increasing and moving closer. Otstott told the leaders of the other three platoons Second Platoon had been overrun, and no more Americans were alive on the south knoll. The company had received a .50 caliber machine gun that day. It was positioned atop the higher knoll, and the commander ordered it turned on Second Platoon's position. The .50 cal opened fire and traversed the area continuously for twenty minutes, breaking the back of the enemy attack. As the night wore on, there was sporadic fire, but the attack was over. Otstott alerted the platoons they would counterattack at first light and retake the knoll. First and Fourth Platoons sent half their troops to the command post. Joining Lt. Anderson and his few survivors, they formed a skirmish line some twenty-strong and moved up the slope, but the NVA were gone. They found six of their own, dead in their defensive positions, and eighteen dead NVA, most armed with AK-47s.

Lt. Anderson took a detail out to search for the missing patrol and soon found "his boys." All were dead, save one. Beneath Ellis' body, they found Porter. He was grievously wounded and unconscious, but he would survive to see his son again and to recount the story of Sparky Ellis' bravery.

Four months later at Vancouver Barracks, Washington, Mr. and Mrs. Aldwin Ellis Sr. were presented with their son's awards: The Silver Star Medal, for "gallantry in action"; The Bronze Star, for "heroism"; two Orders of the Purple Heart, for his battle-related wounds; and the Vietnamese Military Merit Medal and Vietnamese Gallantry Cross with Palm, bestowed by the Republic of Vietnam for "deeds of valor in combat." Ellis also received a posthumous promotion to corporal. Sparky Ellis was eighteen years old.

> Greater love hath no man than this,
> That he lay down his life for his friends.

> —John 15:13

Author's Note

In addition to Cpl. Ellis, the following soldiers from Alpha Company, 2/502nd Infantry, were awarded the Silver Star Medal for their heroism on 7 October 1967: 1st Lt. Leonard G. Anderson; Pfc. Hugh R. Flemister*; Jupiter, Florida, twenty-two years old; Pfc. Robert J. Padgett*, College Park, Georgia, nineteen years old; Pfc. Rodney D. Hill*, Tahoe City, California, nineteen years old; and Pfc. William A. Jateff*, Akron, Ohio, twenty-two years old (*posthumously). Of these six heroes, only Lt. Anderson survived the morning attack (GBB).

17

Thomas James Tomczak

So Much More

Back row: Les Neese, Vince Keeney, Dennis Foreman,
Middle row: Jon Phipps, Tim O'Rourke, Jim Alward,
Tommy Tomczak in front

Tommy Tomczak was two years old when his father, Melvin, married Mary Lou Rork. He was a blue-eyed, bouncing ball of energy and the center of everyone's universe. That would be his role his entire life.

Melvin and Mary Lou had three children of their own (Mark, Cheryl, and Patricia) and then divorced. When Melvin moved on, Tommy remained with his stepmother. He was now the de facto "man of the house" and would do his best to look after his mother and younger siblings.

The family lived on a farm, and the kids delighted in wading in the clear creeks and roaming the woods with their friends during the warm summer months. They spent most of the daylight hours outside, only showing up at the house when their stomachs let them know it was time to eat. They would be outside again late into the evening, chasing fireflies and playing hide-and-seek until bedtime.

There was a trail down which they would ride their bikes at break-neck speeds, whooping and hollering all the way. Patty, the baby sister, was too young to ride a bike, so Tommy would put her on his back and run down the trail as fast as his legs could go. He wanted to give Patty the same thrill the older children were experiencing on their bicycles. With the wind blowing through her hair, the child would scream with delight and hug her brother's neck so tightly as he ran that he could barely breathe. They would collapse in the soft grass at the end of the trail—both of them laughing and trying to catch their breath.

Mary Lou and the children moved to South Milwaukee and lived in a "storefront" for a few years. All four kids slept in the same large room, and their beds were placed side by side, like a dormitory.

The beds were close enough together the children could run into the room and hop from one bed to the next clear across the room, usually with Tommy leading the pack. They had their own gymnasium, as long as Mom was not looking.

When he was younger, Tommy was shy around strangers, especially among crowds of people he did not know. He tended to stay in the background and observe, his keen mind taking in every aspect of what he saw and heard. In high school, however, he began to mature and change. He joined the forensic league and began to debate and make speeches. He enjoyed the give-and-take with his teammates; he relished the competition with other schools; and he was delighted with the impact he could have on people with his quirky sense of humor. He also tried out for parts in school theater productions and was selected for roles in several plays.

In 1964, Mary Lou was in the process of moving the family to a new house in Port Washington, Wisconsin. Located north of Milwaukee, the community was nestled on the shore of Lake Michigan, and the children were excited about living near the lake. Tommy was sixteen years old.

On Saturday, August 22, he went with his mother to haul a load of furniture, bedding, cooking utensils, and dishes to Port Washington in a borrowed truck. The weather was miserably hot and humid, and storm clouds were building up in the west. They hurried to get the last of the boxes and furniture unloaded and moved into the house before the arrival of the expected storm. Thunder was rumbling in the distance, and there was a fresh edge to the breeze. The air was crackling with electricity, and Mary Lou could smell the approaching rain as the two moved inside.

Tommy slumped down on a chair in the kitchen and swiped his sweaty face with the tail of his tee shirt. "Man, it's hot," he said with a sigh. "I hope the storm cools it off."

Rummaging through a box of dishes, Mary Lou found two glasses and filled them with cool water. Handing a glass to her son, she sat down to rest a bit before they headed back to Milwaukee.

Soon, with loud crashes of thunder and wicked lightning, the rain began to fall and build in intensity.

Mary Lou took a long, slow swig of the water. "Maybe we can wait out the storm before we hit the road," she said softly.

Placing her glass on the table, she stood and walked into the living room to look out through the large plate-glass picture window. What she saw froze her in place.

Suddenly Tommy heard what sounded like the roar of a distant train. Sensing danger, he jumped to his feet and ran in behind Mary Lou. The window was filled with a huge funnel cloud bearing down on them. It was jet-black at the bottom, snow white at the top and writhing like a monstrous snake. The roar was now deafening.

Grabbing his mother around the waist, Tommy dragged her away from the window, pulling her back beneath a staircase. A large area rug was rolled up near them—he grabbed a corner of it and pulled it over them, just as the picture window imploded, blasting the interior of the house with lethal shards of heavy glass and large splintered pieces of the wooden facing. The house survived the storm without major damage, and thanks to Tommy, so did Mary Lou. He always seemed to be there when someone needed him.

One afternoon, Patty, the youngest sister, was singing in a school choir concert. Mary Lou had an appointment she could not break; therefore, she had to miss the program. As the children in the choir filed on stage and climbed to their places on the risers, they waved at their parents and other family members, but Patty had no one to wave to, and she began to cry. When the concert concluded, Patty came down the stage stairs still teary-eyed and sniffling, and there was Tommy with his arms outstretched. He had cut his last class and arrived late, but he had heard most of the concert. He was so much more than just a big brother.

After finishing high school, Tommy was unsure what he wanted to do in the future. The war in Vietnam was in all the newspapers and on the television news programs in the evening, and he knew without college, he would soon be drafted. Tommy's cousin, Dougie Benson was a Navy Seal, so he discussed the possibility of enlisting in the military with his cousin.

After considering his options, he made the decision to enlist in the Army. He took the battery of armed forces entrance exams and scored extremely high marks. His family had always known he was smart—they just had no idea how smart.

The recruiter told him his test scores qualified him to join an "elite" group he had never heard of: The Army Security Agency. "I can't tell you what you'll be doing," the recruiter told him, "It's all hush-hush, but you will be doing top-secret work and providing a great service to your country."

Tommy Tomczak was sold!

Part 2

Tomczak enlisted on July 5, 1966, and boarded a plane in Milwaukee bound for Ft. Leonard Wood, Missouri. Known not-so-fondly as "Ft. Lost-in-the-woods," the final leg of the trip was by bus, and the recruits were met by drill sergeants whose primary mission in life was to make their lives a living hell for the next two months.

Fort Leonard Wood had not changed much since the end of World War II. The barracks had been constructed as "temporary" facilities at the start of the war, and there had been little in the way of upgrades since. The men were "marched" to a reception center where they were issued uniforms, given a military haircut (which took about five seconds), given shots for various diseases, and had their personnel files started. Then, they were "double-timed" to their company training area with the sergeants screaming all the way.

When "Reveille" sounded in the morning, the recruits had to be up, showered, shaved, dressed and in formation in about twenty minutes, while constantly being harassed by the drill sergeants. They double-timed to the mess hall (and everywhere else) where they stood at attention as they were lined up at the door, pushed through the chow line, given about five or six minutes to eat, and pushed out the door on the other side. In the field, lunch was always c-rations. The "rats" were leftover from WWII and consisted of a small can of "mystery meat," a small can of peaches or fruit cocktail, a chocolate bar, and a pack of four cigarettes. The men had a few minutes to eat, and then they were off running in step with full back packs to their next exercise.

Tomczak never dreamed southern Missouri could be so God-dammed hot in July and August, and there was no such thing as a fan or AC. His heavy cotton fatigue uniform stayed soaked with sweat. The drill sergeants constantly harped at the recruits to stay hydrated and take their salt tablets, and then they would run them another two miles for more PT. Tommy wasn't sure when the "elite" part of the recruiter's plan was supposed to kick in, but he was ready any time.

After successfully completing basic training, Tomczak and two other soldiers were put aboard a train for Ft. Devens, Massachusetts, where they would receive training as 05H—EW/SIGINT Morse Interceptors, which translated to Electronic

Warfare/Signal Intelligence Morse intercept operators, better known as "ditty-boppers."

At the completion of his Morse intercept training, Tomczak was promoted and informed he had been chosen for even more elite training. If he wanted to volunteer for it, he would join a select group of other ASA volunteers in Okinawa for Special Forces training and jump school. Upon the successful completion of that training, he would become a member of an Army Security Agency Special Operations Detachment and assigned to a Special Forces unit somewhere in the field.

"Holy shit!" Tomczak thought. "What a challenge, what an opportunity—what a helluva ride!"

Tommy Tomczak went home on leave for the first time in almost ten months and looked like a new man. He had always been precocious, but now the boy was gone. An unreserved, confident, young man stood in his place, and so much more. But, the smile was still the same.

"He couldn't tell us much about what his job was," his sister said, "but he would sit in the dining room in the evenings and practice Morse code. He had a book, and he would practice the code over and over. I just sat on the floor at his feet and watched him. He was my big brother and my idol."

When his leave time was up, Mary Lou drove Tommy to the airport in Milwaukee and watched him board the plane for California. She was proud of the man he had become, but she dreaded seeing him head overseas. His next stop would be the US-controlled island of Okinawa, some four hundred miles southwest of Japan. Mary Lou prayed he could avoid duty in Vietnam.

Part 3

Jim Alward, Dennis Foreman, and Les Neese met Tomczak in Okinawa, when he and Tim O'Rourke arrived in June 1967. Jon Phipps, Vince Keeney and others arrived later.

"We were all part of a group fresh from the States, sent to the 400th ASA Special Operations Detachment," Alward said. "Tom was the youngest in the group—nineteen, I think. He was also the funniest and the most carefree, and by his own admission, the one least likely to enjoy strenuous physical activity. We spent every morning of the first several months on Oki getting ready for Special Forces jump school. We had all shaved our heads and went through a grueling series of drills and exercises daily. The thing Tom hated most was pull-ups. He wasn't all that crazy about the five mile run either."

None of the men ever knew why they were offered the opportunity for SOD training.

"I can still see Tom's smile and hear his laugh in my mind," Dennis Foreman recalled.

"Tom and I shared at least one weakness—lack of upper body strength. Prior to jump school in October, we newbies underwent many drills and pretests in preparation for the various physical tests we would have to pass in order to succeed in jump school (timed push-ups, sit-ups, pull-ups, mile run, etc.).

"Tom and I immediately recognized we needed to work on pull-ups in order to proceed with our buddies," Foreman continued. "In the latrine of our barracks in Sukiran, the stall doors were braced by a small wooden beam about seven feet high that ran from wall to wall. We resolved that every time we entered—or walked by—the latrine, we'd grab the beam and do as many pull-ups as we could manage. After several weeks of this self-enforced regimen, Tom and I were able to pass the airborne pull-up test with relative ease."

In addition to the constant physical training, the ASA Green Berets were expected to take part in a variety of other special training courses such as Cold-Weather Survival and Skiing, Jump Master and HALO Parachute, Infiltration and Extraction, and extensive weapons training. Additional academic study was also encouraged. Early in 1968, Tomczak flew to Hokkaido, Japan, for three weeks of ski school, and then returned to Okinawa for additional ASA training at Torii Station in Sobe, Okinawa.

On April 24, 1968, three weeks after Tommy Tomczak's twentieth birthday, several of the ASA Green Berets on Okinawa shipped out TDY to the 403rd Special Operations Detachment (Abn), located at Special Forces headquarters in Nha Trang, South Vietnam. From there, the men were split up and assigned to various SF camps. Alward was assigned to Camp A-239 at Đức Lập; Foreman left for Buôn Mê Thuột; Tomczak went to A-242 at Đắk Pék in Kon Tum Province.

Đắk Pék was the farthest north, the most remote Special Forces camp in II Corps and located in an area totally controlled by the VC and NVA. The main compound sat on a barren hilltop surrounded with six layers of barbed wire, sharpened bamboo stakes and mine fields and was accessible only by air. It was five kilometers from the Laotian border and sat astride the Ho Chi Minh Trail. That is why it was there, and that is why it was a perennial pain in the ass for the North Vietnamese. The camp was also a launch site for top secret MACV-SOG raids into Laos. It was under constant threat of attack but was so strategically important, the Green Berets were ordered to defend it at all costs.

In each SF camp, the ASA ops had their own bunker that was off limits to all non-ASA personnel, including the camp commander. Their intercept equipment and their mission was classified "top secret," and only those with "the need to know" had access to the ASA bunker. There were normally three or four intercept operators in a camp, which allowed for some sort of round-the-clock monitoring of local enemy communications, as well as time for rest and whatever regular camp duties the men were expected to perform. The 403rd SOD had an in-country radio net, and there would be brief contacts with Nha Trang once or twice a week in the evening. The ASA soldiers would gather in their bunker and wait for the broadcast which might include some low-level, unclassified news. As a weak stab at security, each man was called by the phonetic alphabet for their initials. Jim Alward was "Juliet Alpha"; Dennis Foreman was "Delta Foxtrot" and Tom Tomczak was "Tango Tango."

"One night in July, three months after our arrival in Vietnam, we were gathered around the radio," Dennis Foreman said, "and I was horrified to hear Tango Tango was 'Kilo India Alpha!'" (KIA: killed in action).

According to records of the Special Forces Association, Sgt. Tomczak and Sfc. Harry L. Boyle were killed while firing a mortar "w/CHICOM ammo" (Chinese Communist ammunition), which "exploded on exiting tube."

There was speculation by some that the mortar round, which had been captured from the Viêt Công, had been deliberately sabotaged by one or more members of the LLDB (ARVN Special Forces), but the ensuing investigation found no proof of sabotage.

Billy Frank Fuller, another ASA Green Beret and a friend of Tomczak's said, "Tommy always had that mischievous smile and was fun to be with. I spent time with him on several occasions when I was travelling in and out of the camps. I was in Đắk Pék about a week before the accident and drank a few beers with Tom."

"From what I was told later, after dinner on 23 July, Tom went over to help some non-ASA Green Berets who were assigned to the camp. They were firing mortars into the hillside where they sometimes could spot enemy activity. To my knowledge, they were not under fire. The mortar malfunctioned, killing Tom and one of the other Green Beret NCOs and wounding several others."

"I was in Pleiku and was asked to go to Đắk Pék and identify Tom's body for processing back to the USA," Fuller concluded.

Dennis Foreman said, "I have often thought I need to enjoy life in a way Tom never had a chance to. On the other hand, Tom had a grown-up and often off-the-chart-enjoyable life in a short twenty years, and he died during a brave, volunteer adventure ride with his friends."

In 1969, the 400th SOD built a new physical training field in Sukiran, Okinawa, and named it Tomczak Memorial Field. Recalling how Tom hated those long, PT-filled days before their airborne training in 1967, Jim Alward shook his head and smiled. "Tommy would have loved it!" he said.

The Army Security Agency SODs were small, elite units, and their members served our country with distinction and honor. It has been said the SOD units were not just elite, they were extraordinary, and what made them extraordinary was the people. Not only were they good Special Forces soldiers and good technicians—brave, loyal, and dedicated—but most of all, they were trusted and true friends. Only a few hundred SOD soldiers served in Vietnam from 1966 through 1970, but many served in active combat roles. Their awards for heroism in combat include: four Silver Stars; twenty Bronze Stars with "V" Device for valor and fourteen Army Commendation Medals with "V" Device for valor. Twenty-four ASA SOD Green Berets received Purple Hearts for battle-related wounds, and one, Tommy Tomczak, gave his life.

Tommy Tomczak always seemed to get so much more out of life than most people. It was as if he squeezed every last morsel of enjoyment out of everything he did. There were and are no words to describe the sense of total loss—the feelings of total waste experienced by those men who had lived with, trained with, and served with Tommy Tomczak.

> From this day to the ending of the world,
> But we in it shall be remembered—
> We few, we happy few, we band of brothers;
> For he today that sheds his blood with me
> Shall be my brother
>
> "Henry V"
> —William Shakespeare

Tommy had always been there for his younger siblings, and his death devastated the family. "He was so much more than just our brother," Patty Tomczak said. "He was our rock."

Tommy Tomczak came home for the last time in August 1968. He was buried with full military honors at Holy Sepulcher Cemetery in Cudahy, Wisconsin, on the beautiful shore of Lake Michigan. He was twenty years old.

18

Donald Sidney Skidgel

"Armed Savage 33"

Donald "Donnie" Skidgel

Donnie Skidgel did not have to go to war. He had married his high school sweetheart after graduation from Nokomis High School and had two beautiful kids by the time he was nineteen. His draft classification was III-A, but that was not the way it was done in Newport, Maine. And that was not the way it was done in the Skidgel household. His dad, Sid, had signed up for the Army Air Corps in '42. Now it was 1968. It was Donnie's war and Donnie's turn. His country needed him—no excuses. Darlene hated to see him go, but the Skidgels were tough New England stock. There was no point in trying to change his mind. In October, Donnie drove to Bangor and enlisted in the US Army.

After completing basic training, Skidgel was offered the opportunity to join an elite group and volunteered for Armor Recon School at Ft. Knox. The three-month course was physically grueling and mentally challenging. The men trained in armored personnel carriers and received advanced arms training. Their survival training culminated with two weeks sleeping in tents in the snowy mountains of Kentucky. Half the training company came down with pneumonia. It was great preparation for the tropical jungles of Southeast Asia. Finishing his training at the end of March, Skidgel headed home. He had two weeks leave before deploying to Vietnam.

Donnie had written Darlene nearly every day. They had never been apart for more than a few days at a time. He had been her first love, her first kiss, her only love. Now he was leaving for a year. She dared not think beyond that. The fact that Donnie was heading for combat was something she was not ready to face. Terry and Tammy, their children, were two and three years old. Tammy had missed her daddy and was delighted to see him, but it took Terry a while to warm up to him.

April was beautiful in Newport. Winter had finally loosened its grip, and the small town on Sebasticook Lake had that fresh-scrubbed look so typical of northern New England. The weather was unseasonably warm, and Donnie and Darlene made the most of it. They spent hours out with the children. There were Skidgel family gatherings with great meals; Donnie got out with some of his buddies a night or two, and he and Darlene found time when they could be alone. Those times were the best, after the babies were asleep, when they could just be Donnie and Darlene. Darlene would produce frothy mugs of hot "drinking chocolate," put on her Sam Cook and Bobby Vinton LPs, and they forgot about the rest of the world.

The two-week leave flew by, and the day for Donnie's departure arrived. The family took him to Bangor to catch his flight, and the airport scene was tough. His dad clinched his jaw, shook Donnie's hand, gave him a slap on the back, and a "sort of" hug. His mother and Darlene were in tears, and the children did not understand what was going on. Donnie struggled to control his emotions, but damn! It was so hard. He gave Darlene one last kiss, then brushing away a tear, he was gone.

Skidgel landed at the US Army Overseas Replacement Station at Oakland Army Base late in the afternoon. Troops heading to and from Vietnam were being processed there, and after a short briefing, he and the other new men were shown their sleeping quarters. They would sleep on folding cots in a mammoth warehouse. The war in Vietnam was escalating at a rapid pace, and the base was using any space available to accommodate the influx of troops. The men were issued new green jungle fatigues and boots and spent the days standing in line and filling out paperwork.

During free time in Oakland, Skidgel observed many returning from Vietnam and was struck by the sadness in their faces. He thought they should be happy; they were going home, but he saw few smiles. They simply looked old before their time, and he wondered what he was heading into.

After completing his processing, Skidgel and his new buddies were put on board a Greyhound bus to Travis Air Force Base and then loaded aboard a huge C-130 cargo plane. The flight to Vietnam took about twenty-two hours and stopped in Anchorage, Alaska, and Yokota, Japan. Donnie slept as much as possible, but he read some, too. He had become interested in Gen. George Patton while in armor school at Ft. Knox and had picked up his book *War as I Knew It*. "Old Blood and Guts" was someone he could learn a lot from. Patton had held armor in high esteem, and the armored units still worshipped him.

Skidgel's plane landed at Biên Hòa Air Base after midnight. There was no moon, and it was extremely dark. As the aircraft door opened, the soldiers were inundated by a wave of intense heat and humidity. The New Englander had never experienced anything like it. The sweltering air was difficult to breathe, and his uniform was instantly soaked with sweat. As he started down the aircraft steps a breeze stirred, and he got his first whiff of local air: a memorable combo of kerosene, stale piss and rotting garbage, with subtle undertones of Malathion insecticide. Welcome to Vietnam!

The new troops filed into the terminal at Biên Hòa and were herded onto buses for transport to the 90th Replacement Battalion near Long Bình. Skidgel ached in every part of his twenty-year-old body. Upon arrival, the men were assigned to the barracks where they would live while undergoing additional in-processing and receiving their duty assignments. They were marched into a long building with a concrete floor and tin roof. The walls of the building were constructed of angled wooden slats, which allowed air to flow through, and the slats were covered with screen wire on the outside to keep insects out. As Skidgel surveyed the new facility in his exhausted state, it vaguely reminded him of a POW camp he had read about. All that was missing were German guards and lice. Of course, he had not tried out his cot. The men stowed their gear, were ordered "lights out!" and had barely closed their eyes when "Reveille" sounded. The date was April 18, 1969.

After a quick shower and shave, the troops marched to the mess hall for breakfast. They were then marched to the parade ground, where a sergeant read out the names of those who had been assigned to various units. Those formations were held every two or three hours, all day. In between, the men continued to in-process or returned to their barracks to read or play cards. Skidgel's name was not called the first day. He wrote Darlene after evening chow, telling her about his first day in 'Nam, but he could not tell her where he would be going or what he would be doing.

Several of the new men were assigned perimeter guard duty, that night. The perimeter of every US base had defensive bunkers constructed from sandbags, and guards were posted there to watch for enemy infiltration. Skidgel was one of the lucky few tapped for duty, so he spent his second night in Vietnam with little sleep. Following chow the next morning, he fell into formation on the parade ground, and they called his name. Donnie Skidgel was headed for the 1/9th Cavalry Regiment, otherwise known as the 1/9th "Headhunters" of the 1st Air Cavalry Division.

All new infantry troops assigned to the 1st Air Cav were given a week of in-country jungle training before moving on to their new units. The training took place at the First Team Academy in Biên

Hòa, and Skidgel reveled in it. He was issued an M16, spent time on the range zeroing his weapon, rappelled off their forty-five-foot tower, and received refresher training in claymores, trip flares, and other gear. He also learned about VC booby traps and tactics, and the poisonous snakes in the region. Upon completion of his jungle training, Skidgel boarded a Chinook helicopter for a flight to Camp Gorvad at Phước Vĩnh, headquarters for the 1/9th. It was located some thirty nautical miles northwest of Saigon at the edge of the Central Highlands.

When he arrived, he was met by a trooper in a jeep, driven to squadron headquarters to sign in, and then shown to his "hootch." The building had corrugated tin siding and roof, and housed about a dozen troops with bunk beds and mosquito nets. Large barrels filled with rocks and sand bags were piled around the building for protection against rocket and mortar attacks. The Hilton, it was not.

Skidgel was unpacking when he heard the wail of a siren, and someone yelled at him to "git in the bunker." He followed other troopers out through the door and into an underground shelter. The deep hole was dank, musty, and covered with several feet of sandbags. Skidgel did not want to think about what kinds of wildlife might be in the dark hole with them. Mortars began to strike the area as he settled inside; the muffled explosions continued for several minutes. There was a brief period of silence, and then an all-clear siren was heard. Skidgel started to move, but one of the other men grabbed his arm and pulled him back. "Chill man," he said. "Charlie can hear the sirens, too. You never know when he's gonna lob in a few more after the all-clear."

Part 2

The 1/9th Cav was an air cavalry squadron with four combat troops. Alpha, Bravo, and Charlie were air cavalry troops; Delta Troop, however, was a ground cavalry troop, and its members considered themselves to be "the real Cav." Dubbed the "Rat Patrol," they were an elite group and had earned a well-deserved reputation as one of the toughest and best fighting units in the 1st Air Cav. Delta was organized with three ground cavalry platoons mounted on trucks and jeeps. The three platoons were identified by the colors in the US flag: 1st Platoon was "Red," 2nd Platoon was "White," and 3rd Platoon was "Blue." Each platoon had a recon section, an infantry squad, a mortar squad, and an anti-tank section. The senior leadership of each platoon consisted of the platoon leader and the platoon sergeant. Each leader had a jeep with a driver/RTO, and the platoon sergeant was usually accompanied by a combat medic. The troop's main battle vehicles were M-151 jeeps with pedestal-mounted M60 machine guns, M-151 jeeps with mounted 106mm recoilless rifles, three-quarter ton trucks with portable 81mm mortars, and three-quarter ton trucks to carry the infantry squads. Their primary tactic was the element of surprise, and they had a way of popping up whenever and wherever they were needed most, much to the regret of the NVA.

Donnie Skidgel was assigned to the scout section in Delta Troop 3rd Platoon. He was a "Delta Blue" and was ushered in to meet his platoon leader, a young-looking first lieutenant named Buck Ross. After Skidgel reported in, Lt. Ross invited him to sit down and began to speak in a soft Mississippi drawl. He explained the mission of Delta Troop and what he expected from his men. He had an air of quiet self-confidence that was captivating, and he was all business. Buck Ross obviously knew what he was doing. The lieutenant asked Skidgel if he had fired an M60 machine gun. "During training," he replied. The officer turned to a nearby private, told him to "Get Skeets," and a few moments later introduced him to Skeets Trask.

Sgt. Samuel K. Trask, better known as "Skeets," was the M60 gunner and assistant squad leader in the recon squad to which Skidgel was being assigned. He was going to DEROS back to the World in a few weeks. The lieutenant needed a replacement, and Skidgel had the job. He would be accompanying Skeets on every mission until he shipped out. After the briefing, Skeets took Skidgel around and introduced him to some of the other troopers. The platoon sergeant was on a recon mission with about half the platoon, so there were not many around, but he met some of the guys with whom he would be going into the field.

The troops were allowed to go into Phước Vĩnh and hit some of the bars when they had evenings off. There were always bar girls around, ready and eager to relieve the men of their cares, their pay, and anything else they might need relieved of. Skidgel was invited to go to the "ville" with a couple of the Delta troopers, and one of them bought him a bottle of Vietnamese beer called "Ba Mươi Ba" or "33." The men watched with bemused smiles as the newbie held the bottle up to a light bulb. There were various kinds of foreign matter floating around inside the newly-opened bottle. The other troopers called the beer "tiger piss," and it smelled vaguely like formaldehyde, which was not encouraging. Not to be outdone, Skidgel drank the beer, but that was his first and last bottle of "33." It would not, however, be his last encounter with the number "33."

Donnie spent most of his off-duty time writing letters home and reading. He had no interest in the bar scene or the bar girls. He wrote to Darlene and the kids every night. He had finished Patton's book and had started reading *Warrior: The Story of General George Patton Jr.* by the editors of *The Army Times*. He had also picked up two other books on Patton at the PX, so he had plenty to read. In the meantime, he remained the "FNG," and that was not going to change until he went on a mission and had a chance to prove himself.

A few days later, the Blues were assigned a recon mission. Skidgel was finally going to get his baptism in the field. He was filled with a mix of emotions, running the full gamut from excitement to apprehension and some concern about how he would react under fire. The Blue Platoon had a twelve-man recon or "scout" section led by a staff sergeant, and it was divided into two scout squads. Each of the squads had two of the M60-mounted jeeps and a three-man crew: a sergeant who was the squad leader, a gunner/observer, and a driver/RTO.

Early the next morning, the string of "Rat Patrol" jeeps and trucks headed north into the Central Highlands. Two of the scout jeeps served as point squads for the platoon and were several hundred yards ahead of the convoy. Next came the antitank section with their 106mm recoilless rifles. They were followed by the command section and the trucks carrying the four rifle squads. At the rear was the mortar squad and the remaining two scout squads acting as the rear guard. Skidgel was riding with Skeets in the second jeep at the front of the column and in his opinion, they were moving at an insane speed. He was hanging on tightly as the vehicle bucked and leapt through the air.

"This is unreal," he thought. His buddies in Newport would never believe it. Wow! What a ride.

Late in the morning, Lt. Ross halted the convoy along a wooded stream. They were moving into heavier jungle, and the road had all but disappeared. The call sign for Delta Troop was "Armed Savage," and the lieutenant instructed the section leaders by radio to grab some c-rats. They would move out in about an hour. One hour later, the lieutenant's jeep pulled up beside the scout jeeps, and he came striding over to Skidgel. Pointing at a tall tree about a hundred yards away, the officer told Skidgel to climb up behind the M60 and shoot at the tree. Skidgel fired about a hundred rounds before one finally hit the tree.

"Good shot," the lieutenant drawled, jumping into his jeep.

Then, with a "Saddle-up," the platoon leader jumped into his jeep and headed on up the valley with his recon scouts. The rest of the patrol trailed behind in a cloud of red dust.

The terrain was primarily rolling hills surrounded by stretches of dense jungle, and the entire area seemed eerily quiet. The scouts had not seen a person or vehicle in miles. Normally they would see some sign of life, no matter where they were. Children would show up selling bottled soft drinks at all hours of the day and night, unless there were NVA or VC in the area.

By 1:00 p.m., Lt. Ross had dropped back with the command section in the convoy. The scout jeeps were about a mile ahead and moving at a slower speed due to road conditions and visibility. The trail was deeply rutted, and double canopy jungle had closed in to within a few feet on each side. As the lead jeep disappeared over a low ridge twenty-five yards ahead of them, Skidgel and Skeets heard a burst of automatic weapons fire. Flooring the accelerator, the driver of Skeets' jeep cleared the top of the ridge, and the jeep was airborne. Before them was the lead jeep, stopped nose-down along the left side of the road, and the three troopers crouched down behind it were firing into a patch of heavy vegetation. As jeep number two landed and slid to a halt, Skeets began firing his M60 into the thick jungle growth and looking for some indication of where the enemy fire had come from.

Skidgel and the driver piled out behind their jeep and fired into the trees with their M16s. For Skidgel, everything was a blur of noise and confusion. The jungle canopy seemed to hold in and magnify the horrendous noise of the weapons, and that was compounded by the shouts of troopers, the raucous screeches of hundreds of birds, and the screams of dozens of small monkeys in the upper reaches of the forest. Donnie crouched lower behind the right front wheel as AK-47 fire raked the left side of the jeep.

At that moment, Skeets swung the M60 sharply right, screamed "Donnie!" and blasted an area of low grass and vines ten yards to their right. Out of the corner of his eye, Skeets had spotted an NVA soldier rising up out of a spider hole and taking dead aim at Skidgel.

For a brief moment, Donnie slumped down against the hub of the wheel. His face was bathed in sweat—his heart was about to beat its way out of his chest, and he could not breathe. He glanced up at Skeets who had immediately resumed firing into the jungle. Then he managed a deep breath to calm his nerves and resumed firing his M16. The enemy fire ended as suddenly as it had begun. The entire episode had lasted about a minute—a lifetime in a minute—almost his lifetime.

The rest of the convoy had not yet arrived on the scene. The Delta troopers looked as each other and slowly rose from their cover. No one had been hurt. Several of the men moved cautiously into the jungle growth from where the main attack had emanated. Crouching low, Skidgel moved toward the spider hole on the right to check the body of the man Skeets had killed. It was the first dead body he had seen in Vietnam, and the first he had ever seen hit with machine-gun fire. Staring at the still form, he shivered and broke out in a cold sweat; tears began to flow down his face, and he vomited. Pulling a towel from around his neck, he wiped his face and mouth, then he felt a strong hand squeeze his shoulder.

Glancing around sheepishly, he saw the concerned face of Krist, the medic who rode in the first scout jeep. Krist was small and blonde, and looked like he was fifteen years old, but he had been in Vietnam six months and was a seasoned trooper. The young man did not say a word. He simply patted Skidgel on the shoulder to reassure him and let him know he understood exactly what he was feeling. Then he turned and walked back to his jeep. At that moment, his compassion was just what Donnie Skidgel needed.

Skidgel made his way back to the number-two jeep just as Skeets returned from checking out the enemy bunker. "Hey, Sarge, thanks!" Skidgel said.

"Forget it," Skeets replied. "You'd do the same for me. Besides, if I get my replacement KIA on his first mission, the old man will chew my ass off—and he might not let me go home."

Donnie could not believe how near he had come to dying in his first combat action. Trask had saved his life, and there was a bond there. He might not have an opportunity to repay Skeets, but he could help someone else. There were all colors and creeds in Vietnam, and the men were from all over the country, but they were bound together by the same needs to survive and to help each other survive.

The jeeps pulled back on the trail to continue their journey, and there was a burst of static on the radio. A voice said: "Armed Savage 10 here. Everything okay?"

"Armed Savage Two-Three," Skeets responded. "A-OK—all clear! Over and out!"

Moving deeper into the jungle, Skidgel recalled something George Patton had said: "No man ever won a war by dying for his country. He won it by making the other dumb bastard die for his."

Part 3

Over the next six weeks, Donnie Skidgel shadowed Skeets Trask on mission after mission. He gained valuable experience and was promoted to corporal. On June 14, 1969, the scout section held a huge going-away party for Skeets, and he shipped out, seriously hungover, for home the next day. Skidgel was now the gunner.

Two weeks later, Delta Troop moved its base of operations from Phước Vĩnh to Fire Support Base Buttons. Buttons was located northwest of a two thousand-foot mountain called Núi Bà Rá and four miles west of the village of Sông Bé. It had an airstrip long enough to handle aircraft as large as C-130s and was headquarters for the 5/7th Cavalry and an Army artillery battery with six 105mm howitzers. The M102 howitzers provided fire support for the 5/7th's Infantry companies, Echo Company 5/7th's Scout Platoon, and Delta Troop.

During the day, Delta conducted ground operations in the jungle and rubber plantations surrounding the fire base and mounted reconnaissance and security missions along a vast network of trails and roads spread throughout Phước Long Province. At night, they carried out ambushes and occupied defensive positions for a large section of the fire base's massive perimeter. This area of the province was a major infiltration route for NVA forces moving down the Ho Chi Minh Trail through Cambodia. It was estimated over a thousand enemy troops per week were pouring into South Vietnam along this route and into the 1st Cav's Area of Operations. Delta Troop's services were in constant demand; the men rarely had a day off.

By early September, Donnie Skidgel had been promoted to sergeant and was the senior squad leader in the second scout squad of the 3rd Platoon "Blues." He had been on the job five months and gloried in what he was doing. He had never been involved in anything so exciting. He thrived on the adrenalin rush as the scouts sprung an ambush or launched an attack. He had become proficient with the M60 and seemed to defy death. He was not foolhardy, but luck always seemed to be with him. To the other recon troopers, Skidgel was simply the best at doing everything they did. Patton had taught him there is "no such thing as luck, merely opportunity meeting preparedness." He made certain he always had a "plan B" ready if he needed it, and his squad-members counted on that. Still, he felt luck played a part, too. He had long considered "33" to be his lucky number, aside from his run-in with the Ba Mươi Ba beer. His radio call sign was "Armed Savage Three-Three," and he took that as a lucky sign.

Early on Saturday morning, September 13, Delta Troop, led by its commander, Capt. Andrew Hudson, departed Buttons with the White and Blue Platoons. Red Platoon was on detached duty providing security for Bravo Troop 1/9 and was located at a fire base near An Lộc. White and Blue, including Skidgel's scout section, were going to establish strong points along Road 311. They were accompanying a detachment of Vietnamese provincial police whose mission was to check papers and inspect all vehicles and pedestrians moving along 311. The policemen were not looking for VC or NVA; they were searching for bandits and contraband, and the Delta troopers were there simply to support them.

Three weeks earlier, all of Delta Troop's 106mm recoilless rifles and its antitank section troopers had been airlifted to the top of Núi Bà Rá. There was a major communications complex on top of the mountain, which housed radio relay towers for all of the infantry and support units operating in the 1st Cav AO. The complex was also home to a detachment of the Army Security Agency's 371st Radio Research Company and their top-secret surveillance and communications intercept equipment. The 371st was ASA's direct support unit (DSU) assigned to the 1st Cav and was tasked with monitoring the continuous flow of NVA forces into the area. Infantry platoons from the 5/7th at Buttons provided defensive security for the communications complex, and the 106s had been moved there to bolster their defenses against a possible NVA attack.

The day spent with the provincial police was quiet and uneventful. Sgt. Skidgel and his squad were manning a strong point, and other Delta Troop elements were stretched out for a couple of miles along Road 311. Each strong point was located so the troopers manning it had a 360-degree view and could provide supporting fire in any direction. They could also see the next manned strong point in each direction. The Vietnamese policemen and a squad of Blue Platoon riflemen were manning a reinforced inspection point at the top of a hill just north of a major curve on 311. Skidgel was taking his turn at watch. The day had been long and boring, but he had set up a rotating schedule with his driver, Sgt. Sal Silva, and another trooper that required each of them to be on watch for thirty minutes and then have an hour off. It had made the time go faster and had allowed each of them time to read, write letters, or do whatever. Stretched back in the passenger seat of the jeep with his M16 in his lap and a straw of grass in his mouth, the young sergeant scanned the surrounding area with field glasses, but saw no sign of life except the Delta troops on the other strong points. He laid down the glasses, pulled the frayed camo boonie off his head, and ran his fingers through his short-cropped hair.

"Man, I'm tired," he said, to no one in particular. "Hope there's water for a shower when we get back to Buttons." He had written his letter for Darlene, so all he had to do was clean up, eat, and hit the rack. "Settin' around kills me," he said with a yawn.

It was getting late in the day. Capt. Hudson was ready to call a halt to the operation and head back to base with his troop. The section of road the team was working had been eerily quiet. The scout squads had not seen a bicycle, truck, farmer, or water buffalo in hours. The road was asphalt and wide enough to handle two-way traffic. It wound northwest from the Sông Bé area through rolling hills, bordered by jungle and rubber plantations. US Army engineers had used Rome plows to clear away the jungle from the sides of the road. The downed trees had been pushed back to the treeline, but it had not taken long for tall grass and brush to sprout up again along the road. It could provide cover for enemy troops, so they had to remain alert and keep their eyes open.

The commander gave the order over the radio for the platoon leaders to saddle up and head north. One of the scout jeeps was with Capt. Hudson and followed his jeep as they began to move north toward Skidgel's position. Hudson saw Skidgel's jeep pull onto the road, move slowly forward over a low ridge, and disappear. At that moment, there was an explosion of AK-47 and machine gun fire.

Hudson shouted "Go!" and his driver gunned the jeep forward. Flying over the ridge, they saw Skidgel's jeep twenty yards away stopped along the right side of the road. Hudson's jeep slid to a halt behind it, and he jumped out. Skidgel was kneeling behind the right front wheel of his jeep and firing his M16 across the front of the vehicle. His gunner and Sgt. Silva were also behind the jeep and firing into the trees across the road. Enemy fire was coming from behind some fallen trees to the west. As Hudson crouched down behind Skidgel, the young man turned and looked back. Recognizing the troop commander, a grin flashed across his face, and he nodded.

"Glad to see you, sir," he said. He told the captain he estimated enemy strength to be about a dozen, and no one in his squad was hurt.

Suddenly, two more scout jeeps flew over the ridgeline with guns blazing and poured a hail of rifle and M60 fire into the western tree line.

The firing died down, and the Delta troopers cautiously moved forward to search for the enemy. They found foxholes, abandoned equipment, and evidence of wounded or dead, but no bodies. The enemy had obviously spent time in the area, building and improving their installation. The sun was setting as the search of the enemy position concluded, and the troopers resumed their trek back to Buttons. Air Force fighter-bombers were called in and directed to bomb south and west of the attack location. When Capt. Hudson arrived back at HQ, he submitted a battle report, and during a command briefing, it was decided the Echo Company 5/7th Scout Platoon would infiltrate the area west of the attack site, attempt to locate the NVA force, and determine its size. When that was accomplished, an infantry company would be air-lifted in to engage and destroy the enemy force.

Part 4

Delta Troop was assigned to pick up the Echo Company 5/7 Scout Platoon and transport them to the site of the previous day's attack. It was Sunday, September 14, 1969. The fifteen Scouts would ride on White Platoon's jeeps and at an agreed-upon point, quietly slip off of into the tall grass as the slow-moving jeeps proceeded south down Road 311. When all the men were in the jungle, they would consolidate their group and pick up the NVA's trail. The Delta squads would reestablish their strong points and respond in case of trouble. The total American force consisted of sixty-six men.

The units began moving down Road 311 at 11:30 a.m. White Platoon was led by its platoon sergeant, Sfc. Baxter, who was a seasoned combat veteran. The Scouts' platoon leader, Lt. Thomas, and his assistant, Pfc. Halladay, rode with him. Thomas sat on the radio mounted atop the right rear fender behind the platoon sergeant, and Halladay sat on top of the radio on the left rear fender behind the driver with one of the Scouts' radios strapped to his back.

The convoy crossed a creek near the hamlet of Ap Binh Lan. There was a Vietnamese Regional Forces/Provincial Forces (Ruff-Puff) camp located along the creek, and the families living there came out and waved as the Delta convoy drove by. The two White Platoon lead jeeps climbed to the high ground south of the creek, and Sgt. Baxter requested permission to conduct a reconnaissance by fire with his lead scout's mounted M60 machine gun—Capt. Hudson radioed his approval a few seconds later. The White Platoon infantry squads were behind their platoon sergeant; Hudson's jeep was behind the infantry. The Delta Troop forward observer was next, with his assistant, and then came the mortar squad in their three-quarter ton truck. The second pair of White Platoon scout jeeps brought up the rear. There was a gap, and then Blue Platoon followed White Platoon.

The lead White scout jeep disappeared over the crest of a hill and headed down into a small valley. There was no sign of life as far as they could see. The jeep crossed the valley, and as it ascended on the other side, the gunner began firing his M60 in a sweeping 180-degree arc. The gunner in the second scout jeep also began firing into a clearing near the road, and then in sweeping motions across the tall grass and along the tree line. The lead jeep topped the hill and approached the curve on 311, just north of the previous day's attack. The column slowed in preparation for the Scouts to begin slipping off the vehicles—and their world exploded into a wild melee of noise and flame.

The entire Delta Troop column was engulfed in a massive wave of AK-47 and heavy machine-gun fire. Small arms and rifle fire, combined with a barrage of B40 rocket propelled grenades, came from the tall grass and brush along both sides of the road. The reconnaissance by fire of the two lead scouts' machine guns had prematurely triggered what would have been another "Custer at the Little Big Horn" massacre at the hands of over 600 NVA regular infantry. The Americans were outnumbered ten to one. It is ironic that the Echo 5/7 Scout Platoon was 7th Cavalry, Lt. Col. George Armstrong Custer's command in 1876.

As a result of the ambush being launching early, some of the Delta units at the end of the column had not yet reached the northernmost enemy positions along the sides of the road. That prevented the huge enemy force from closing the jaws of their trap and surrounding the small band of Americans; however, a deadly wall of machine gun and AK-47 fire had hit the two lead scout jeeps and the platoon sergeant's jeep. Sgt. Baxter and his driver were grievously wounded. Lt. Thomas and Pfc. Halladay, who were perched on top of Baxter's jeep died instantly in the fusillade. Eight other White Platoon troopers and several Scouts were also wounded. A rocket exploded alongside Capt. Hudson's jeep as he and his driver jumped out and took cover along the right side of the jeep. The enemy fire was devastating. Hudson retrieved a portable radio and then crawled into the tall grass some distance from the jeep, expecting the vehicle to be hit by an RPG at any moment.

Using the radio, Hudson called the 5/7th Cav tactical ops center at Buttons. He reported heavy enemy contact and requested helicopter gunships. Col. Healy, commander of the 5/7th, got in his command ship with his copilot and door gunners and headed south to the scene. Hudson also contacted "Cavalier Red," the 1st Platoon leader of Charlie Troop 1/9, and he was also on the way in a Cobra gunship armed with cannons and rockets. Hudson was still unsuccessful in establishing contact with anyone in the White or Scout Platoons ahead of him. There was no way to know that everyone in the lead units with access to a radio was either dead or severely wounded.

The commander could see the infantry squad truck and the platoon sergeant's jeep, which was ablaze. The second scout jeep was also on fire. He could not see the lead scout jeep or any of the other White Platoon troopers; however, he could hear their M60s and M16s firing, combined with long bursts from a host of AK-47s and exploding RPGs. His boys were putting up a fight against overwhelming odds. Delta Troop's primary "ambush-busting" weapons were their 106mm recoilless rifles. When loaded with flechette rounds, they fired hundreds of deadly darts with each shot and could quickly break up an enemy force, but their 106s were sitting atop Núi Bà Rá, ten miles away.

Looking back down the valley, Hudson saw the Blues' lead scout jeep and troopers firing into the trees on both sides of the road. Led by Lt. Buck Ross, the Blues had dismounted and sought cover.

Skidgel was in the second scout jeep with his driver, Sal Silva, and a gunner. Piling out of their jeep, they began to fire into the trees to the west. Most of the enemy fire was toward the front of the column, and Skidgel could see the lead jeeps and trucks were in major trouble. The scene was total chaos. They had to act quickly, or many good men were going to die today.

As the battle progressed, Capt. Hudson contacted Lt. Ross and asked if the Blues could provide covering fire for him and his driver to move out of the kill zone. Sgt. Skidgel was behind the rear wheel of his jeep below the radio and heard the commander's request. Silva was in front of him and also heard the brief transmission above the noise of the battle.

For a brief moment, Skidgel pondered what he should do, and then a portion of a humorous poem written by George Patton flashed through his mind: "In war just as in loving, you must keep on shoving, or you'll never get your reward, for if you are dilatory, in the search for lust or glory, you are up shit creek and that's the truth, oh, Lord."

With a slight smile, Skidgel yelled, "Hey, Sally, you want'a do this?" and nodded down the road.

Without hesitation, Silva crawled into the front seat behind the steering wheel. Skidgel slipped up over the back fender of the jeep behind the radio, and crouched at the base of the pedestal-mounted M60. Hudson and Ross both heard the radio response:

"Armed Savage Three-Three on the way, sir—over and out!"

As the jeep slowly moved out onto the asphalt, Donnie thought about his family back in Newport. "Things may get hairy in the next few minutes, Darlene," he said softly, "but this is something I gotta do. This is my time, and I gotta keep on shoving. I can't sit here and let those men die."

Silva pulled the jeep to the left to get around the lead scout jeep—then he hit the accelerator and the jeep shot forward. Skidgel reached up with his right hand, stretching to reach the pistol-grip and trigger of the M60—then he hauled himself up and felt the familiar pressure of the gun stock as he pulled it into his shoulder. Standing now, in full view of the enemy, he began to fire the weapon into the trees in wide sweeping arcs. Ignoring the AK-47 rounds ricocheting off the front of the jeep, Silva straightened out the vehicle and headed down the road past the stalled convoy. Fearlessly ignoring the hail of enemy machine gun and rocket fire, Skidgel continued to fire into the enemy positions, and the enemy fire abruptly decreased. Two rockets impacted behind the jeep, spraying both Skidgel and Silva with deadly shrapnel, but they continued to pick up speed and appeared unstoppable. Other Blue Platoon troopers saw what was happening and shifted their fire forward to provide a withering barrage of cover fire for the young sergeant as his jeep careened down the road.

God, how they loved this kid!

At that moment, Skidgel felt red-hot stabs to his legs. The shock of the blows knocked him to his knees, but he caught himself, and held on to the mounted M60. Silva heard the M60 stop firing, glanced back, and slowed a bit.

"Keep going, Sally," Skidgel yelled. "Forward!"

Exerting all his strength, he pulled himself back up behind the gun and resumed firing. He was severely wounded, but adrenalin overpowered most of the pain. The NVA were focusing all their attention on the "Ma quỷ Mỹ" (American devil) and were determined to stop him. This man was "điên cái đầu" (crazy). Skidgel fired another short burst of deadly fire into the tree line and then felt a sharp, painful blow to his upper body that knocked the wind out of him, and he could not breathe.

The young sergeant slumped down behind his gun and continued to hold on to the pedestal of the M60. He was sitting on the right rear fender—his chin was resting on his chest; his eyes were closed, and he had to fight for every breath he took. Opening his eyes, he saw the front of his flak vest and it was covered in blood. He slowly raised his head—Silva was looking back at him with a look of concern. Their eyes met for only a moment, and then a final burst of gunfire knocked Skidgel off the back of the jeep. The vehicle immediately veered off into the tall grass and ground to a halt. Silva crawled out alongside the jeep and stared back at the still form lying in the middle of Road 311. Tears welling in his eyes, he searched for any sign of life, but Donnie Skidgel did not move.

Capt. Hudson had observed Skidgel's courageous actions and immediately called for a medic to try and reach the man lying in the road. Skidgel's short-lived counterattack had quelled enemy fire and allowed many of the troopers to move to better cover, but after he fell, the fire intensified again, and no one could get near him.

At that moment, Col. Healy arrived overhead in his gunship. His door gunners poured M60 fire down into the enemy positions, and a Blue Max aerial rocket artillery gunship provided supporting fire. The "Cavalier Red" Cobra attacked the enemy bunkers with its rockets; its mini-Gatling guns chewed wide swaths through the jungle vegetation. An Armored Cav troop arrived from the 11th ACR with guns blazing. The armor unit was being loaded aboard a C-130 on the airstrip at Buttons when its commander was notified of the attack, and he rushed his troops in to help. Each of the unit's APCs was mounted with a .50 caliber Browning heavy machine gun, a devastating weapon against NVA troops on the ground. With the combined firepower of the Delta troopers, the Armored Cavalry troop, the Charlie Troop Cobra, the Blue Max Cobra, the Huey gunship, and two sorties by Air Force F-4E Phantoms with napalm, the battle ended. Enemy fire died out, and the NVA troops that had survived melted into the jungle. Col. Healy ordered a 5/7th Cav Infantry Company in to pick up their trail, close with them, and destroy them. When the unit swept the area, they found 240 NVA bodies.

Blue Platoon troopers began to slowly move up from the valley, and in twos and threes, they surrounded the still form of Donnie Skidgel. Each man in the scout section said good-bye in his own way, and then they silently wrapped him in his poncho.

When the first chopper landed with its contingent of infantry soldiers, it was used to transport Sgt. Skidgel's body out of the battle area. Tenderly, his fellow soldiers lifted him and carried him to the Huey, placed him on board, and stood silently at attention as the bird lifted off the ground for the short flight to FSB Buttons.

The following day, Capt. Hudson wrote the citation recommending the Medal of Honor for Sgt. Donald S. Skidgel. It was immediately signed by Lt. Col. James Booth, the 1/9th Squadron Commander, and forwarded to the Secretary of the Army.

A memorial service was held for Skidgel on FSB Buttons a few days after the battle, and as many troopers attended as security would allow.

On December 16, 1971, at the Old Executive Office Building in Washington, DC, Vice Pres. Spiro T. Agnew presented the Skidgel family with Donnie's Medal of Honor and other decorations, including the Bronze Star for heroism; the Purple Heart; and the Vietnam Gallantry Cross with Palm, awarded by the Government of South Vietnam.

"He was so very young," Capt. Hudson said. "In thirty days he would have celebrated his twenty-first birthday. He was so young."

REQUIEM FOR A HERO

Donnie Skidgel

On July 6, 1973, a new building was dedicated at Ft. Knox, Kentucky. The mammoth brick and glass structure would house the Weapons Department for the post's Armor School and was the most modern weapons training facility in the nation. The name of the building was Skidgel Hall, and it was dedicated to the memory of Sgt. Donald S. Skidgel of Delta Troop, 1/9th Cav, 1st Cavalry Division. The keynote speaker for the dedication was Maj. Andrew J. Hudson, Skidgel's former troop commander, and the man who had recommended him for the Medal of Honor in 1969. Maj. Hudson was surprised and honored to speak. He had not known Sgt. Skidgel received the award until he read the dedication invitation over three years later.

Maj. Gen. Donn Starry was the Commanding General of Ft. Knox. The Deputy Commander and Commandant of the US Army Armor School at Ft. Knox was Brig. Gen. George S. Patton, IV, son of the famous WWII general. Sgt. Skidgel's parents were seated between the two generals for the service, and Maj. Hudson sat next to Gen. Patton. The former 1/9th Cav Squadron Commander, Col. James "Pete" Booth, came next, followed by Congressman Romano Mazolli of Kentucky.

During the ceremony, Maj. Hudson related the story of Sgt. Skidgel's courageous one-man assault against an NVA battalion and his fearless bravery in the face of the enemy's overwhelming numbers. It was an incredible story, and most of the large audience had not heard it before.

Following the ceremony, Mr. and Mrs. Skidgel were escorted on a tour of Skidgel Hall and then taken to a large open room where they were the guests of honor for the official reception. Sometime later, Maj. Hudson was talking with Gen. Patton and some of the dignitaries when the Skidgel's escort approached and asked to speak with him. The young officer told the Major that Sgt. Skidgel's parents had requested a private meeting with him.

Hudson accompanied the escort and was introduced to the Skidgels, then the three were taken to a small second-floor office for their meeting. In the speech he had given earlier in the day, Maj. Hudson had spoken directly to the Skidgels. He had been complete and detailed in his story of their son's heroics and the lives he had saved, possibly including his own, and he had hoped to provide answers to most of their questions. When they were alone, Maj. Hudson spoke:

"I will do my best to answer any questions you may have. I am very proud to have known your son. It was an honor to have served with him."

It is extremely rare for the family of a soldier who dies in combat to be able to talk with someone who was there at the time of his death. They might hear from one or two of his buddies. They might even meet some of them, although that too, is rare, and in most cases, the buddies were not present when their loved one died.

Mrs. Skidgel looked directly at the Major, and then asked, softly: "Did my boy suffer?"

Mr. and Mrs. Skidgel were in their mid-forties and immediately impressed the Major as "down-to-earth, good people." Modest and conservative, Mr. Skidgel looked slightly uncomfortable in his suit and tie, and Mrs. Skidgel had seemed uneasy as the center of attention, but these were the kind of people he would expect to bear a son like Donnie Skidgel. The questions they asked and the comments they made showed how deeply they loved their young son and how desperately they missed him. It had been nearly four years since his death, but for them, it was yesterday. Their emotions remained raw.

Maj. Hudson understood he was talking to parents, whose son had been killed far from home, and he sought to reassure them— Donnie did not die alone. He was part of a close-knit brotherhood of men who were with him and cared deeply about him. And he told them how Donnie's buddies had wrapped him in his poncho, and then tenderly and carefully lifted him into the helicopter that would transport him back to their base camp. Mrs. Skidgel listened intently with tears in her eyes and nodded her head slightly. Mr. Skidgel remained silent with his arm around his wife.

The Major concluded by telling them about the memorial service for their son that had been held on Fire Support Base Buttons a few days after his death. It had been conducted by the Delta Troop chaplain and every trooper who could possibly be spared had attended the service.

There was a knock on the door, and the meeting ended. The conversation had been special, and the Skidgels thanked the Major for meeting with them. He expressed his sorrow for their loss, knowing he could do little to ease their grief.

Maj. Hudson and the Skidgels walked downstairs together. The young escort opened one of the doors into the spacious alcove and stood quietly in the doorway. Skidgel Hall was beautiful and state of the art with towering glass windows to let in the light.

There on the wall before them was a large painting of Sgt. Donald Skidgel, standing in his fatigue uniform. The painting had just been completed, and the artist had perfectly captured Donnie's youth and honesty, and his hope for the future.

The three paused, and there was total silence as they stood looking up into the eyes of the twenty-year-old hero.

"I do so miss my boy," Mrs. Skidgel whispered.

"I was a combat hardened Cavalry soldier," Maj. Hudson said, "but his mother's whisper was so powerful, so poignant, tears welled in my eyes. And, they do again as I remember."

In 2011, a new bridge was build spanning the Sebasticook River in Newport, Maine. It was named "The Donald Sidney Skidgel Memorial Bridge" and was dedicated to the memory of Donnie Skidgel. On Memorial Day 2014, the Nokomis High School JROTC led the Newport parade with the National Colors, and the Nokomis Junior and Senior High Bands provided the music. The parade stopped on the Skidgel Memorial Bridge, where the National Anthem was played followed by a prayer, a twenty-one-gun salute, and "Taps." The parade ended at the Barrows-Skidgel American Legion Post 105 in Newport. There is an old proverb that says: "We live as long as we are remembered." In Newport, Maine, Donnie Skidgel still lives.

"Let us not ask God why men such as this should die in war.
Rather let us thank God that such men lived."

George S. Patton Jr.

19

Stanley Claus Campbell

"Stoney"

Stanley Campbell

The toddler reeled his way across the kitchen floor, his tiny bare feet slipping and sliding on the wet linoleum. His mother, Donna, stopped her mopping and smiled at her mischievous son.

"You look like a drunken sailor," she said, laughing.

The small boy continued his ungainly trek across the floor, as his mother watched. Upon reaching her mop bucket filled with warm suds, he stopped and stared into it. Then flashing his mother a toothy grin, the small boy turned and plopped his diapered bottom into the bucket, splashing soapy water all over her clean floor.

"That's my boy," she said, shaking her head. It would seem to have been preordained that spring day in 1948—Stan Campbell would join the US Navy.

Stan had a sister who was two years older. Named for her father, and a true "daddy's girl," Phyllis resented her little brother when they were small. He was "just so darn cute, and got all the attention." Unable to say "Stanley," big sister called him "Stoney," and it stuck. Successful in business and seeking a better environment for his young family, Phillip Campbell moved them to "the country." Their beautiful new home was in a wooded area of Portage, Michigan, and the children delighted in roaming the forest and climbing the trees. They would rush home from school in the afternoon to watch cowboy movies on TV and then run outdoors to reenact them.

As teenagers, Stoney and Phyl became best friends. His friends were hers—her friends his, and they often double-dated. They went everywhere together and even shared a paper route delivering the *Kalamazoo Gazette* during their high school years. "We blacked each other's eyes over who would get the short half of the paper route," Phyl said, laughing.

Handsome and intelligent, Stoney was the jokester within their social circle. With his keen sense of humor and ready smile, the party usually started when Stoney Campbell arrived.

In the mid-sixties, many young men were called to serve their country. Most of their fathers and uncles were WWII veterans, and their patriotism was reflected in the family values they had been taught throughout their lives. Across the nation, if called, it was unquestioned—they answered the call. After graduating in 1964, Stan made the decision to enlist in the Navy. He turned eighteen in October and headed for Great Lakes Naval Training Center in Great Lakes, Illinois. It was located about four hours from his home across the southern tip of Lake Michigan. With high scores on his aptitude tests, Campbell opted for the Seabees, and after completing two months of basic, he headed west to Port Hueneme Naval Base in California.

The Seabees were the Naval Mobil Construction Battalions, the US Navy's construction arm, and its members were trained to go anywhere and build anything that could be built, often in harm's way. Their official motto, "Construimus, Batuimus," means "We Build, We Fight." Created during WW II, the Seabees trained alongside the Marines, followed them ashore, and built roads, bridges, gasoline storage tanks, hospitals, warehouses— whatever was needed to further the Allied cause. There were seven Seabee ratings: BU (Builders), CE (Construction Electrician), CM (Construction Mechanic), EA (Engineering Aid), EO (Equipment Operator), SW (Steelworker), and UT (Utilitiesman). Each was a specialist in his own area; however, each man also learned enough about the other ratings to do basic work.

Stan Campbell's MOS was SWE-Steelworker (Erector), and the twelve-week "A" school at Port Hueneme was a combination of classwork and hands-on training involving steelwork (welding, cutting and fitting), and learning to build and assemble projects such as pontoon bridges, watch towers, and water tanks.

Campbell graduated from training school in June 1965 and was assigned to Mobile Construction Battalion Seven, based at the Naval Construction Battalion Center in Davisville, Rhode Island. The living conditions there were not ideal. The barracks were WWII vintage, with some ninety men sleeping in the open bays on each floor, but Stoney made the best of it. He liked the camaraderie of the other men in his unit and usually managed to keep his buddies laughing.

Campbell did not get to enjoy Rhode Island for long. On July 13, 1965, the battalion began loading men and equipment aboard the USNS *Buckner* and deployed to Southern Spain. The Seabees constructed ninety-six prefabricated homes for dependent housing at the US Naval Station in Rota which included streets, sanitary systems, water systems and utilities. Stan finally had the opportunity to do real work in his chosen field, and it gave him great satisfaction.

The Seabees were a building unit but were never allowed to forget they were also a fighting unit. Their organization was structured like the Marines. Unlike the Navy, they had battalions, companies, platoons, and squads, and sixty days after they arrived at Rota, the Marines conducted a rigorous inspection of the Seabee battalion. The men were individually quizzed on their personal weapons, as well as the assigned recoilless rifles and mortars. It was tough, but MCB-7 came through with high marks. The 7th spent four months in Spain and earned the Navy "E" (Excellence) for their efforts. The "E" was great for morale, and the men were proud of their work. The unit headed home on November 30, and the shipmates were back in Davisville in time for Christmas.

In February, the entire 850-man battalion deployed to Camp Lejeune, North Carolina, for three weeks of Marine Advanced Infantry Warfare School. The winter weather in Carolina was cold, wet, and miserable, and the training was tough. Many were the nights in the field when Stan wished he were back in sunny Spain, but he would not remain cold for long. By the end of March, he was in tropical South Vietnam and wishing for a cool breeze. Before leaving home, he had made Phyl the beneficiary on his Navy life insurance policy, just in case.

MCB-7's base of operations was a place called Phú Bài, which was located sixty miles south of the DMZ. Variously described as a "death-trap," a "hell-hole," and a "Việt Cộng campground," Phú Bài was not beautiful. The men were housed in twelve-man tents, which were erected on top of a Buddhist cemetery. There were burial plots and elaborate tombstones in every direction and getting to their tents could be hazardous after dark, especially if one had imbibed an alcoholic beverage or two.

There was no chow hall. The men existed on c-rations left over from WW II. The boxes were dated "1942." Stoney had never seen Lucky Strike cigarettes in a green pack, but he was always up for a new adventure. He was not quite as adventurous when it came to what he ate. The "docs" told them not to eat the food if the cans were rusty or leaking. They did not have to worry about that. Stoney did not like the idea of eating twenty-five-year-old meat, so he traded it away and lived on chocolate bars, crackers, and canned fruit. He had weighed 150 lbs. when he arrived in

Vietnam. With his diet, hard physical labor, and the hellish heat and humidity, he was down to 125 lbs. by the Fourth of July.

The 7th had deployed to Phú Bài to build a new Marine base; however, the men soon found themselves on all kinds of reconnaissance patrols: foot patrols, jeep patrols, and squad patrols. MCB-7 was attached to the 3rd Marine Division, and the Seabees rode shotgun on the Marine/Seabee resupply convoys. They also transported construction supplies to a detached platoon at the Marine Combat Camp in Đông Hà. It was three hours north of Phú Bài and three miles south of the DMZ. Seabees provided part of the security for that too.

The Americans owned the daylight hours, but the VC ruled the night. And nighttime was long and totally dark. The men worked all day, and then took turns manning their perimeter defenses until morning. Việt Cộng sappers attacked the Seabee camp about every other night. Occasionally, the men got a break with two quiet nights in a row, but that was usually made up for with two or three straight nights of attacks. The pressure on their perimeter was unrelenting, but the VC were never able to penetrate their defensive line.

"We may not be Marines, Stoney said soberly, "but dammit, we're Marine-trained. When the VC try to come through our lines, we give'em hell." Then, he broke into his usual grin and elbowed the buddy next to him. His smile was never far below the surface.

The Seabees pissed off the local Việt Cộng leadership to the point they were mentioned on Hanoi Hanna's radio propaganda broadcasts. She announced a regiment of NVA infantry was being sent especially "to annihilate MCB-7 at Phú Bài," but it never happened. Borrowing a bit of swagger from their Marine compatriots, the battalion's unofficial motto became: "We fear no evil 'cause we are the meanest muthers in the valley."

Part 2

Over the next few months, the Seabees were busy. They constructed living quarters and an air strip for the Marines, facilities for themselves, and a causeway that jutted 1,500 feet into the South China Sea. The causeway served as an unloading ramp for cargo-laden landing ships. They also built forty-four thousand cubic feet of cold-storage space, steel observation towers, a massive antenna field, and a top-secret electronics building for the 8th Radio Research Field Station (ASA) at Phú Bài. The men worked from sun up to sun down most days with a half-day off on Sunday. If a man was on a mortar squad and fired mortars at night, he might be permitted to sleep in a little later, but it was usually too hot to sleep after the sun came up. Stoney looked forward to Sunday afternoons. Sometimes the men would grill out, if they could find the steaks and beer. Beer was ten cents a bottle in the "Punji Pit," their enlisted men's club.

The Army MARS radio station at Phú Bài was located inside the 8th RRFS compound. The station equipment and antenna field were maintained by Army Security Agency personnel and could be used to place calls home. The "Spooks" were quite willing to barter their access back to the World for whatever they could get, so they traded a month of priority placement on the call list to the local Seabees for a concrete patio and BBQ grill pit next to the station. The Army MPs were surprised when a concrete truck and a squad of Seabees pulled up to the front gate of the top-secret facility. They were even more surprised when they were ordered to let the sailors inside. The ASA sites were some of the most highly classified and closely guarded in Vietnam. The MPs were not permitted inside the gate. So much for security!

Stoney had the opportunity to call home about once a month. The MARS guys would patch him through to a ham radio operator in the States. The radio op would get the Campbells on the phone, and Stoney could talk to them. There was a twelve-hour time difference between Phú Bài and Kalamazoo, so if he called at 1900 hours (7:00 p.m.) in the evening, it was 7:00 a.m. the same day at home. Their only problem was saying "over" when you were through talking, so the person on the other end of the line could talk. His mother never got the hang of it. He would tease her, and they would laugh.

By August, Stan Campbell had been promoted to the rank of Steelworker (Erector) 3rd Class (SWE3) and was running the welding shop. If there was a need for general welding or structural repairs on the batch plant, asphalt plant, or rock crushers, he was on it, anytime, day or night. If something broke, there was no place to go for spare parts; Stoney improvised and made his "creative" fixes from whatever he could find. He was challenged by the job and delighted in impressing the "old salts" with his ingenuity.

It had been four months, and Stoney was still not acclimated to the climate. The wind blew constantly and sand sifted into everything. His eyes were full of it; his clothes were full of it. For someone who had spent his entire life in the lushness of Michigan, Phú Bài was truly a miserable place. The monsoon season was almost upon them. He had heard horror stories about the endless rain, but there was a bright side. At least the air would be clean.

Work had been completed on their quarters, outside toilets and showers, so living conditions had improved. Their hootches were strongback-style buildings with concrete floors, plywood sides and corrugated tin roofs with wide eaves. They were screened under the eaves for ventilation, and sandbagged outside up to the screens for safety. The huts were hot during the day, but were cooler than the tents. There was a trap door in the floor that opened into a ditch leading to a bunker in case of a rocket attack. Enemy action continued at night, and it was not unusual for the camp to receive thirty or forty rockets or mortars during an attack. Often, that was followed by harassment rounds fired into the camp every half hour, for the rest of the night. Everyone dragged out of bed in his skivvies, scrambled in the dark for his weapon, helmet and flak vest, and crawled into the bunkers. That ensured the men got little rest, and they were all a bit jumpy. A security squad had taken out a water buffalo the night before. It strayed too close to the camp perimeter in the dark, and that was a dangerous place to be.

Stoney wrote to his family every week. He knew they worried about him, but he kept the mood light. He rarely mentioned the military action occurring around him, or his involvement in it. He sent home photos of himself, his buddies, and some of the projects he helped build. He told funny stories about happenings around camp and came up with a joke or two. They expected nothing too serious from him, and he happily obliged. His letters always brought a smile to their faces.

"That's my boy," his mother would say, smiling through her tears. She missed him so much.

By August, there was an influx of new men coming into MCB-7 from the States. Many of the "newbies" (or "new Bees") were just out of "A" school and having a tough time. They were young, homesick, and receiving the usual newbie harassment from some of their more senior shipmates. If they complained, the old salts told them: "Quit griping, you sound like a f——king fleeter!" Stoney was too soft-hearted to give them a hard time and tried his best to lift their spirits.

The monsoon season was almost upon them, and the camp had begun to receive downpours every few days. There had been a corresponding increase in humidity and morning fog in the gullies and low-lying areas around the perimeter. Early on August 25, Campbell's platoon drew early guard duty on the defensive perimeter. There had been a sapper attack a few hours earlier, and everyone was a bit uneasy. Stoney had worked to relax the men in his squad, telling stories and reminiscing about home. A layer of ground fog had moved in from the sea, and he thought about the old saying that it is darkest just before the dawn. The sky and the surrounding area were totally black.

A few moments later, Stoney announced to those near him he needed to go relieve himself and was going behind some nearby bushes. Staying low, he quickly moved out of sight and disappeared into the misty darkness.

About ten minutes later, Campbell's squad heard a desperate voice yell "halt!" three times, followed by a blast of M14 fire. When they got to Stoney Campbell, he was already gone. An M14 round had pierced his heart, and he was dead before he hit the ground. One of the new men was on sentry duty on the outer perimeter, and his nerves were on edge. He had yelled "halt"—there was no immediate response, and for whatever reason, Campbell kept moving. The man fired.

No one knows what Stoney's intentions were. He may have been playing a prank on his buddies and moving in to scare them, but no one will ever know for sure. For those working in the communications center at the battalion command post, there was the unforgettable call coming in, frantically pleading for help and shouting, "Stoney Campbell's been shot!" That call would haunt them forever.

For the Campbell family, there was that terrible knock on the door at 2508 Vanderbilt Avenue in Portage, Michigan. They were told only that their son had died as the result of "an accidental gunshot wound while returning to camp."

For Phyl, part of her died that day too. "He was my incredible brother," she says, "who did so much for so many in so little time."

The impact one young man had on an 850-man battalion was incredible. His constant efforts to entertain and uplift those around him had made Campbell a popular figure his entire life. It seemed there were few of his shipmates, even at the battalion level, who did not know him. During the toughest, dirtiest jobs and the longest, darkest nights, Stoney Campbell was the one who had always been there to boost the morale of everyone around him.

Campbell's death was devastating, not only to his company, but to the entire battalion. On October 30, 1966, the assembled personnel of US Naval Mobile Construction Battalion 7 paid tribute to him. In a brief, twenty-minute ceremony, their new camp was formally dedicated and named in memory of their lost shipmate, SWE3 Stanley C. Campbell, "who died in the service of his country."

Rear Adm. W. M. Heaman, Commander, Construction Battalions, US Pacific Fleet, spoke the dedicatory words and noted that an appropriately inscribed plaque would be mounted permanently in the center of the camp Stoney and his shipmates had built.

Also in attendance were Rear Adm. H. N. Wallin, Deputy Commander for Acquisition, Naval Facilities Engineering Command; Maj. Gen. W. B. Kyle, Commanding General, Third Marine Division; and Navy Capt. P. E. Seufer, officer in charge of Construction, RVN.

"Camp Campbell"—Stoney would have loved it!

"We'd have done anything for each other," Phyl said later. "We each traveled a lot. You could bet that wherever he went, I would wind up, and where I landed, he was sure to make a show-ing. I wasn't able to follow him to Vietnam. So many times I've wished we could have fought that one together. I can't think how much different our lives would have been now, had he come home. He had a way of fixing everything."

Stan Campbell was buried at Riverside Cemetery, Kalamazoo, Michigan, in September 1966. He was nineteen years old.

This be the verse you grave for me:
Here he lies where he longed to be;
Home is the sailor, home from sea,
And the hunter home from the hill.

"Requiem"
—Robert Louis Stevenson

20

The Boys of Nui Vu

"Howard's Indians"

1st Platoon, Charlie Company, 1st Reconnaissance Battalion, USMC

This is a tale many Marines have heard, but most outside the Corps have not—a testament to unsurpassed bravery and the sheer determination of a band of young Americans who refused to die. They fought to stay alive, and they fought to save each other, despite overwhelming odds, during one dark, bloody, interminable night.

Early in June 1966, intelligence from radio intercept and radio direction-finding, gathered by the 1st Radio Battalion (USMC) and other intelligence sources, indicated a combined force of Việt Cộng and North Vietnamese Army troops were gathering by the thousands in the Hiệp Đức Valley northwest of the Marine base at Chu Lai. Hidden by rugged mountains and areas of dense jungle, the communist units were massing and preparing for attacks against the heavily populated coastal towns and government bases in I Corps, south of Đà Nẵng.

For security and defensive reasons, the enemy commanders kept their units spread out over a large area, moving mainly in squads and platoons. Lt. Gen. Lewis W. Walt ordered the 1st Reconnaissance Battalion of the 1st Marine Division to covertly scout the mountains, determine enemy strength, and locate the main enemy units. The recon Marines were to move in small teams of eight to twenty men. If they located a large unit, Marine infantry would air-assault into the area. However, if the recon teams saw only small groups of VC and NVA, they would remain concealed and call in air strikes and artillery to destroy them.

The recon battalion was an elite unit. Lt. Col. Arthur J. Sullivan, the commander, had set the highest standards for his Marines and had full confidence in their abilities. Every man had received schooling in forward observer techniques and recon patrol procedures, and many had additional specialized training. In response to Walt's orders, Sullivan sent eight teams into the highlands surrounding the valley in a major reconnaissance operation titled "Operation KANSAS."

Staff Sgt. Jimmie Howard, from Burlington, Iowa, was the acting platoon leader of 1st Platoon, Charlie Company, 1st Recon. A tall, athletic man in his mid-thirties, he had been a star football player and later coached at the San Diego Recruit Depot. He looked like he could still play. He had earned a Silver Star in Korea at age twenty-one, along with three Purple Hearts. He was a born leader, and his men idolized him.

As darkness fell, a flight of three Marine H-34 helicopters descended slowly toward the verdant slopes of a grassy mountain. The area was twenty-five miles west of Chu Lai, and the H-34s were escorted by two Huey gunships. The troop-carriers hovered low, and Jimmie Howard and his team jumped out, quickly climbing the steep incline toward the top. The choppers lifted up out of small-arms range and disappeared over the horizon. The date was Monday, June 13, 1966.

Howard's seventeen-man team, code-named "Carnival-Time," consisted of: Cpl. Jerrald R. Thompson, First Squad Leader, twenty-four, Raleigh, North Carolina; Lance Cpl. Ricardo C. Binns, Second Squad Leader, twenty, The Bronx, New York; Lance Cpl. Robert Martinez, radioman, twenty, Garden City, Kansas; Lance Cpl. Daniel Mulvihill, radioman, nineteen, Chicago, Illinois; Lance Cpl. John T. Adams, twenty-two, Covington, Oklahoma; Lance Cpl. Alcadio N. Mascarenas, twenty-two, Sapello, New Mexico; Lance Cpl. Joseph Kosoglow, twenty, Greensburgh, Pennsylvania; Lance Cpl. Thomas G. Powles, twenty, Vacaville, California; Lance Cpl. Raymond S. Hildreth, nineteen, Tulsa, Oklahoma; Lance Cpl. William C. Norman, nineteen, Sedona, Arizona; Lance Cpl. Ralph G. Victor, eighteen, Ogden, Utah; Pfc. Ignatius Carlisi, twenty, New York, New York; Pfc. Charles W. Bosley, nineteen, Greencastle, Indiana; Pfc. James O. McKinney, eighteen, Monroe, Louisiana; Pfc. Thomas D. Glawe (pronounced "Glave"), eighteen, Rockford, Illinois; and two Navy corpsmen: Hospitalman 1st Class Richard J. Fitzpatrick, Senior Corpsman, thirty-five, Vacaville, California, and Hospitalman 3rd Class Billy D. Holmes, twenty-three, Madison, Tennessee. Howard referred to the team as his "Indians."

The small mountain, called Núi Vú (Hill 488), was nearly 1,500 feet high and dominated the terrain for miles. At the top of the peak, narrow strips of level ground extended out in three directions for several hundred yards before falling steeply away. The crest was only about twenty-five yards across at its widest point. The three strips of ground roughly resembled the prongs of an inverted letter "Y," with the main prong pointing north, and the other two prongs pointing southwest and southeast. Sgt. Howard established a command post below a huge boulder that sat at the base of the north prong and posted a four-man fire team at observation points on each prong. It was an ideal vantage point for the teams to survey the surrounding area.

Enemy troops had used the hilltop previously and had dug foxholes across the top of the peak. Designed for the smaller Vietnamese, one hole was barely large enough for two of the huskier American Marines to squeeze into. Each hole had a small cave scooped out at one end that was about two feet under the surface. Howard's men took turns using the one-man caves during the day to stay out of the hot sun and avoid enemy detection. There were no trees to conceal their position. Their only cover was knee-high grass and low scrub brush that thinned to rocks and boulders surrounding the huge crag at the crest of Núi Vú.

Mascarenas was the fire team leader on the southwest prong and shared a fighting hole with Hildreth. Adams and McKinney shared the other hole. Ric Binns was team leader on the north with Powles, Norman, and Kosoglow. Victor was the southeast team leader with Bosley, Glawe, and Carlisi. The two corpsmen, two radiomen, Cpl. Thompson, and Sgt. Howard manned the command post at the top.

The surrounding valleys and villages were full of enemy troops. For the next two days, Howard's team saw small enemy units almost every hour and constantly called for fire missions. Most of the attacks on targets located by the platoon took place when there was an observation aircraft in the area so the enemy commanders would think the plane was responsible. Headquarters at Chu Lai was considering pulling the team out after two days. The risk increased greatly with each day the men remained on the hill, but the observation post was in an ideal location and had encountered no difficulties. It was believed the team had a reasonably safe escape route along a ridge to the east, if they were spotted, so it was decided to leave the platoon on Núi Vú for one additional day.

Unfortunately, the North Vietnamese commanders were well aware of the recon platoon's presence and were quietly moving small units of troops into place to eliminate it. By late afternoon on June 15, a battalion-size force had been secretly massed at the base of the mountain, and several hundred well-trained North Vietnamese regular infantry began to climb up the three prongs.

The enemy commanders hoped to wipe out the small contingent of Americans in one overwhelming attack. They suspected there were other American observer teams in the area, and they intended to make an example of the interlopers on top of Núi Vú.

Part 2

Luckily, for the Marines, two US Green Berets spoiled the NVA's surprise party. Sgt. 1st Class Donald Reed and Spc. 5 Hardey Drande were leading a Montagnard CIDG patrol within a couple miles of Núi Vú that afternoon. The patrol spotted sizeable NVA units moving into the area surrounding the mountain and radioed the information back to their camp at Hội An. For security purposes, Sgt. Howard's radio was always set on the Special Forces frequency. He was alerted about a possible attack and had time to draw up a plan of defense. Gathering his two squad leaders and four fire team leaders, he briefed them on the situation and instructed them to put their teams on alert. The fire teams were to be split into two-man listening posts and placed twenty yards out from the command post, completely encircling the top of the hill. The teams were to withdraw at the first sign of enemy troops, meet up at the big rock, and then, if possible, they would make their escape across a ridge to the east.

Other than Sgt. Howard, most of the team members had little or no combat experience. A few of them had been out on an uneventful mission or two; three of them were new to the team. They had all had the training, but for the most part, the men were untested, and the sergeant had no way of knowing how they would react during an attack. He hoped he did not have to find out.

Mascarenas crept back down the southwest prong and informed Adams, Hildreth, and McKinney about the attack, and what their plan was. If the recon team was able to "bug out" to the east, his team would take point, with Hildreth in the lead. Then he moved his fire team, positioning Hildreth and McKinney in a fighting hole east of the command post. He and Adams moved around the hill toward the south.

As darkness settled over the peaceful-looking valley below, the Marines saw the twinkle of lights in the small villages and scattered farms in the distance. McKinney turned his head and stared back across the hills to the west. The setting sun had left the darkening sky tinged with shades of mauve and pink, and the young man thought of home. A shy, gentle Cajun boy from the poor-side of Monroe, Louisiana, James had not excelled in high school. He had been content to remain in the background and watch others be the star athletes and the "popular" kids. That was not his thing. Then one day, he decided he "wanted to be more," so he joined the Marines. Now, James was like everyone's little brother; his older teammates teased him about being a virgin, just to see him blush, and then they would tease him more. He had a thick "Looziana" accent and had grown up hunting and fishing in the swamps and bayous along the lazy Ouachita River. Volunteering for recon had been the most natural path for him to take. "Jis like fallin' off a log," as his "grandpap" used to say.

Swiping away a bead of sweat from the corner of his eye, McKinney turned and looked at Ray Hildreth, the Marine he was now paired with. McKinney and Hildreth had been buddies since recon school, along with Bill Norman and Joe Kosoglow. The four had made the trip to Vietnam together three months before, aboard the USS *Whitfield County*. Hildreth's mother had died when he was fifteen, and he'd had a tough time dealing with it, eventually getting into serious trouble in Tulsa, where he grew up. The Marine Corps was the answer, and he had thrived. Taking every opportunity to better himself, he had volunteered for recon school and then sniper training, finishing at the top of his class. There were four snipers on their recon team, but no one could outshoot Ray Hildreth.

McKinney could just make out Mascarenas and Adams in the dwindling light, some twenty yards away. Adams was a big muscular guy and rarely had much to say. Some considered him a bit of a bully. Scuttlebutt said he had a black belt in martial arts, but James had never been able get him to say much about himself, or anything else. Since they had been on the hill, though, Adams had opened up a bit and promised to teach McKinney some karate moves when they got back to camp. Mascarenas, their team leader, was another quiet guy. He was a natural leader, sharp and tough as nails, but so soft-spoken his men could barely hear him. They had celebrated his twenty-second birthday the week before this mission. The team had celebrated; Mascarenas had just smiled and quietly watched.

Vic Victor was the youngest fire team leader. He was eighteen years old, from Utah, and spoke with a slight stutter. Staying low, Victor made his way back down the southeast prong to Glawe, Bosley, and Carlisi, and briefed them. Tommy Glawe was a skinny, good-natured kid from Illinois and always had a smile on his face. He had joined the Marines when he was seventeen and then shipped to 'Nam after he turned eighteen. Bosley was another Midwestern teenager from a small town in Indiana and was married. Natty Carlisi was the son of a wealthy Italian family from New York City. He was small and baby-faced and had obviously been raised in a cultured and protective household. He did not look like a Marine, but seemed determined to prove himself to everyone, especially his dad. He was one of the "cherries" on the team and had been in-country two weeks. This was his first mission. Victor moved his team to the west and paired up with Carlisi. Glawe and Bosley were twenty yards to their right.

The shorter north prong of the hill sloped downward from the big rock at its base and was considered to be the most likely route for an enemy attack. Ric Binns was of Jamaican descent and had grown up in a tough neighborhood in The Bronx, New York. He had enlisted at 18, and his first year in the Marines had been a struggle. He had finally settled into the Corps after two years, becoming a dependable leader, and Jimmie Howard relied on him. Binns and Powles were buddies. He hurried back to brief Powles, Kosoglow and Norman. Tom Powles was a laid-back Northern Californian and married. Joe Kosoglow was a Yankee from Pennsylvania with a funny sense of humor and a honking laugh. He was also married. He and Bill Norman were two more of the team's trained snipers. Norman was an Arizona cowboy who enjoyed playing chess. Highly intelligent, he strategized the enemy's moves like they were chessmen on his board.

Around 10:30 p.m., Jerry Thompson, the First Squad leader, left the command post and moved quietly from team to team making sure the men were awake and alert. Thompson had just recently arrived in Charlie Company but seemed to be a squared-away Marine. He was married with his wife and two little girls back in Raleigh, North Carolina. The night was pitch-black, aside from a few stars. There was no moon. A light wind blew across the face of the hill, rustling the dry grass. McKinney and Hildreth were crammed together in their fighting hole, M14s at the ready—eyes straining to see through the darkness toward every sound.

"Man, it was so dark," Hildreth said, "If I scratched my nuts, I had to ask James if they were mine or his!"

Binns and his team were lying prone in a low depression, forming a firing line, with rifles and grenades ready. Norman, Powles, and Kosoglow were nervously whispering back and forth about the impending attack and their escape plan. Binns was quiet, his eyes focused on the area in front of him. He casually reached up to wipe the sweat from his eyes. Then, in an easy, natural motion, he propped himself on his elbows and placed the butt of his rifle on his right shoulder. Without uttering a word, the young Marine squeezed the trigger of his M14 and fired into a tall bush that was barely discernible about four yards away. The "bush" screamed, pitched backward, and disappeared into the darkness.

Binns' teammates jumped up with their weapons—each man threw a grenade in the general direction of the "bush," and they scrambled up the hill toward the command post. Behind them, the grenades split the night with a thunderous roar and brilliant flashes of light before the hillside was plunged back into total darkness. There were more screams, followed by the sound of automatic weapons fire.

The battle of Núi Vú had begun.

Part 3

Upon hearing the sounds of battle, the Marines on the other listening posts jumped to their feet, grabbed their weapons, and ran through the darkness toward the command post atop the rocky knoll. The first unit of NVA infantry was less than fifty yards behind them and climbing steadily. Binns had killed one of their scouts. Additional units of regular infantry and main force Việt Cộng were also moving up the other two prongs of the "Y." The Marine recon team was surrounded. There would be no escape across the saddle to the east. The time was 11:00 p.m. on June 15, 1966.

The rocky field at the top of the peak provided only limited protection. Sgt. Howard had stationed his two radiomen behind some larger boulders below the big stone crag and had set up a tight perimeter about twenty yards across. He had selected a firing position for each man, placing a Marine about every ten to twelve feet. If his team could not escape, he had to be able to mount an effective defense at the top of the hill until they could be rescued.

The Marines fell into their assigned spots as quickly as possible, laid out spare clips of ammo and grenades so they could find them easily in the darkness, and prepared to make their stand. They were equipped with eighteen M14s, one M79 grenade launcher, and eighteen K-Bar combat knives. The Navy corpsmen were both carrying .45 caliber pistols. Each Marine had at least four hand grenades and three thousand rounds of ammunition; some carried more. Sgt. Howard and Cpl. Thompson tried to calm and reassure the young men. "Be sure to fire beneath the muzzle flashes," Thompson told them. That's where they were most likely to hit a vital spot on an attacking enemy soldier.

As Howard had watched these eighteen- and nineteen-year-olds over the past two days, he had felt like a grizzled old man at thirty-six. God, they were so young. Bosley had the wide-eyed innocence of a schoolboy; he didn't think Glawe even shaved yet; and Carlisi looked like a choir boy straight out of St. Pat's. All he needed was the lace collar. And here they were, lying ten feet apart on a God-forsaken hill, twelve thousand miles from home, waiting for four hundred enemy troops determined to wipe them off the face of the earth. Alone with his thoughts in the darkness, Jimmie Howard slowly shook his head and tried to think what else he could do to save these boys—his Indians.

James McKinney was hunkered down with his M14 pointed out between two boulders. He could feel a cold shiver creeping down his backbone—he knew the shit was about to hit the fan. He cleared the sweat from his eyes and licked his parched lips with the tip of his tongue. He took a deep breath and tried to relax, resting his cheek against the cold steel of his weapon. It had been about a minute since he hit the deck, but it seemed like an hour. Raising his head slightly, he felt the coolness of the breeze on his face and reached up to adjust the sweat-stained boonie on his head. At that moment, AK-47s opened up and rounds began to rake the ground a few yards below McKinney's position.

Courageously, Tom Powles stood in the midst of the incoming fire and began to fire his grenade launcher. Again and again, he fired the M79, as the automatic weapons zeroed in on his position. Rounds ricocheted off the boulders, and then there was a loud slapping sound. Powles was thrown backward, screaming in agony.

"Corpsman! Corpsman!" someone yelled, as Binns dragged the wounded grenadier behind the big rock. Some of the Marines were firing back, but Howard ordered them to stop and save their ammo. There were no visible targets.

Powles thrashed and continued to scream horribly as the two corpsmen attempted to help him. Billie D. Homes administered a shot of morphine, and Fitz Fitzpatrick tried to ascertain the extent of his wounds by running his hands over Powles' torso in total darkness. He had been shot through the abdomen and was in serious danger of bleeding to death. As the morphine took effect, the young man gradually ceased his anguished cries and lost consciousness.

The Marines were on edge as they remained huddled in their assigned positions and waited for the NVA's next move. They peered into the inky blackness looking for any sign of movement, listening for any sound. But there was only the sound of the wind, like a huge snake slithering through the dry grass. Without warn-ing, Hildreth heard a yell and an M14 fired into the darkness a couple of yards to his left. The muzzle flash of the Marine weapon was met immediately with the explosion of an enemy grenade. Shrapnel and rocks rained down on Hildreth and Mascarenas, fol-lowed by the return of almost total silence.

James McKinney

Softly, Hildreth called McKinney's name and got no response—only the sough of the wind in the grass, and a low moan that seemed to come from within the mountain itself. "McKinney," he pleaded softly, not wanting to attract a second grenade. "Are you all right? Oh God, no—not James."

The team was down two men, and the real attack had not begun. Sgt. Howard was on the radio quietly and calmly calling in artillery, flare-ships, gunships and whatever other assistance he could muster to help his team. Then, he crawled on his belly around the tight perimeter, from man to man, touching each of them, patting their backs, reassuring them, and calming them. He promised them he would do whatever he could to get them out. They just had to hang on for a little while. "And stay alive," he thought to himself.

At that moment, a loud clacking noise rent the silence. The sharp crack of bamboo sticks was like breaking bones and sent shivers down the spines of the young Americans. As more joined in, it sounded as if there were hundreds and the unnerving clamor was coming from all around them. Abruptly the noise stopped; however, it was soon replaced by the nightmare caterwauling of shrill whistles and tin trumpets. The horrendous noise seemed to emanate from the very bowels of hell.

For Jimmie Howard, it brought back visions of screaming hordes of North Koreans and Red Chinese coming out of the darkness in Korea, fourteen years before, and he knew it preceded an all-out attack. After a few moments, the whistles stopped, as if turned off by a single switch, and the Marines heard the sound of objects hitting the rocks and the ground all around them. Then the objects began to explode.

"Grenades!" someone screamed out of the darkness. Some of the grenades bounced off rocks and rolled back down the slope, exploding among the massed ranks of NVA; a few did not explode; but some landed right on top of Marines and exploded with tremendous force, throwing out waves of shrapnel and splintered rock. The scene was utter chaos.

"They were within twenty feet of us," Billie D. Holmes said. "Suddenly there were grenades all over. Then people started hollering. It seemed everyone got hit at the same time." Some of the young Marines began to scream, and the corpsmen crawled toward them to help. Natty Carlisi had a finger shot off. As Holmes dressed the young Marine's hand in the dark, a grenade landed between them and exploded, knocking the corpsman unconsciousness. Coming to his senses, Billie D. realized he was not seriously hurt, aside from contusions and multiple small cuts on his forehead. Carlisi, however, had two badly wounded legs to go with his missing finger. Wiping away the blood that was trickling into his own eyes, Doc Holmes patched up the boy, and Carlisi dragged himself back to his position on the firing line. "I still have my trigger finger," he quipped.

Four NVA .50 caliber machine guns opened up from four different directions and began firing in support of the assaulting units. The rounds ricocheted off the monolith violently. Large chunks of rock were torn loose and showered down on the young Marines hunkered at its base. Streams of bright green tracer rounds from enemy light machine guns split the black sky, pointing directly toward the position of the Marines' command post, and identifying it for hundreds of NVA and VC reinforcements still gathering in the valley below; 60mm mortar rounds smashed into the mountaintop, filling the air with deadly shards of rock and shrapnel. The onslaught lasted for some twenty minutes as the NVA commanders sought to soften up their target and inspire their troops before delivering the final coup-de-grace.

The barrage ended, and the North Vietnamese infantry pushed up the final yards of the steep incline toward the Marine positions. They were firing AK-47s, throwing grenades, and screaming at the top of their lungs. They were certain of their imminent victory and felt invincible. For a moment, the situation looked hopeless for the recon team. The young Marines had been shocked by the ferocity of the grenade attack and the screams of their own teammates. They were confused and disoriented. They had hugged the ground during the enemy barrage and prayed for it to end. Then they saw the NVA infantry charging toward them, and they were filled with anger. They were enraged at these men who were killing their buddies and were so intent on taking their lives. Training and instinct took over, and the youngsters responded with a savage fury Jimmie Howard could have only dreamed of.

The first ranks of the human-wave attack rushed forward. They were dimly illuminated by flickering flames from burning grass and brush set afire by their own grenades. Taking a final step forward, every man was mowed down, falling in one long, bloody pile. The second wave pushed forward and was cut down on top of the first wave. The assault began to falter as the forward ranks of the attacking force lost their enthusiasm to face the American firing line and began to turn back into the ranks of those pushing them from behind. All semblance of military discipline disappeared, in spite of their screaming commanders. The attack ground to a halt and descended into chaos. The infantrymen struggled to retreat back down the slope, clambering over the bodies of their fallen comrades, and the Marines continued to fire into the churning mob.

Part 4

Nearly every Marine had been wounded in the grenade attack. Young Vic Victor had been blown completely out of his firing position. He had painful shrapnel wounds in both legs, but managed to crawl back onto the firing line. His hearing was nearly gone from the blast, but his mind was clear and focused as he calmly fired his M14 into the advancing NVA infantry. Billie D. crawled to him, but Vic refused treatment. There were others more seriously wounded; the doc needed to care for them first. Besides, he was "too busy shooting Cong to stop." Adrenalin had overwhelmed any pain he might have felt. He told Billie to come back after they had beaten off the attack, and he continued to fire at the enemy.

Ralph "Vic" Victor

Doc Fitzpatrick, the senior corpsman, was crawling forward to help patch up another wounded Marine when a grenade exploded in his face. He was unconscious and in critical condition.

Billie D. got to him and dragged his colleague to the limited cover of the big rock. He gently pulled him in next to Powles, who was also unconscious, and attempted to dress his terrible wounds. His face was a bloody pulp.

Thomas "Tommy" Glawe

Tommy Glawe had taken over Powles M79 "blooper" and was firing grenades as fast as he could load the single-shot weapon. He kept yelling, "We gotta get outa here," but there was no place to go. Leaning against the big rock in full view of the enemy troops, he fired grenade after grenade down the hill. He was firing a variety of grenade types including "willie pete" (white phosphorus) and high explosive rounds that were exploding three hundred yards down the mountainside. He called for more ammo—Sgt. Howard pulled a bandolier of the 40mm rounds from Powles body and handed it to him. The young Marine was single-handedly wreaking havoc among the NVA ranks, making him a prime target for their gunners. Automatic weapons fire raked the boulder, hitting Glawe in the head, and he pitched forward into the darkness. Someone yelled for Doc Holmes, but the eighteen-year-old was dead before he hit the ground. Billy D. searched for a pulse, but knew Tommy was gone. Handing Howard the M79, the corpsman grabbed the boy's thin shoulders and dragged him in behind the big rock next to Fitz.

The NVA troops continued to probe the perimeter, seeking weaknesses. They crawled close, under cover of the tall grass, and then attacked with a burst of gunfire and grenades. The Marines used grenades, too, and the American grenades were not only more reliable, they were twice as powerful as the Chinese "potato mashers" the NVA were tossing. In addition, the Marines could throw farther and were more accurate than the NVA troops. After an hour, the North Vietnamese pulled back to regroup.

About midnight, the Special Forces camp at Hội An began to fire artillery in support of the Marines on the hill. The rounds exploded to the side of the hill and were generally ineffective. Then they began to fire flares that exploded overhead. As the flares slowly descended on their parachutes, the entire area was bathed in an eerie, yellow light. For the first time, the Marines saw what confronted them.

"Holy shit!" someone croaked, his voice breaking.

"Oh my God," someone else exclaimed. In the strange, flickering light, the spectacle before them resembled the battle scene from some B-movie epic: endless combinations of squads, fire teams, and platoons maneuvering, marching, running, reserve units standing off to the side, as far as the light extended and beyond—and hundreds of enemy troops moving up the hill toward their command post.

"It looks like an ant hill that's been ripped apart," Joe Kosoglow said, staring down at the terrifying scene. "They're all over the place."

The NVA had been massing for another human-wave attack, when the flares caught them with their pants down. Like rats caught in the glare of a switched-on light, the enemy soldiers froze and then scurried for cover.

The Marines seized the opportunity and began to pick off the enemy soldiers, one by one. They could finally see what they were shooting at; however, there was also a negative side to the illumination. For the first time, the teammates could see each other and the carnage within their own fortification, and they reacted in horror. There was blood and gore everywhere. There were pools of blood on the ground; the big rock was splattered with it. Almost all of the Marines were wrapped somewhere with bloody bandages, and their uniforms were soaked with the blackened stains of their own blood and that of their buddies. Billie D. had been busy. The blood-soaked bodies of Powles, Fitz, and Tommy Glawe were laid out side-by-side near the big rock, and all three appeared dead. Some of the men made eye contact for only a split-second, then they turned back to the job at hand—staying alive.

Sgt. Howard saw the reaction on the faces of his young Indians. He took the PRC-25 radio from Bob Martinez and contacted Lt. Col. Sullivan at Chu Lai. Their escape route was blocked, and his team was facing overwhelming odds, so the sergeant kept his message simple. "You've gotta get us out of here, Skipper. There are too many of them for my people to handle."

Sullivan tried. He was well-known at the Direct Air Support Center of the 1st Marine Division. He called near midnight and did not waste words: "I want flare-ships, helicopters, and fixed wing aircraft dispatched to Núi Vú immediately." However, for some reason, the response was delayed, and shortly after midnight, the enemy rushed forward in their second human-wave attack.

A grenade landed in front of Hildreth and Adams, exploding violently. That was followed by several enemy troops who appeared only a few feet away. As Hildreth struggled to clear his head, he saw Terry Adams spring forward, swinging his M14 by the barrel. He heard the sounds of violent hand-to-hand combat, and in a few moments, Adams dropped back into his position behind the rocks. Another enemy soldier charged forward, and Hildreth shot him. At that moment, a .50 cal machine gun opened up on their position. It had been hauled in and set up during the dark period between flares. It was a devastating weapon, especially at point-blank range. It had to be knocked out.

The .50 cal continued to rake the southeast side of the hill, exploding rocks and plowing deep furrows in the earth. Suddenly, Hildreth heard Adams grunt, and yell, "I'm hit!"

"Is it bad?" Hildreth asked.

"Bad," Adams replied weakly.

Hildreth called for the corpsman as the heavy machine gun raked the area again; the big man was hit a second time, tearing him apart. Billy D. would not be needed.

John "Terry" Adams

Coolly and calmly, Ray Hildreth aimed his weapon, and as the enemy gunner continued to fire, he zeroed in. Hildreth was the ace shooter, and he intended to use every bit of his extensive skill. The rear sight of his M14 was set at 250m, which would put the center of impact about three inches high at three hundred feet. Allowing for windage, he moved the muzzle slightly to the left. "This is for Adams and McKinney," he said to himself with a grim smile, and he squeezed the trigger. He had tracers mixed in with his ammo, and he watched as the red streak flew straight into the chest of the NVA gunner, throwing him backward away from the machine gun. Before the assistant gunner could react, Hildreth killed him too, and the deadly weapon was silenced.

The flares died out, and the area was once again plunged into darkness. When the next flare exploded, Hildreth saw enemy troops had moved the .50 cal a few yards farther away and were setting up a mortar position to protect it. Before the NVA could react, Hildreth killed them all, and the .50 cal remained abandoned the rest of the night. Adams was dead; McKinney was dead. Hildreth had called for Mascarenas several times, but had gotten no answer, and he had seen no sign of him since they had moved to the command post. How long ago was that? An hour and a half? It seemed like a lifetime. It had been a lifetime for McKinney and Adams. Now Hildreth was the last member of his fire team left to cover their side of the hill.

Ray Hildreth

A grenade exploded spraying Natty Carlisi's back and legs with shrapnel. He screamed in pain. Vic Victor dragged him behind the big rock, calling for Billie D. As the corpsman dressed his new wounds, another grenade landed nearby, and Holmes threw himself over Natty to protect him from the blast, sustaining additional wounds of his own. Recovering from the blast, Holmes finished bandaging Carlisi, and the young man moved back to the firing line with his M14.

Ric Binns moved around the perimeter distributing ammunition he had collected from the dead and severely wounded. He was bleeding from numerous wounds, but had no time to stop and take care of himself. Jimmie Howard had taken up the M79 after Glawe was killed and fired it until he ran out of ammo. He then returned to the radio, pleading with headquarters to send help.

"My boys can't hold out much longer, Colonel," he said. "We've got to have some support."

On the northwest side of the hill, Jerry Thompson had his hands full, too. He had been firing as fast as he could fire; however, the enemy troops continued to gain ground. He was knocked down by a grenade, and as he struggled to his knees, two hands reach in from the grass and dragged him off. Managing to pull his K-Bar knife from its sheath, a vicious fight ensued before Thompson finally killed the enemy soldier. He crawled back into his position behind the rocks and called for the corpsman.

Jerrald "Jerry" Thompson

As Billie D. crawled toward the injured corporal, a grenade exploded between them, knocking Holmes unconscious. The flare burned out, plunging the area into complete darkness once again. The corpsman began to regain his senses just as another flare illuminated the area and watched in horror as two NVA dragged Thompson into the tall grass and disappeared. Then he felt someone take hold of his collar and begin to drag him away on his back. Still groggy from the grenade, he could do nothing to prevent it. He rolled his head back and stared into the face of a Vietnamese soldier. He was still looking into those piercing black eyes when the man's head exploded. Ray Hildreth had come to his rescue. Billie D. painfully crawled back to the comparative safety of the big rock and wiped the gore from his face. There was no sign of Jerry Thompson.

The Marines were careful with their ammo, firing on semiautomatic and relying on accuracy to make up for the overwhelming number of enemy troops. They threw the last of their grenades, and the NVA fell back. Every Marine had been wounded—most numerous times. Several were dead, or near to it. Sgt. Howard continued to contact headquarters on the radio, calling for support. Binns repositioned Bill Norman and Dan Mulvihill to cover the gaps left by the loss of Adams and Mascarenas and pulled the perimeter in to form a tighter defensive ring around the big rock.

Harassing probes continued and about 1:00 a.m., a grenade came flying in. It landed behind Sgt. Howard, who was focused on the radio and did not see it. Joe Kosoglow threw himself forward and kicked it away, taking most of the shrapnel meant for the sergeant. Binns called out, asking Kosoglow if he was okay. There was a pause, and then Joe responded with a groan and his usual dry humor: "I'd rather be fishing."

Natty Carlisi, the "choir boy" who didn't look like a Marine, continued to fight like one. He was so wounded he could barely stand. He had been shot in both his left leg and his left foot, along with many shrapnel wounds and his missing finger. He had propped his M14 across the top of the big rock so he could lean against the rock and fire the weapon with one hand. A grenade landed behind him and Victor, and Carlisi was unable to get away due to his wounds. The blast blew him off the rock and down on top of Powles. The youngster dragged himself over near Binns and slumped forward with a groan. A few moments later, Binns realized the boy had not moved and leaned back to check on him. There was no pulse.

Ignatius "Natty" Carlisi

Binns had grown up in one of the most violent Jamaican neighborhoods in The Bronx and had a well-deserved reputation for toughness. There was no one better to have by your side in a firefight because Ricardo Binns was always cool—no fear, no emotion. Binns was always in control.

Staring down at the young man's face in the flickering flare-light, tears welled in Binns' eyes. He could not allow himself the luxury of emotion, not here, not now. Swiping his hand across his face, Binns reached down and flicked a blade of grass and some red dirt off Carlisi's cheek. Then, he reached across and picked up the end of a poncho that was lying at Powles' feet. He pulled it over Carlisi and tucked it in around him as if he were tucking in a sleeping child for the night. "Rest well, my friend," he said softly. "Rest well."

Ricardo Binns

Victor had dived away, but had been hit in midair by the blast and thrown into the rock. Bosley had escaped the first grenade, but both were soon hit by shrapnel from another one that exploded nearby. Victor was seriously wounded on his left side, but dragged himself back to the rocky crag and continued to fight on until he passed out. Billie D. came to him and patched him up, then moved on to help someone else. Victor woke up, shook his head to clear it and crawled back to his defensive position to resume firing.

Howard continued to plead for help. "Skipper," he said. "Do you have a reactionary force or something? We're almost out of ammo. I don't care for myself, but I've got good Goddamn men here, and I'd like to get them out."

Every ear in I Corps was listening to Carnival Time's tactical channel. It was the most compelling show in town. And finally they heard the tough Marine sergeant's voice break as he said, "Skipper, just in case, tell my wife I love her."

At that moment, everyone in headquarters heard the loud crack and whine of a ricocheting bullet. And they heard Sgt. Howard scream.

"Jimmie, talk to me!" Col. Sullivan shouted, but there was no response.

"Jim!" There was only silence...

305

Part 5

The sergeant was badly wounded and barely conscious. Ric Binns crawled to him and attempted to take the radio headset, but Howard was clutching it firmly.

"Dammit, Binns! I'm not dead yet," he growled. Howard had been shot through the lower back and could not move his legs.

"How long was I out?" he asked.

"A couple of minutes," Binns replied.

"How we doin'?" Howard asked weakly.

Binns hesitated, and then replied, "The men are hangin' in there, Sergeant." In truth, morale had plummeted when word was passed that Howard had been hit. He was their rock and for most of them, their only hope of surviving to see another sunrise. Without Sgt. Howard, they had no hope.

Billie D. came to dress the sergeant's wounds and offered him a shot of morphine.

"You takin' it, Doc?" Howard asked.

"No," Holmes replied softly. "The men need it worse."

"I need to be alert," Howard responded, and the discussion on morphine was over.

Automatic weapons fire continued to periodically rake the top of the hill. Binns dispensed the last of the ammunition from the dead Marines and continued to talk to the men as he moved among them. "Hang in there, Jarhead," he said. "We're gonna walk out'a here come daylight."

The men lay under the moonless sky, wishing for the next flare to explode and wondering when and from what direction the next assault would come. Each time a flare lit up the mountain, the Marines were reminded how tenuous their continued existence was. They need only survey what they faced and then look around at the bloodied remnants of their platoon. Jimmie Howard knew they could not withstand another assault. This was literally their last stand unless they got help from outside.

There would be no surrender. They all knew what the Việt Cộng and NVA did to Marines they captured alive. The American prisoners ended up with certain masculine appendages lopped off and other atrocities done to them while they were butchered alive and kept awake to die by inches. It was too horrible to contemplate. They would all die fighting; they would all die together; and they would take as many of the bastards with them as they possibly could.

From past experience, Jimmie Howard knew the enemy was listening for any sound which indicated his men were demoralized or weakening in their will to fight. Like a tiger circling its prey, they watched and listened for any sign of weakness, then they would strike with a vengeance and without quarter. The NVA commanders intended to destroy the Americans and send the message that this was their territory. Those who dared enter it would die. Howard could already hear the high, singsong taunts coming up the dark slopes of the mountain. They were the same taunts other Marines had heard in other wars—in places like Guadalcanal and Chosin Reservoir. "Marines, you die tonight!" the voices screeched. "Marines, you die in an hour." Howard had heard it all before. He had heard the exact same words on the perimeter at Outpost Bunker Hill, the night he almost died in Korea.

Howard's men asked him if they could yell back. "Sure," he said. "Yell anything you want—give 'em a little of your Marine vocabulary." And the nine Marines let out every bit of rage and hatred that had built up inside of them over the past few hours. They shouted every curse, racial epithet, and insult in every language they knew, including Spanish, German, Jamaican, a smattering of Vietnamese, and every profanity they could remember from their vast, collective repertoire. From every quarter of the mountain's crest, Marines who were so wounded they could barely pull a trigger, gave full voice to the most vile insults aimed at the enemy troops, their wives and girlfriends, and especially their mothers, and the NVA screamed back. They quickly used up their limited English and French and yelled in pure Vietnamese. The enemy troops were obviously annoyed by the insolence of these "Người Mỹ" (Yankees), and it gave Jimmie Howard the opportunity to deliver a master stroke in psychological warfare.

"Awright, Marines," he yelled, "let's give 'em a horse laugh."

One by one, the exhausted, bloodied Marines began to laugh at the North Vietnamese. And it was contagious, and infectious, and genuine. They laughed until tears ran down their cheeks, and they rolled on their backs and held their sides because it hurt and still they continued to laugh. As the laughter rang down the slopes of Núi Vú, there was only silence from the Vietnamese. They must have thought every man on top the mountain had gone completely mad.

Howard keyed the button on the radio microphone so headquarters could hear the laughter. An incredulous smile spread across Col. Sullivan's face, and he shook his head.

"Those crazy, magnificent bastards," he said.

As the laughter died away, a new voice came on the radio. "Carnival Time, this is Smoky Gold." It was a US Air Force flare ship, and as Sgt. Howard talked to the pilot, the plane dropped its first flare, illuminating the entire mountainside.

Another voice came on the radio. An A-4 Skyhawk flight leader radioed: "Carnival Time, we are approaching your position now."

And suddenly, helicopter gunships were overhead. "Carnival Time, this is Klondike-Zero-Three. We have some special delivery for your guests."

Sgt. Howard pulled the perimeter in even tighter, and the survivors were all within about ten paces of the big rock. They had found Mascarenas. He was alive, but in bad shape with shrapnel wounds to his head. He had been hauled up to the big rock with the other casualties.

Arcadio Mascarenas

The major problem with the tactical air support was how to use it. From the aircraft, it was impossible to tell where the enemy lines ended and the Marine lines began, so close coordination was essential. They also had to coordinate between the various types of aircraft, insuring that each was able to do its job without endangering the others.

Klondike-03 and Klondike-04, Marine Observation Squadron Six, were finally able to pinpoint Carnival Time's location and attacked the NVA with a vengeance. They spotted a large concentration of troops on the northern slope and came over the big rock with M60 machine guns blazing and rockets firing. It was what the Huey pilots called a "target rich environment," and they tore up the NVA troops on the ground. The Marine A-4s flew in low over the crest of Núi Vú, dropping their 250-lb. bombs and were gone before the bombs and the roar of their engines hit the ground. If the recon Marines had been standing up, the force of the blasts would have knocked them down, and they wanted to stand up and cheer. The acrid stink of thick black smoke, jet fuel, cordite, and burnt meat was almost overpowering as it flowed up the hill and into the Marine positions surrounding the big rock.

"It was terrible—It was wonderful," Ray Hildreth said.

As soon as the A-4s left, the gunships were back. One of them remained overhead at all times, like guardian angels. Flying as low as twenty feet, they skimmed the surface of the mountain, firing their machine guns in long, sweeping bursts and exterminating any enemy troops who dared raise their heads. The gunships pulled back, and the A-4s moved in again, releasing bombs and napalm as directed by the gunships. Then the Hueys returned to pick off stragglers, survey the damage, and direct the next A-4 run.

On the perimeter surrounding the big rock, the fight continued. Two of the .50 cal heavy machine guns opened up on the Hueys. Sgt. Howard got on the radio and warned them away. Dan Mulvihill took aim and fired at the nearest gun in an attempt to take it out. Then, a grenade landed next to him and exploded, painfully wounding him for the third or fourth time. The nineteen-year-old lay quietly on the ground for a few moments, trying to clear his pounding head and determine if he still had all his moving parts. Slowly he rose to his knees, pulled himself up to his firing position, and resumed targeting the gunners on the .50 cal.

The pilots were afraid of hitting the Marines and had to leave a twenty-five-yard safety zone in front of the Marine lines. The North Vietnamese, fleeing uphill to escape the carnage of the combined Huey and A-4 attacks, soon found themselves within that safety zone, and Howard's team had their hands full fighting them off. The .50 cals and light machine guns continued to pour fire toward the big rock, hoping to get some of the Marines with ricochets, and one hit Bob Martinez in the back, knocking him down. The radioman called out and Dan Mulvihill came to help him. Billie D. was caring for someone else. Pulling up his blouse, Mulvihill inspected the wound. It was a bad one and next to the young man's spine.

"Can you move your legs?"

"Yes," Martinez groaned. "Patch me up, Dan."

In any normal firefight, this would have been a disabling wound, but not tonight. Mulvihill dressed the wound, and the two Marines returned to the fight.

Howard radioed in the casualty report: "There are seven so severely wounded they are either unconscious or unable to move; although, some are still fighting. Six more are wounded and still fighting. At least five are dead. This is one hell of a bunch of men, Skipper. The good Lord never put a better crew on this earth. I don't wanta see any more of them die."

"Neither do I, Jim," Sullivan replied.

It was still three hours until daybreak, and having expended the last of their grenades, the Marines relied on cunning and marksmanship. Howard ordered redistribution of their small supply of ammo. They made sure they had retrieved all ammo from the bodies and weapons of the dead. The men were told to fire only when they had an identified target—and then one shot at a time. The enemy fired all automatic weapons; the Marines replied with single shots. Then the sergeant quietly made a strange suggestion. He told his men to throw rocks.

It seemed like a crazy idea, but it proved to be a good tactic. A Marine heard a noise and tossed a grenade-size rock in that general direction. The NVA soldier thought it was a grenade, dived for another position, and a Marine sharpshooter took him out with one shot. The range was generally less than thirty feet. For the Marines, it was like shooting fish in a barrel.

Occasionally the flares burned out, and the aircraft in the area had to break off contact. During those times, artillery from the Special Forces camp at Hội An, three miles south, filled in the gap. South Vietnamese Army gun crews manning 105mm howitzers threw in concentration after concentration of accurate artillery fire and punished any enemy forces gathering at the base of Núi Vú.

"I'm out of ammo," one of the Marines called out. A few minutes later, that was echoed by a second man. Bill Norman fired the last of his rounds; Hildreth had three rounds left in his M14. "Please God; don't let 'em hit us now," he said.

About 5:30 a.m., the darkness began to lift. The men searched the gray sky toward Chu Lai, anxiously watching for any sign of rescue choppers. Surely they would come soon. Marines always came for their own.

Sgt. Howard looked at his watch, and then for the benefit of any English-speaking NVA in the area, he shouted: "'Reveille' in thirty minutes, Marines!" He made it sound as if they were so little concerned with the enemy, they had all been sleeping.

A short time later, amid a flurry of whistles and the clacking of bamboo sticks, the NVA forces began to withdraw and disappear into the surrounding jungle, taking a sizeable number of their dead and wounded with them. Only a token force remained to delay pursuit.

At 6:00 a.m., Howard yelled, "'Reveille'! 'Reveille'! Get yer asses up Marines!"

Victor gave out a loud groan, as if he were just waking up, and called out, "Chicken-shit to the end!"

Part 6

The morning sun gradually broke through the fog to the east, turning the gray sky to vivid shades of pink and orange. For the boys of Núi Vú, it brought a mix of feelings. For some it brought a flood of emotions: tears of relief at having survived the longest, blackest night of their lives, and guilt for having survived—tears of pain and of sorrow for the buddies they had lost, that slowly coursed unashamedly down young faces covered in dirt and grime and blood.

The men still lay in the firing positions to which they had been assigned. All sides of the command post were strewn with enemy bodies and abandoned NVA equipment. The North Vietnamese and VC normally raked the battlefield clean when they withdrew. It was always difficult to get a correct body-count after a battle, because they left no bodies behind. This time, however, the firing line of the recon team had been so deadly the NVA left unclaimed those who fell within twenty-five or thirty yards of the perimeter. It would have been suicide to try and collect them.

The firing had slacked off, but the small force of NVA and hardcore VC remaining on Núi Vú had the recon Marines pinned down and did not intend to leave. They slipped into their spider holes and waited, intending to attack and delay any Americans who came to rescue the men on top of the hill. Occasional bursts of fire from light machine guns continued to chip off chunks of the crag that towered above the Marines' heads. Firing uphill from their concealed holes, the enemy guns would cut down any man who silhouetted himself against the skyline, and two of the .50 cal machine guns were still firing sporadically.

Jimmie Howard remained at his post by the radio talking to Col. Sullivan. "All my people will need help when you extract us, Colonel. Only three can walk, and they are wounded, too. The only way we'll get out is with troops."

"They're on the way, Jim," Sullivan said. "They are in the air."

"We are out of ammo, Skipper. We're dead if these snipers decide to come up the hill. I have seven men that can pull a trigger, and we've got eight rounds between us."

An unarmed Huey medevac circled Núi Vú. It was waiting to come in for the wounded as soon as it was deemed safe enough for it to land. Klondike-03, who had been overhead much of the night, had been relieved by Maj. William J. Goodsell, the new commander of VMO-6. Maj. Goodsell flew in low over the hill-crest, while Klondike-04 hovered to one side, ready to pounce if the enemy took the bait, but no one fired. Then, Klondike-04 made a couple of low passes across the gouged and scarred face of the mountain, with the same result. Everything seemed to be quiet in the bright, early-morning sunshine.

Maj. Goodsell made the decision to try for the evacuation.

"Carnival Time, this is Klondike. We're bringing in the medevac. Can you get your whiskeys (wounded) ready?"

"Roger, Klondike," Sgt. Howard replied. Powles, Mascarenas, and Fitz Fitzpatrick had somehow managed to hang on through the night. If they could get them to a hospital, they might make it. But Howard had a bad feeling about this. It was too quiet and too easy—nothing had been quiet or easy since the NVA had attacked the night before.

"Klondike, this is Carnival Time. Maybe you should wave off," Howard said. "It's too risky."

"We are coming in, Carnival Time," Goodsell responded.

The Huey gunship slowly descended and hovered—Goodsell's copilot, 1st Lt. Stephen Butler, opened a window and dropped a yellow smoke grenade to mark the spot for the medevac to land. Goodsell waved to Howard, and then the ship skimmed north over the forward slope. The Huey was about ten feet above the ground, whipping up a cloud of red dust and dried grass with its blade wash—the M60 machine gunner watching warily from the open door.

At that moment, the chatter of NVA machine guns drowned out the sound of the helicopter's engines, and green tracers flew toward the Huey, ricocheting off the undercarriage and striking Maj. Goodsell. The helicopter rocked and veered sharply to the right and then zigzagged down the mountain, trailing black smoke and streams of white hydraulic fluid. Lt. Butler grabbed the stick and managed to crash land the bird in a paddy east of Núi Vú. None of the other crewmembers were seriously hurt. Klondike-04 landed beside the downed chopper and rescued the crew, but Maj. Goodsell was critically wounded. One round had gone through the chin bubble striking him in the right leg and severing an artery. He bled to death before reaching the hospital at Chu Lai. He had commanded Squadron VMO-6 for less than a week.

The medevac helicopter did not hesitate and would have attempted to land, but Howard frantically waved it off. Medevac pilots were brave, but they were not invulnerable. The pilot saw the sergeant's signal and turned away as machine gun rounds clanged off his chopper's undercarriage. Jimmie Howard was not going to have another bird shot down. The recon team watched the medevac as it disappeared over the next mountain, and the last wisps of yellow smoke were carried away by the wind. Sgt. Howard and his team would have to wait for ground troops.

After the shoot-down of the gunship, Marine Corps A-4s were scrambled from Chu Lai, and they, along with gunships from VMO-6 and VMO-2 attacked the enemy positions with renewed fury. Flying lower and lower, the gunships crisscrossed the slopes, searching for the machine gun emplacements. They offered themselves as targets, daring the enemy to shoot, and one of the VMO-2 gunships was hit. It crashed, and its crew chief, twenty-year-old Leo Buckholdt, was killed. During the attack, however, the positions of the two .50 cal guns were exposed, and they were immediately silenced.

Assisted by a forward air controller in a Cessna, the A-4 Skyhawks pounded the hillside with bombs and 20mm exploding rounds. Núi Vú shuddered and groaned like some gargantuan beast as the recon Marines hugged the ground at the top. Jimmie Howard helped the FAC direct the strikes.

The pilots flew as low as they dared; pouring everything they had into the suspected location of the NVA machine guns and snipers. However, after each attack, the enemy gunners popped back out of their holes like some sort of indestructible gophers. Apparently they also had a limitless supply of ammo to go along with their immortality. It was going to take ground troops to root them out; in the meantime, they remained a deadly threat to any and all who dared to move on or over the northern slope of Núi Vú.

Escorted by gunships, dozens of UH-34 transports loaded with over 300 Marines flew out of Chu Lai as soon as the morning fog lifted, but enemy gunfire around the base of Núi Vú was too intense for the choppers to land. They circled for forty-five minutes while A-4 jets and artillery blasted a secure landing zone.

The recon team watched from their mountaintop hold as the armada of choppers approached Núi Vú. Framed against the pink morning sky, they looked like a glistening swarm of dragon flies; soon the men began to hear the roar of their engines. It seemed they should be exhilarated to see their rescue so near at hand, but most were too numb from exhaustion, dehydration, and blood loss to feel much of anything. Each man watched quietly, alone with his thoughts—reflecting on what the team had endured.

Charlie Company, 5th Marines, the recon team's own company, was transported in from Hill 54 and inserted on the southern slope of the mountain. Led by 1st Lt. Buck Darling, the fresh troops climbed fast. They ignored sniper fire and quickly wiped out small pockets of resistance. Their 60mm mortar team knocked out an NVA mortar with the first round it fired, and Sgt. Frank Riojas, the weapons platoon commander, cut down a sniper at five hundred yards with a tracer round from his M14.

Marine machine gun sections were detached from the main body and sent up the flanks of the hill to support the company's movement. The NVA had now become the hunted. Marines scrambled around the sides of the mountain, as well as up the slope, in order to shut off all avenues of escape for those enemy troops still on the hill. They could surrender or die. None would be allowed to flee.

Charlie Company's main column climbed straight up the mountain. Their point squad saw the recon position on the crest of the mountain while they were still a quarter mile away. The monolith which served as their command post was the most prominent feature on the peak. The Marines were not sure what they would find at the top. They only knew the guys on "Howard's Hill" were in a bad way, and the lead platoon hurried forward. Those were their brothers up there.

When the platoon reached the rock, the Marines had to crawl over piles of enemy bodies to enter the recon team's perimeter. "My God!" someone said, "This must have been one hell of a fight."

"Get down!" Sgt. Howard yelled. "There are snipers right in front of us." The recon Marines looked back to see what their sergeant was yelling about and found themselves looking into the clean, fresh faces of the relief Marines who had crawled in from the South.

One of the guys let out a whoop.

Another man said, "Hey, you got any cigarettes?"

Joe Kosoglow asked for water.

Some of the fresh Marines crawled forward and replaced the wounded men on the perimeter. Others helped the wounded move back near the big rock and began preparing them to be transported out as soon as possible. There seemed to be corpsmen everywhere.

Staff Sgt. Richard Sullivan was one of the first Marines in, and gave Joe Kosoglow a drink from his canteen. "I never thought

I'd see the sun rise again," Kosoglow told him, "but once it did, I knew you'd be coming."

Billy D. Holmes

Corpsman Billy D. Holmes was in bad shape. He had so many wounds to his hands, legs, and buttocks he could barely move. His face was a ghastly mask of dried blood and dirt. Tears mixed with the blood as a relief Marine reached him. "Christ, man, I can't believe you're here," he said.

"We're here to help you out," the Marine responded.

Bob Martinez had gradually lost the use of his legs due to the bullet that grazed his spine. "We're gettin' your tough ass out of here," his replacement said and dragged him out by his feet to the south side of the big rock, away from the snipers.

Sgt. Howard reported in to Col. Sullivan and told him: "Skipper, we have friendly troops with us, but I'm not leaving yet." He would not consider evacuation until all of his boys, alive or dead, had been evacuated first.

Ray Hildreth asked one of the Marine point men if he could spare a mag for his M14.

"Sure," the young man said.

He started to move forward, and Hildreth yelled, "Stay down! Snipers have us pinned down."

The kid handed Hildreth the magazine. He was clean-cut, gung-ho, and looked to be about eighteen. Hildreth was eighteen, too, but felt much older after the past twenty-four hours.

"Where are the snipers located?" the kid asked eagerly.

"About twenty yards down the hill," Hildreth replied.

Without warning, the boy rose slightly to look down the hill and a shot rang out. His helmet flew off and his body fell across Hildreth, spurting blood and jerking reflexively. Hildreth was splattered with gore and began to scream. After all he had been through—after losing McKinney and Adams, and all the other guys, and going through an endless night from hell, this pushed him over the edge.

"Dammit, dammit, GODDAMMIT!" he screamed, pounding the ground with his fists, tears streaming down his face. "I told him to keep his head down—I told'im—I TOLD'im...," and his voice trailed off to a soft whimper. "I told'im."

Two corpsmen ran low to Hildreth and moved the young Marine's body away from him. They then moved Hildreth and his teammates further back by the big rock. They would become spectators until they could be evacuated.

Sgt. Howard watched quietly as 2nd Lt. Ronald Meyer deployed his platoon along the crest of Núi Vú. Meyer had graduated from the Naval Academy a year previously and was planning on making the Corps his career. A champion wrestler from Dubuque, Iowa, Meyer had been a member of the varsity wrestling team at Annapolis and had acquired the nickname "Stumpy" due to his short, muscular build.

Like most Marine officers, Meyer wore no visible rank in the field, and Howard, assuming he was a corporal or sergeant, shouted orders to him. Respecting the sergeant's knowledge and performance, the lieutenant obeyed. He never mentioned his rank, so Sgt. Howard, refusing all offers of assistance, proceeded to direct the tactical maneuvers of the relieving company. He was determined to wipe out the band of hardcore NVA that were dug in some twenty yards downslope. This was the primary group that had shot and harassed his boys for hours. He planned to make them pay.

Meyer hollered for members of his platoon to pass him grenades, and he lobbed them down toward the snipers' holes. Peering around the base of the big rock, Howard directed his throws. "A little more to the right on the next one, buddy. About five yards farther. That's right. No, a little too strong." The grenades had little effect, however, and the snipers kept firing.

Lance Cpl. Terry Redic asked to fire a rifle grenade at the snipers' nest. Redic was only eighteen years old but was an experienced sharpshooter and had several kills to his credit. In firefights he often disdained to duck, preferring to suppress hostile fire by his own rapid, accurate shooting. The young Marine rose up on one knee, sighted downslope and was killed instantly.

Terry Pete Redic

Meyer swore vehemently. "Let's get that sonuvabitch! You coming with me, Sotello?"

"Yes, Stump." Lance Cpl. David Sotello turned to get his rifle and some other men, but Meyer did not wait. He started forward with a grenade in each hand.

"Keep yer head down, buddy, they can shoot," Howard said.

Meyer crawled for several yards and threw a grenade into a hole, killing an enemy sniper. He turned, looking back up the hill, and another sniper shot him in the back. Sotello heard the shot as he started to crawl down.

2nd Lt. Ronald Meyer

So did Hospitalman 3rd Class John Markillie, one of the platoon corpsmen. Markillie immediately crawled down toward the fallen lieutenant.

"For God's sake, keep your head down!" Howard yelled. Markillie reached Meyer, rose slightly to examine the wound, and a sniper shot him in the chest.

Corpsman Doc Holloday and Cpl. Melville, a Marine squad leader, were next to go. Sgt. Howard called for the relief Marines to provide cover, and the two men crawled forward. Holloday could feel no pulse on Lt. Meyer; however, Markillie was still breathing. Ignoring the sniper fire, the men began dragging and pushing his body up the hill.

Suddenly, Melville was hit in the head and his helmet bounced off. The other Marines continued their covering fire as the corporal lay still on the ground. Then, miraculously the Marine shook his head and continued to crawl. The round had gone in one side of his helmet and blown a hole out the other side, just nicking the corporal above his left ear. Reaching the perimeter, Melville and Holloday dragged Markillie behind the rocks and collapsed beside him.

Billy D. Holmes was rejuvenated by the arrival of the relief platoon and supervised the other Charlie Company corpsmen as they administered to the wounded. With the fire fight still occurring on the northern slope of the mountain, helicopter extraction was not possible. Holmes moved back and forth, in complete charge, making certain all his buddies were accounted for and cared for. No one dared question his authority, regardless of rank. In spite of his own serious wounds, he had singlehandedly kept many of these men alive during the darkest night of their lives.

Part 7

Lt. Philip Freed was the forward air controller attached to Charlie Company. He was on his way up Núi Vú with the command staff when he heard the lead platoon needed air support. He ran the last quarter mile up the hill and crawled in beside Cpl. Melville on the northern perimeter. With machine gun rounds zinging over his head, Freed needed no additional briefing.

Marine lieutenants Richard Deilke and Edward Menzer were cruising down the coastline in their F8 Crusader jets. They were returning to Chu Lai from a mission during which they had not been utilized, and their aircraft were fully armed.

Menzer said, "We called DASC (Direct Air Support Center) and asked for another mission. We got diverted to the FAC Cottage 14. He told us he had a machine gun nest right in front of him."

"This is Cottage 14," Freed said. "Bring it on down on a dry run. This has to be real tight. Charlie is dug in right on our lines." Freed had flown F8s and could talk to the pilots in a language they understood; however, he was not certain they could help. He was afraid they could not fly in close enough to get the machine gun, without hitting the Marines on top the hill. Deilke and Menzer flew in on a test run, and Freed deliberately called them in wide so he could judge their precision and technical skills. He was impressed—these guys were good.

He called for them to attack, but the pilots were concerned. The target was only twenty yards from the FAC.

"As long as you're flying parallel to the people, it's okay," Menzer said, "It's a good shooting bird. But even so, I was leery to fire with troops that near."

The two pilots were about to fly one of the closest direct air support missions in the history of fixed-wing aviation. They approached from the northeast with the sun behind them, cut across the ridge parallel to the friendly lines, and strafed with no room for error. The gun-sight on an F8 looks like a bull's-eye with rings marked in successive 10-mil increments. When the pilots aligned their sights while three thousand feet away, the target lay within the 10-mil ring; the Marine position was at the edge of the ring. The slightest variance of the controls would rake the Marines with deadly cannon fire.

Each pilot made four strafing passes, skimming by at ten to twenty feet above the ridge. Their wings dipped so close to the top of the hill, Freed was afraid they would crash. The impact of the cannon shells showered the Marines with dirt, and they swore they could see the color of the pilots' eyes. During the eight attacks, the pilots fired 350 20mm explosive shells into an area sixty yards long and ten to twenty yards wide. The side of the mountain was plowed up as if a giant bulldozer had moved across the ridge.

The FAC cautiously lifted his head, and a round zipped by, ricocheting off the top of the big rock. Every NVA sniper on the hill had been silenced, but one. A Marine shouted that the shot had come from the same location as the shot that killed Stump Meyer. The lieutenant's body was still lying several yards down the side of the hill. No one had dared try to retrieve it. "And the SOB that shot Stump is still down there," Melville snorted.

The F8s had spent their ammo, but had ample fuel left. Menzer called to say they could make dummy runs over the position if the Marines thought it would be useful. Freed asked them to try it.

Buck Darling, the Charlie Company commander, had arrived on the scene and was watching the jets. The NVA gunner stopped firing when the planes roared past. The planes would be his cover. "I'm going to get Stump," Darling said. "Are you coming, Brown?" he asked the nearest Marine.

Lance Cpl. James Brown was not known as the most squared-away Marine in Charlie 1/5. His superiors generally thought his off-beat sense of humor was inappropriate, if not downright disgrace-ful, and his mouth kept him in trouble. During one fire fight, when the enemy caught Brown's squad in crossfire, rounds were passing high over the Marines' heads. As the rest of the squad returned fire, Brown strolled over to a tombstone, propped himself on it with one finger, crossed his legs and yelled, "You couldn't hit me if I was buried here!" The squad leader nearly shot Brown himself.

On Núi Vú, however, Brown had been all business. He had emptied several rifle magazines and hurled grenade after grenade. When he ran out of grenades, he threw rocks to keep the snip-ers ducking. And through it all, he screamed, cursed, and shouted every insult and blasphemy he could think of. Jimmie Howard was impressed, both by his enthusiasm and his vocabulary.

The F8s came over, and Darling and Brown began to snake their way through the grass down the side of the hill toward Meyer's body. Tugging his company commander's boot ahead of him, Brown quipped, "Don't sweat it, lieutenant, they can only kill us." The commander did not reply.

The two Marines reached Meyer and tried to pull him back while crawling on their stomachs, but he was just too heavy to move in that fashion.

"All right, let's carry him," Darling said.

Now Brown was at a loss for words, and that rarely hap-pened. He knew what had happened to every Marine on the slope that raised his head—and his CO was suggesting they stand up and carry Stump.

"We'll time our moves with the jets," Darling continued.

When the jets passed low, the two men scrambled forward a few feet with their burden. Then, they hit the deck as the jets pulled away. The sniper took shots at them after every pass—rounds chipped the rocks and kicked up sprays of red dirt all around them. They had less than ten yards to climb, but it took over a dozen passes by the F8s, and when they rolled behind the rocks at the top with Meyer's body, they were exhausted.

Now the time had come to deal with the sniper on the slope.

Cpl. Samuel Roth quietly led his eight-man rifle squad out the back and around the left side of the slope. On the right, Sgt. Riojas, the weapons platoon commander, set up a machine gun near the big rock to cover the squad. A burst of automatic fire struck the tripod of the gun, and a strange duel developed. The sniper would fire at the Marine gun. Riojas would lay low until he fired, and then reach up and loose a burst downhill, forcing the sniper to jump back into his hole.

Riojas managed to keep the NVA sniper's attention. The gunner did not hear the Marine squad moving through the brush to his right. Roth brought his men on line facing toward the sniper's hole, and with fixed bayonets the Marines began walking forward. There was no visible movement in the torn clumps of dry grass and plowed earth.

Riojas had to stop firing as the Marines moved in, and the sniper heard the squad. He spun around with his gun and fired. Bullets flew by the Marines heads and Sam Roth's helmet spun off with a loud clang. Roth fell, and the other Marines hit the deck. The corporal, however, was uninjured. The steel helmet had saved a second Marine's life within an hour, and he was not aware he had lost it.

The Marines finally knew exactly where the sniper was located.

"When I give the word," Roth said, "kneel and fire."

"Now!" he yelled.

The Marines rose as one and their rounds kicked up dust and clumps of earth in front of them, but they missed the sniper. He had ducked back down into his hole. The Marines lay back down, and Roth swore.

"All right," he said. "We're gonna get this sonuvabitch. Put in fresh mags and let's do it again."

"Now!" Roth yelled.

As the Marines rose for the second time, the sniper popped up like a target in a shooting gallery. A round knocked him backward against the side of his hole, and Roth charged, with his squad behind him. He dived into the hole and drove forward with his bayonet. A grenade rolled from the sniper's left hand. Roth froze, and then saw the release pin was still in place. He jerked his bayonet free, and the sniper slumped forward over his gun.

Núi Vú was quiet. In the distance, birds began to sing. It was noon. Buck Darling declared the objective secure and ordered the Charlie 1/5 Marines to fan out across the mountain. They would search the enemy dead for documents and collect their weapons.

Chuck Bosley slowly rose to his feet. It was the first time he had stood in an eternity. His knees shook as he placed his hand back against the stone edifice to steady himself. He felt more like he was ninety than nineteen. His eyes were sunken into dark holes in his once-boyish face; his skin was covered in layers of dust, grime, and dried blood. His filthy uniform was tattered and bloody from the blasts of enemy grenades and shrapnel. Sliding the boonie back on his head, he revealed surprisingly white skin on his forehead and a shock of golden hair. Taking a few hesitant steps forward, the young man looked down the slope toward the sniper's lair and then surveyed the dozens of enemy bodies, strewn where they had fallen. The bodies were beginning to swell in the midday sun. Spitting out a mix of dirt and bloody phlegm, Bosley closed his eyes and bowed his head.

At that moment, he felt a hand on his shoulder and turned to look into the equally worn and battered face of nineteen-year-old Ray Hildreth. Hanging onto Bosley for support, Hildreth crept forward and stared down the hill at the carnage. Tears welled in his eyes, and he struggled to speak. "Oh, my God," he finally forced out. "Oh, my God!"

Hildreth's knees began to buckle, and Bosley grabbed him under his arms, backing up until both of them were once again supported by the solid face of the big rock. "Hang in there, Ray," Bosley said. "We're almost home."

Dan Mulvihill, appearing equally gaunt and abused, made his way around the rock to stand beside Bosley and Hildreth. Of the eighteen men in their patrol, these three teenagers were the walking wounded. Ten of their teammates were in serious to very critical condition on stretchers; five were dead, so far.

Beyond them, Jimmie Howard lay on a stretcher by the big rock with his eyes closed. There were deep grooves in his cheeks and dark bruises under each eye showed through the dirt and blood—his hair seemed to have turned white overnight. His head was pounding, and he hurt in every part of his body, but he still refused Morphine. He knew he had done everything he could to save his men, but he deeply regretted those he had lost. He felt the emotion building within him and turned his face toward the rock, away from the others, as tears seeped from under his eyelids and slowly coursed down onto the stretcher. It had been his decision to stay on the mountain one more night, and it had nearly killed them all.

Part 8

During the long, terrible night on Núi Vú, the Carnival Time Marines fought as a team; however, each man also fought alone. Each man witnessed events and experienced things none of the others were privy to.

Ric Binns was the only witness when Natty Carlisi died, and Ray Hildreth was the only one to know when McKinney and Adams were hit. No one knew when Mascarenas was wounded by the grenade, but there were several dead NVA near him when they found him unconscious. The enemy soldiers had been killed hand-to-hand and attested to the brave fight the quiet man put up before he fell.

No one will ever really know how some of the men died. There is no question, however, that they all died heroically. As the relief Marines located and removed the bodies of their recon brothers, they found remarkable scenes.

Several of the team, including Sgt. Howard, witnessed young Tommy Glawe being shot through the head as he fired the M79 grenade launcher. Billy D. had dragged his body beside the big rock with the other casualties. However, when the Charlie 1/5 Marines found him the next day, Glawe was propped against the rock and lying in front of him was a dead NVA soldier. Each man was holding a weapon with the muzzle touching the other man's chest, and the enemy soldier had been killed by a shot to the chest.

The Marines recovered two Marine entrenching tools amid a circle of mangled NVA bodies; both shovels were covered with blood and gore. No one knows which member of the recon team fought and won that round in the darkness of that horror-filled night.

Jerry Thompson had fought like hell until he was seriously wounded and was last seen being dragged off alive by several NVA troops. When they found him, he was heavily bandaged around the head and chest from previous wounds and had been shot in the face. Beside him lay a dead NVA soldier who had been stabbed to death. A second NVA soldier lay firmly embraced on top of him, and Thompson's hand was frozen around the hilt of the Marine Ka-Bar combat knife that was buried in the enemy soldier's back.

Medevac helicopters were called in and began to land on the crest of the mountain. Some of the dead were loaded first, followed by the most critically wounded. Mascarenas was still alive when the chopper lifted off, but died en route to Chu Lai.

Sgt. Howard and Billy D. Holmes still refused to leave. James McKinney had not been found, and they would not leave without him. Finally, after repeated assurances from Lt. Darling that he would not leave until they had recovered everyone, Howard and Holmes agreed to leave Núi Vú. Their jobs were done.

The stretchers with the two men were carried aboard a waiting medevac, along with Fitz Fitzpatrick and several more dead wrapped in their ponchos. As the medevac chopper lifted off, the grizzled Marine sergeant and the tough Navy corpsman reached across and gripped hands. And, as they left Núi Vú in the distance, tears began to flow for both. It had been that kind of day.

A Charlie 1/5 squad found James McKinney. He was lying peacefully in a patch of the remaining tall grass below the command post and appeared remarkably untouched by the terrible battle that had been fought around him. He was wrapped in his poncho and placed aboard a chopper, along with his honor guard of Bosley, Mulvihill, and Hildreth.

Honors and recognition soon began to come in for the men of Charlie Company 1st Recon Platoon. Lt. Gen. Lewis W. Fields, commander of the 1st Marine Division, visited those in the hospital, pinning purple hearts on their hospital gowns.

"The NVA were well-trained, well-armed, well-disciplined," Sgt. Howard told the general. "They were the best we'll ever run up against, but their best just ain't good enough, sir."

"Sergeant," Gen. Fields said, "You've seen enough for one man. I'm ordering you to knock it off and stop making a habit of getting wounded."

Of the eighteen original team members, only Bosley, Mulvihill, Hildreth, Norman, and Kosoglow remained in Vietnam. All the rest, including Howard, Binns, Martinez, Powles, Victor, Fitzpatrick, and Holmes were so seriously injured they were shipped to the US Naval hospital at Subic Bay, and then on to the States for surgery and long-term hospitalization.

The five left behind were treated for their wounds at Chu Lai and assumed they would form the core to rebuild their shattered platoon; however, they were soon advised otherwise. The company sergeant major spoke to them and said, "You men survived something that happens once in a lifetime. We will not take a chance of it happening again. None of you are going back into combat."

If the action atop Núi Vú had centered around only one man, it could be considered a unique incident of exceptional bravery on the part of a remarkable man, and it was that. Without Jimmie Howard, every Marine on the mountain would probably have died in the initial attack. But, it is also something much more. On June 13, 1966, few people would have noticed anything special about the 1st Recon Platoon of Charlie Company 1/5. Now, however, in reading the names of its heroic dead, and those who fought for survival and each other, we see that here were the typical and the average, who, well-trained and well-led, rose above the norm to perform an exemplary feat of arms. These eighteen men took on the elite troops of an entire NVA battalion and, outnumbered twenty-five to one, fought them to a standstill. In the following months, the 1st Recon Platoon would become the most highly decorated unit of its size in US military history.

Lance Cpl. Alcadio Mascarenas, The Silver Star and the Purple Heart (Posthumously)

Pfc. Ignatius "Natty" Carlisi, The Silver Star and the Purple Heart (Posthumously)

Pfc. Thomas "Tommy" Glawe, The Silver Star and the Purple Heart (Posthumously)

Pfc. James O. McKinney, The Silver Star and the Purple Heart (Posthumously)

Lance Cpl. Raymond "Ray" Hildreth, The Silver Star and the Purple Heart

Lance Cpl. Joseph "Joe" Kosoglow, The Silver Star and the Purple Heart

Lance Cpl. Robert "Bob" Martinez, The Silver Star and the Purple Heart

Lance Cpl. Daniel "Dan" Mulvihill, The Silver Star and the Purple Heart

Lance Cpl. William "Bill" Norman, The Silver Star and the Purple Heart

Lance Cpl. Thomas "Tom" Powles, The Silver Star and the Purple Heart

Lance Cpl. Ralph "Vic" Victor, The Silver Star and the Purple Heart

Pfc. Charles "Chuck" Bosley, The Silver Star and the Purple Heart

Hospital Corpsman 1st Class Richard "Fitz" Fitzpatrick, The Silver Star and the Purple Heart

Cpl. Jerrald "Jerry" Thompson, The Navy Cross and the Purple Heart (Posthumously)

Lance Cpl. John "Terry" Adams, The Navy Cross and the Purple Heart (Posthumously)

Lance Cpl. Ricardo "Ric" Binns, The Navy Cross and the Purple Heart with OLC

Hospital Corpsman 3rd Class Billy D. Holmes, The Navy Cross and the Purple Heart

S. Sgt. Jimmie Earl Howard, The Medal of Honor and the Purple Heart with OLCs

Jimmie Howard stood proudly at attention in his dress uniform. Next to him were his wife and children. The extraordinary story of his heroic stand on Hill 488 was read, and then Pres. Lyndon Johnson placed the Medal of Honor around his neck. With tears in his eyes, the Marine sergeant stepped forward and gave all the credit to his team.

Sgt. Howard with six of his Indians: (L to R)
Ray Hildreth, Billy D. Holmes,
Howard, Tom Powles, Joe Kosoglow, Bill Norman, and Ric Binns

And the team survivors were all there—nine young Marines and two Navy corpsmen who had fought with Sgt. Howard during that incredible night of horror and heroism on Núi Vú. After a brief speech, Howard took Pres. Johnson by the hand and led him to the edge of the stage where he introduced him to each of his men—the men to whom he felt the Medal of Honor belonged more than it did to himself—the team Jimmie Howard had always called his "Indians."

The siege on top of Núi Vú received little or no publicity in the States. June 1966 was slightly before the major influx of war correspondents, and the American public was not as absorbed in the Vietnam conflict as it would become later. One cannot help but wonder what effect news of this amazing victory might have had if the American people had known about it, on a home front that was not yet swayed against the war. Would the liberal media have told the story honestly if it had come a year later, or would they have spun it in a negative way? We will never know, but we must never forget the boys of Núi Vú.

They went with songs to the battle, they were young,
Straight of limb, true of eye, steady and aglow.
They were staunch to the end against odds uncounted;
They fell with their faces to the foe.

"For the Fallen"
—Laurence Binyon

Epilogue: USS *Jimmie E. Howard*

The US Navy commissioned the USS *Jimmie E. Howard* (DDG 83) on 20 October 2001. The ship was the 33rd Arleigh Burke-class guided missile destroyer in its fleet.

On June 17, 2016, the sailors on board her were treated to a firsthand account of the Battle of Hill 488 from the last four survivors: Ray Hildreth, Joe Kosoglow, Dan Mulvihill, and Bill Norman.

Their visit coincided with the fiftieth anniversary of the June 15, 1966, battle and was the first time in nearly fifty years the group had seen each other since the war. The former members of

1st Recon Battalion shared stories with the *Howard's* crew and the Howard sisters, the daughters of 1st Sgt. Jimmie Howard.

"We are truly honored to have been able to take part in this event," said Cmdr. Amy McInnis, *Howard* commanding officer. The group gathered in the ship's wardroom alongside Yvonne, Yvette, Barbara, Linette, and Darlene Howard and shared memories of Sgt. Howard and the tremendous events of the historic battle on Hill 488.

Guests later toured the ship, visiting the ship's bridge, forecastle, helicopter hanger, and flight deck. The last stop was the Medal of Honor Passageway, a hallway which houses the history of USS *Howard* and memorabilia from Sgt. Howard's military career.

"It was a tremendous honor to serve under Sgt. Howard," Mulvihill said.

"I probably would not be here if it were not for him," Hildreth added.

As they moved down the passageway, each guest studied the mementoes, medals, and photos lining the bulkhead. The deck is painted bright red, paying homage to the Marine Corps, and there is a tangible spirit of honor that fills the space.

The visit concluded on the *Howard's* quarterdeck where Cmdr. McInnis traded hugs and handshakes with the Howards and the Hill 488 veterans.

"I am confident stories of the heroism displayed on Hill 488 and the memories created during this visit will endure with the crew," Cmdr. McInnis said. "I hope we can honor the memories of those that served on Hill 488 in all of our future endeavors."

21

Michael Blanchfield and Duane Keil

Out of the Clouds

Michael Blanchfield   *Duane Keil*

They came from America's heartland, two children of the Great Lakes—one born in Minnesota and raised in Chicago's northwest suburbs—the other a son of southern Michigan.

Michael Blanchfield dropped out of Wheeling (Illinois) High School after first semester of his sophomore year. He turned seventeen in January 1967 and left for Army basic training the next week. With dreams of being a paratrooper, Michael excelled during basic training and AIT, and volunteered for airborne training at Ft. Benning, Georgia.

Jump school was tough, both physically and mentally. "We double-time everywhere," Michael wrote in a letter to his mother. Those who quit or washed out were lined up on the parade ground the following morning, and the entire class double-timed past them in one final gesture of humiliation before they were shipped out.

"I'll never end up on quitter's row,'" he wrote. "I'd die, first."

The school consisted of two weeks of ground training and then a week of jumps. "The first jump was the best," he said. "I can't believe how much I like it. All I can hear is the sound of the wind as it blows through the cords of my chute. I have never felt so free. I just want more." There were two additional jumps the next day and two final jumps on the third. Some four hundred recruits had started the course—less than two hundred graduated.

Successfully completing jump school, Blanchfield was assigned to the 173rd Airborne Brigade and shipped out for Ft. Campbell, Kentucky. He was too young for deployment to a combat zone, so he remained on duty in the States. He would not turn eighteen until the following January.

> Out of the clouds I tumble
> To survey the earth below.
> With a snap of my billowing canopy
> I glide like a bird, and slow.*

Duane Keil was a typical tall, gangly teenager. Growing up in Adrian, Michigan, he would spend the day sprawled on the couch, watching old movies, and eating everything in sight. He had an old '55 Chevy he called "Fu Man Chu" and the name was scrawled in red paint on the rear fenders. The back of the driver's seat was broken, so he crawled into the car, stretched his long legs straight out and rested his seatback against the seat in the rear of the car. His head was barely visible above the car windows, but somehow it worked. With his long, blonde hair blowing in the breeze, he and his buddies cruised around town, waving at the girls and being "cool." Duane loved his car.

After graduation from Tecumseh High School, Keil got a job with Tecumseh Products, the area's big manufacturing company, but he knew he was facing the draft. After a year at Tecumseh, he enlisted in the Army, volunteered for airborne training, and was assigned to the 173rd Airborne Brigade.

Returning home for a brief leave, Duane enjoyed a few days with family and friends in the fall of 1968.

"It's great to have Duane home," his sister Toni said, as she sat and watched him roll around on the carpet with their little brother, Ronnie. Duane had put on a few pounds, but he was still just a big skinny kid. He would lie on the floor with Ronnie and play with toy cars or build things with blocks. "He's always loved kids," she said. I can't wait until he has some of his own. He'll be a great daddy."

With his sense of humor, Duane enjoyed a wide circle of friends and spent time with most of them while he was home. He always had a smile on his face and joked around with his buddies. He was popular with the ladies too.

"Of course, he's never liked any boy I liked," Toni said. He's a typical big brother. "He thinks they're all losers," she continued, "and he's usually right, which makes me even madder. We used to fight a lot—guess that's normal, but I miss him so when he's away. He's my big brother and my best friend."

Part 2

Duane Keil arrived at the airport in Oakland, California, on October 23, 1968. As he walked into the terminal, he was met by a sergeant who directed him into a holding area where several others were waiting. When the sergeant had gathered a dozen more, the group was moved into a crowded auditorium, where the soldiers were issued preliminary orders for their new units in Vietnam. A few of the men in the room did not know where they were being assigned, but many already had division patches displayed on their uniforms. The vast majority of them, including Keil, were on their way to the 173rd Airborne Brigade and proudly sported the winged "Sky Soldier" patch on their sleeves. A senior NCO who was in charge of the orientation looked over the close-cropped group of new troops and remarked, "We can always tell who's taking it on the chin in 'Nam by whose patch we see the most." The new 173rd troopers all laughed, nervously, but Keil wasn't sure how funny the remark was.

Most of the new paratroopers appeared to be barely eighteen, which automatically made Keil feel like the old man (at twenty). Several looked like they had never used a razor. Keil smiled to himself and shook his head. After getting their orders and a short briefing, the men were moved into the main terminal. Duane hoped they were going to board their plane, but it was the same old "hurry-up and wait." Most of the men settled in to nap, smoke, read, and BS—the usual ways to cope with downtime in the military.

The soldiers were eventually herded onto their plane, a civilian Boeing 707, and were off on their way to Hawaii. There were five stewardesses on board, and the raucous load of young GIs was loud and boisterous. They teased the attendants continuously; however, the women were more than capable of taking care of themselves. Landing in Honolulu, the plane parked some distance from the terminal. It was refueled, resupplied, and a new crew came aboard. The soldiers were allowed to get off the plane, stretch their legs and enjoy the warm, balmy air, but the large, civilian terminal was strictly off limits. Departing Hawaii, the aircraft headed for its next stop on the island of Guam.

Arriving in Guam some eight hours later, the men were permitted to leave the plane and go into the terminal for breakfast. They were stiff, sore, and tired from the long trip. With his long legs bent sideways for most of the trip, Keil could barely walk as he struggled to make his way along the aisle of the plane and down the metal steps. The weather was overcast with light drizzle and a cold wind blowing across the tarmac. Most of the soldiers went inside, and the crew joined them while their aircraft was serviced.

After their break, the men reboarded for the last and longest leg of their journey. The plane departed over the deep blue waters off Guam and was soon flying in sunshine above a thick layer of clouds. Most of the men read or slept during the long day, and Keil watched the sun finally disappear into the endless sea of clouds below them in a blood-red display. As the soldiers neared their final destination, the once-rowdy group of men became increasingly quiet and introspective. They would be landing at the huge US base at Cam Ranh Bay. It was located in an area that was considered safe, but Keil had the impression many of the youngsters surrounding him felt they would be in immediate danger when they disembarked the plane. And most of them had the same thought on their mind: "How many would make the trip home alive, a year from now?"

The seatbelt lights came on, and the pilot announced passengers should fasten their belts and prepare for landing. Duane shivered slightly as a cold chill went down his spine. He had a tightness in his chest and his palms were sweating as he stared intently out the window. It had gotten dark, but there was a full moon and brilliant stars gleamed in the deep blue sky above them. The plane began to descend through the thick clouds, shuddering and jerking as the young soldiers held onto the arms of their seats, and then the pilot extinguished all the internal lights on the plane. The interior of the plane was plunged into total darkness.

"This is it," Keil thought. "The war zone—we are here."

Darkness seemed to increase the noise and vibration of the aircraft as it descended through the turbulence. The fuselage shuddered violently, rattling trays and coffee pots in a nearby galley. Duane screwed his eyes shut and pressed himself back into his seat. Would they ever get on the ground? Opening his eyes slightly, he peeked out the window and saw runway lights below them through the rain-streaked plexiglass.

"Well, so far, so good," Keil said to himself. "We haven't been shot down, yet."

As the aircraft touched down with a hop and a bump, there was an audible sigh of relief. It was as if all the soldiers onboard had been holding their collective breath and had begun to breathe again at the same time. The plane taxied to the terminal building, and the door was opened. The men stood quietly and began to file off. When Keil got to the door, he was hit by a wave of humidity and a fetid breeze that reeked of jet fuel and open sewers.

"Wow," he said, covering his nose and mouth with his hand. "I could've gone all day without this."

The soldiers were moved into the terminal building, formed up for a roll call, and then moved outside to buses that carried them to the 22nd Replacement Battalion, a few miles away. That is where they would be inprocessed. The men collected their duffle bags, handed their personnel records to a clerk, and then stood in line to draw two sheets, a pillowcase, and a blanket from the supply room. They were then marched to a one-story wood and screen-wire barracks with a tin roof. It was about twenty feet wide and one hundred feet long, with a concrete floor, and was lined with metal bunk beds. It was nearly midnight local time. Keil had no idea what time it was in Michigan.

"Get some rest," the NCO said. "Lights out in five minutes—'Reveille' at 0600!"

Keil made up his bunk, undressed quickly and crawled into bed. He would shower in the morning. Right now, he was too exhausted to do anything but sleep. The sheet and pillow case felt damp from the humid air, but he did not care. It was wonderful to be able to stretch out his sore legs. As he buried his face in his pillow, he could hear the sound of the pre-monsoon rain beating against the metal roof above.

In the next day or two, Duane and the other troopers would fly north to Camp Radcliff at An Khê, where he would be assigned to Alpha Company, 4th Battalion, 503rd Infantry.

"I wonder if these camps are ever attacked," he thought as he began to drift off. "Welcome to Vietnam, Duane," he said to himself softly. "Welcome to hell."

The wind kisses my face
Like a welcoming friend—
Takes my hand to lead the way.
The other hand grasps St. Michael's wings,
In the exhilarating game we play.*

Part 3

Michael Blanchfield flew into Chicago's O'Hare Field a week before Christmas 1968. The weather was typical for a December night in Chicago: around thirty degrees and spitting light snow. His mother, Jeanette, met him at the airport, loaded him and his duffle bag into the car and headed north for the half-hour drive to Wheeling. His younger siblings, Jimmy, William, Patty, and Bobby Jo, along with his step-father, Leo, would be waiting for him. Fran, his high school sweetheart, might be there too. It was great to be home, especially for Christmas.

Jeanette glanced at her son's silhouette in the street lights. It was difficult to believe this was the same boy she had signed over to the recruiter back in January 1967. She was sure he had grown at least two inches in height, and he had put on thirty pounds of muscle. This ruggedly handsome young soldier was her son, and she was so proud of him. Bright holiday lights twinkled every-where, breaking through the drizzle and gloom of the dark, stormy night. Michael turned to look at her, broke into his easy grin, and she saw the boy again. It was so good to have him home. She tried not to think about what loomed in his future—his next duty assignment.

Richard Blanchfield, Michael's dad, lived in Des Plaines, twenty minutes away. Michael would see him tomorrow and intended to spend a lot of time with him.

Michael had thirty days to enjoy family and friends and the freedom to go and come as he pleased. He would be home for New Year's and his birthday celebration on January 4. Then he would fly back to Ft. Campbell toward the end of the month and have a few weeks to get his affairs in order before he shipped out for Vietnam. His deployment date was 20 February 1969, and he would be assigned to Alpha Company, 4th Battalion, 503rd Infantry, based at An Khê.

> The thunder of the silence
> Soothes my soul
> As I drift in laughter's wake,
> And I dance on the air
> With the earth my goal,
> All for my country's sake.*

Blanchfield stepped off the plane at Cam Ranh Bay on February 22, 1969. He was not much older than many of the newly-minted paratroopers he had flown over with, but he had been in the Army for over two years. He had used his time well, getting his GED and taking a few college courses. He knew he would need a college degree regardless of whether he remained in the Army or opted for civilian life.

The rebuilding process for the 173rd AB continued as the Brigade replaced not only combat casualties but also those who had completed their twelve-month tours and were ready to DEROS back to the States. The arrivals went through two days of inprocessing at the 22nd Replacement Battalion and were issued all the necessary equipment for their airborne infantry assignment: rucksack, poncho liner and blanket, jungle uniforms and boots, steel helmet and liner, pistol belt, first-aid kit and insect repellent, water purification tablets and canteen. Most of the equipment was specially designed for jungle warfare in Vietnam. The boots had stainless-steel plates in the soles to protect the wearer from Việt Cộng punji stakes and the insoles had vent holes for draining out the water when they slogged through mud holes and streams. They would be issued weapons when they joined their assigned units.

After the inprocessing was completed, the men were transported back to Cam Ranh Bay where they were loaded on board a C-130 Hercules and flown to Camp Radcliff, 150 miles north.

Blanchfield stepped off the plane at An Khê in pouring rain. He was wearing his poncho and slipped his helmet on his head as he exited the plane. The winter monsoon season was nearly over but had refused to ease its soggy grip. There was a sea of mud everywhere Michael looked. Through the downpour and low clouds, he could barely make out the hulk of a huge mountain in the distance.

As the young man waited for his duffle bag, he heard someone call out: "Hey! Are you Blanchfield?"

Mike turned and stared up into the face of a tall, skinny soldier with a big smile. He nodded and said, "Yes."

"Hi," the soldier said. "My name's 'Keil' and you're in my platoon. Welcome to Alpha Company. You don't have to wait here with these 'cherries.' Come with me—I'll take you to the orderly room to sign in, and then we'll send our houseboy back to pick up your bag."

That was Michael Blanchfield's first encounter with Duane Keil. Blanchfield would soon learn he had been in the Army over a year longer than Keil, but right now, in this place, that was completely irrelevant. Most importantly, Keil had been in Vietnam for four months, and the experience he had gained during that time was an invaluable asset for someone who had just arrived. In addition, Keil was a squad leader and an all-round nice guy. Everybody liked him.

Keil soon had Blanchfield processed into the platoon and moved him into his squad, along with one of the "nugs." His squad had been short-handed for a month. Michael moved into the locker and cot next to Duane. David Noblett, one of the "cherries," moved in on the other side.

Noblett was small, wiry, and blond. "Man, I've seen some young ones," Keil said softly to Blanchfield, "That kid looks about twelve years old. I can't believe he made it through AIT and jump school without some DI having him for breakfast."

Blanchfield laughed, but he had to admit this must be one tough little sonuvabitch. The boy had piercing blue eyes, unlike anything Michael had seen before, and there was a hardness there that belied his obvious youth. When he looked into those eyes he knew this was a kid you did not mess with.

Keil and Blanchfield soon became close friends. They were the two oldest men in the seven-man squad (at twenty and a very mature nineteen), and they spent most of their time together. They were rarely alone, however. "Nob" Noblett had decided it was to his advantage to stick close to Mike and Duane. The youngster was intensely shy and resisted talking about himself, but as he became more comfortable around them, he began to relate his story.

"Ah ain't never had no real fam'ly," he drawled. "Nobody cared where Ah went 'r what Ah did. Ah dropped outa school when Ah was 'bout fourteen—nobody noticed." The boy had joined a gang of Fort Worth street punks, was arrested and jailed for a few weeks on suspicion of armed robbery, but no one cared. Narrowly avoiding one of the infamous Texas "schools for boys," he ran away. He headed for California at age sixteen, but was jailed again. Authorities in Los Angeles advised him to return to Texas and "never come back." Finally, at seventeen, he joined the Army, "'cause Ah thought it'd make me a man."

As the days went by, Duane and Mike developed a liking for the quiet, youngster. If they headed out of the barracks, they called Nob's name, and he tagged along. Then, after an altercation with some drunken Aussies, the two "old" guys decided it was a good idea to keep the boy around.

Mike, Duane, and Nob had gone to a local watering hole one stormy evening. The bar was crowded and noisy as the three troopers talked and enjoyed a few beers. Keil got up from the table sometime later and headed for the WC (toilet). A huge Aussie soldier rose from a nearby table at the same time, tripped, and stumbled into him.

"Piss off, dirt dart!" the drunken Aussie yelled, and he shoved the paratrooper to the floor. The Digger was a half-foot taller than Keil and outweighed him by at least eighty pounds. Several other Aussies at his table, equally as drunk, cheered him on. "Shirtfront th' wanker, Chopper," one of them yelled, jumping up from his chair.

Before Blanchfield realized what was happening, Nob sprang from his chair and rushed to Duane's defense. Seeing the teenaged boy heading his way, "Chopper" placed his hands on his hips, reared back like the "Jolly Green Giant," and burst into loud, derisive laughter.

And then Nob attacked. Striding directly toward the big man, he hit the surly Goliath with a vicious kick to the groin, and as the man staggered forward, Nob finished him off with a savage uppercut. With a stunned look on his face and blood streaming from his nose and mouth, the huge man fell backward with a thunderous crash, smashing a table and turning over several chairs.

There was complete silence in the dark, smoky bar. Every eye in the room was focused on Nob. Stretching to his full "almost five foot" height—fists clinched, jaws tight and eyes ablaze, he stood white-faced over the fallen behemoth. The big man's mates quickly stepped forward, pulled the unconscious soldier up by his shoulders and dragged him out the open door into the muddy street.

David "Nob" Noblett

Without a word, Nob sat back down at the table, lit a cigarette and took a long swig of his beer. Duane had forgotten about going to the toilet and slowly sat back down. He and Mike looked at each other, then both sat quietly, drinking their beer and staring dumbly at Nob. This was one tough little bastard, and he was afraid of nothing—at least nothing he could see.

Part 4

An Khê, RVN
20 March 1969

Dear Mom:

I got your letter today. We went through 10 days of jungle warfare training after we got here. It was pretty interesting. They taught us about enemy tactics and booby traps, and stuff in the jungle like snakes and leeches, and some nasty ants. We also had plenty of PT and rappelling to make sure they got all the rust off of us.

I'm sure you're buried in snow. Our weather's gotten better. It's really hot, but at least it's stopped raining all the time. It just rains when we are in the field. It was dry for a week—then my platoon went out on a three-day operation and it rained all three days. We got back last night, and I'm tired. I don't sleep much in the jungle. I can't relax. It's really dark and spooky. My little buddy, Nob, says the jungle's "hainted," but I've not seen any ghosts yet. I'll let you know if I do.

When we move through villages, we're surrounded by children. They're cute and dirty, and beg for cigarettes and candy. My friend Duane loves kids and would play with them all day, if he could. They don't speak English, but it doesn't matter. He towers over them, makes funny faces and they laugh. They love it. We laugh at him, too. He's crazy.

The water in our canteens tastes bad when we're out on patrol. The guys put Kool-Aid or instant coffee in the water so it tastes better. Duane likes iced tea, so he carries a jar of instant tea with him. Send some Kool-Aid, if you can. Cherry or grape would be fine.

I can't think of anything else. Try not to worry and write soon. Tell everyone hello.

Michael

The 4/503rd Airborne Infantry continued to operate out of Camp Radcliff during the first three weeks of March 1969. As part of Operations STINGRAY and DARBY PUNCH III, Alpha Company conducted operations south of An Khê. There were no large VC/NVA main force elements in their AO, so their primary objective was to keep Highway 19 open and comparatively safe. Alpha platoons and squads patrolled the jungle and lowland trails throughout the area, keeping an eye on enemy activity, preventing large-scale enemy attacks, setting up ambushes, and uncovering stashes of enemy food and weapons.

Duane, Mike, and Nob headed out on combat patrol every three or four days and spent many nights in the jungle with their squad. They talked long into the night about life and girls and cars. Duane told them about "Fu-Man-Chu" (his old '55 Chevy) and they had a good laugh, then he told them about the new sports car he was going to buy when he got back to the States. He sent money home every month for his dream car. He also bragged about the young lady who sent him the sweet-smelling letters every week and how she would be waiting for him when he got home. Mike commented occasionally, but Duane did most of the talking, as usual.

Nob sat in the dark smoking a cigarette, and listening quietly to the stories of a world that was as foreign to him as 'Nam. Blowing out a long stream of smoke, he traced the deep engraving on the new lighter in his hand. Across the top was the Combat Infantry Badge—across the bottom were jump wings, and in the center was engraved his nickname: "NOB."

Nob's lighter

Listening to the interaction between Mike and Duane, the boy felt emotions rise in him he had seldom felt and which made him quite uncomfortable. Wiping tears from his eyes, he was thankful for the darkness. His daddy was dead—he had no idea where his mama was—probably shacked up with some low-life. He had not seen her in five years. When he was old enough to fight back, she had kicked him out for good. He had met Mike and Duane only a few weeks before, but friendships developed quickly in combat. This was the nearest thing to a family he had ever known in his life.

Squad members took turns standing two-hour guard shifts at night, and Keil soon discovered Nob was terrified of the dark jungle. "That boy would take down the devil himself, if he could see him," Keil said. The total blackness of a Vietnamese jungle at midnight, however, was another matter, and when it came Nob's turn to stand guard, Duane sat up with him. In a soft voice, he identified the different night sounds and taught the youngster what to listen for.

"Keil teaches me the steps that'll get me home," Nob told Mike one morning.

Blanchfield tried not to think about the danger that constantly surrounded them. They rarely encountered the enemy, but knew he was there. They heard him creeping through the dense foliage and slithering through the tall elephant grass. Sometimes, they could almost hear him breathing. As the troopers moved along the jungle trails, they were spaced apart so a booby trap or burst of gunfire was less likely to kill more than one, and they watched each step they took. If a trip wire or a hole filled with punji stakes was missed, a buddy behind might pay the price. An actual encounter with enemy troops was almost a relief from the day-to-day stress of their combat patrols.

Keil was the designated cook for the squad when they were in the field. His mother was into "experimental" cooking when he was growing up, and he had helped her in the kitchen. The other men turned their c-rations over to him and he whipped up gourmet-style meals on his "boonie stove." He had made the stove from a "B" unit c-rat can, carried it in a pocket of his combat fatigues, and fueled it with small chunks of C-4.

"It was amazin' what he could do with a can a ham n' lima beans," Nob said. "Ham n' muthas never tasted so good."

Then there was the time the squad was on patrol, and Duane cooked up something that did not agree with him. It turned into a long, tough night. Blanchfield and Nob rolled with laughter, listening to Keil's misery off in the brush.

"We honestly felt sorry for him," Mike said, "but then Duane would stagger back into camp all green in the face—sweat pouring down his cheeks, and we'd lose it. Nob would look at me; I'd look at him, then we'd both look at Duane, and we could not hold it inside. We'd crack up again and laugh until we had tears running down our cheeks. Duane would stare at us for a second and then head back into the brush."

"'Tween Duane's awful groans and our crazy laughin,' we musta frightened away everythin' around, includin' the VC," Nob said. "We call it 'Montezuma's Revenge, in Texas," he drawled, "Ain't sure that name works in 'Nam, though."

Despite his usually sunny disposition, Keil failed to see the humor in the situation. By morning, however, he was feeling better and greeted them with a sheepish grin.

On March 24, 1969, the 4/503rd Airborne Infantry moved from An Khê to Qui Nhơn. The first units departed Camp Radcliff by C-130 at 2:00 p.m., and the last units arrived at Qui Nhơn some five hours later. The 4/503rd joined one ROK (Korean) battalion and one ARVN battalion and commenced search & clear operations in the villages and countryside surrounding Qui Nhơn. The troopers also provided security for the major supply areas attached to the busy seaport. That continued until April 8 when the 4/503rd moved sixty miles north to LZ North English, near the village of Bồng Sơn.

Part 5

In front of the small HQ building at North English was a sign driven into the dusty, red soil: "Welcome to the Home of the Geronimo Battalion. Don't Count the Days, Make the Days Count. Stay off the Grass!"

Keil, Blanchfield, and Noblett had a few days to settle in, and then their platoon was loaded aboard choppers and moved west into a range of rugged mountains in the Central Highlands. From their chopper, the men could see steep slopes, deep valleys cleft by rushing streams and dense jungle. There were a few thatched roofs along the bigger streams, but it was mostly an endless sea of green.

Soon the choppers descended toward a clearing on top of a mountain. When the birds were a few feet off the ground, the troopers began to jump off amid a whirlwind of red dust and rotor wash. Lt. Hayword, their new platoon leader, was met by a sergeant who was already onsite. The lieutenant was escorted through an opening in the perimeter and shown where his men were to dig in. They were relieving another platoon that would rotate back to Tam Quan for a few days of rest, hot food, and clean, dry beds.

Over the next two days the platoon set about doing what all infantry units do in the field: digging or reworking old foxholes, rigging sunshades over them, eating, cleaning weapons, and any combination of smoking, chatting, playing cards, or all three.

On the third day, Keil and his squad left the perimeter and headed west on a short patrol. It was early morning, but despite the altitude, the air was hot and oppressive. The squad humped its way through jungle for three hours. Seeing nothing of interest, Keil gave his men a break along a shaded mountain stream. They would rest, grab a smoke, and fill their canteens before returning to camp.

Noblett unscrewed the cap from his canteen and sank it into the cool, clear water. He yearned to drink directly from the flowing stream, but understood the need to add the iodine tablets to the water before he drank it. None of the local water was safe for Americans to drink, regardless of how remote the site might be. Mike had given him packets of grape Kool-Aid, so he dropped in two of the purification pills and poured in the purple powder. He had no sugar, but the Kool-Aid would help cover up the medicinal taste.

Removing his helmet, Nob tugged the sweaty towel from around his neck and soaked it in the creek. Then, he squeezed out the excess water and tucked the wet cloth back in around his neck with a slight shiver. "Damn, it's hot," he thought. Opening his flak jacket, he pulled out his lighter and a soggy pack of c-rat Luckies and lit a cigarette. Lazily running his fingers over the engraved letters on his lighter, he blew a plume of blue smoke into the heavy air, took a swig from his canteen, and made a face at the sour taste. Then he leaned back against a large boulder and closed his eyes.

Keil and Blanchfield had moved further down the stream. Michael had been having problems with his feet. Slogging through rice paddies, fording streams and wearing his jungle boots for days at a time had caused his feet to crack and bleed. He was taking precautions to keep his feet dry, including carrying a supply of extra socks. Duane filled his canteen, stirred in instant tea, and rambled on with his usual inane banter as he watched Mike remove his boots and slip on a pair of dry socks.

Keil stopped talking, leaned back and surveyed their surroundings. This spot was a veritable paradise. They were surrounded by dense rain forest. Giant ferns shaded the stream and water striders the size of his hand glided across the water of the fast flowing creek. They reminded him of ice boats sailing across the frozen lakes in Michigan where he had grown up. His sister, Toni, would be in awe of this place. There were lavender and yellow orchids blooming along tree limbs that extended out over the water, and colorful fungi grew along the banks and up the trees. Tiny monkeys and brilliant parakeets jumped and flitted through the trees with a clamor. Flowers along the stream were alive with bright butterflies and dragonflies. It was hard to believe they were in the middle of a war.

This entire area had been Montagnard land, but the indigenous people had fled deeper into the mountains to escape the fighting. The troopers had hiked for hours and not seen a single human being. Of course, that did not mean they were alone.

"Saddle up!" Keil called out, "Time to head back to camp."

The squad members reluctantly rose from their reveries, grabbed their weapons, and fell into their usual line of march. Two members of Keil's squad had just DEROSed back to the States, and two cherries had arrived to replace them. One was a New Yorker named Chavitz, and he was walking point. Nugs always pulled point duty, and it was a stressful job. Nob had walked his share of it during his first few weeks at An Khê. The other man, Daniels, was from some little town in North Carolina. He was their rear guard.

Per orders, Keil took a different route back to the platoon's encampment. There were fewer trees and the undergrowth was heavy—thick with elephant grass and bamboo. Keil was in the middle of the seven-man squad, followed by Noblett and Blanchfield. It was nearly impossible for each trooper to see the next man who was ten feet ahead.

The squad was three hundred yards from the platoon's perimeter, following a barely discernible path, when there was a violent explosion. Due to the dense vegetation, Keil heard shrapnel slicing through the tall bamboo above his head before he felt the force of the blast. For a moment, there was silence as shredded leaves filtered down from above.

Then, Keil, Noblett, and Blanchfield rushed forward through the brush. The man ahead of Keil was Robles, the RTO. He was down, but not seriously injured. He had flesh wounds on his right cheek and right shoulder, but his helmet and flak jacket had taken the worst of the blast. Leaving Blanchfield to care for the trooper, Keil and Noblett moved on. The next man, Caruso, was bleeding badly and unconscious. Nob stayed with him as Keil hurried forward to find Chavitz.

The point man had stepped on a trip wire, detonating two fragmentation grenades. He had been blown ten feet through the air, landing deep within the bamboo thicket. Keil heard him groan and fought his way in to him. The trooper was barely conscious; his legs were mangled and shrapnel had struck every unprotected part of his body. He was bleeding profusely. Opening his first aid kit, Keil grabbed compresses and tied off the man's legs in an effort to control the worst bleeding. They were not far from camp, but if help did not arrive soon, Chavitz would bleed out before they got there.

Hurrying back down the path, Keil found Nob holding Caruso, who was conscious and had a serious chest wound. Caruso outweighed Nob by a hundred pounds, and Keil could barely see the boy. He had gotten under Caruso's back and was holding him up. He had his right arm around Caruso's neck and his left hand over the hole in the big trooper's chest trying to help him breathe. Caruso was gasping frantically; air was whistling out between Nob's fingers, along with sprays of blood. Nob looked up at Keil with tears in his eyes, silently pleading for him to do something. Keil plugged the wound with a compress, placed Nob's hand back over it and squeezed his shoulder. "You're doin' good, Nob," he said. "Help will be here soon." Then he hurried back to Chavitz.

Blanchfield had taken the radio from Robles and contacted the platoon. Within minutes they heard the sound of rotor blades overhead, and the bird was able to set down in a clearing twenty yards from their location. Chavitz was unconscious. Keil had applied a tourniquet to his left leg, which was the most severely injured, but held out little hope for the young man's survival. There were just too many wounds for him to deal with. Medics came running with stretchers, forcing their way through the brush. They quickly loaded the wounded troopers on stretchers and carried them to the chopper.

The medevac departed, and Keil, Noblett, Blanchfield, and Daniels were left standing silently in the bamboo. The episode had taken twenty minutes, but seemed much longer. Keil and Nob were covered in blood—all four were in shock. Lt. Hayword arrived with a reinforced patrol and escorted the four troopers back to camp. Hours later, Keil was notified Caruso would recover. Chavitz had died.

For the next week, Keil stayed to himself. He was carrying a heavy load of guilt for what had happened. He was convinced he was at fault and wanted nothing to do with anyone who might disagree with him, especially his closest buddies.

Mike and Nob were bewildered by the change in Duane, but left him alone. He performed his squad duties in stony silence, refusing to even acknowledge their presence unless it was required. He was not sleeping or eating, and his tall, skinny frame became haggard and gaunt. His once bright eyes were dull and lifeless. Finally the two troopers reached the end of their patience and cornered Keil.

With his usual air of quiet diplomacy and tact, Nob opened the discussion: "Duane Keil, Ah'm gonna kick the shit outa you if you don't shape up! Yer no more responsible for Chavitz' death than anya us. We'll be headin' back out on patrol soon—you can carry 'round a load a guilt, n' pity, n' shit 'n get the resta us kilt 'n go to hell, or you can get offa yer ass and quit cryin'. Ain't nona us gonna make it outa here alive if ya don't."

Duane stood looking at the boy in stunned silence—then reluctant tears welled in his eyes and began to course down his cheeks. He reached down and pulled Nob's head to his chest and began to sob. Finally all the guilt and pain and shame came out.

Michael stood by and watched silently—astonished that this tough little Texan had become such a force in their lives—and touched by how much the boy cared.

Part 6

In mid-June 1969, Lt. Hayword's platoon rotated back to LZ North English. The area was comparatively safe, at least during the daylight hours, and a certain amount of boredom set in. The troopers were accustomed to patrolling the mountains, never knowing what they would encounter moment to moment, so life in the base camp required some adjustment. The days were long; the heat was sweltering; and there was not much to do in Tam Quan. Michael Blanchfield missed the mountain air. The ambiance of the local benjo ditches (open sewers) on a ninety-five-degree afternoon was an unforgettable experience—one could smell the town from ten miles away if he were downwind.

Keil recovered from the trauma of Chavitz' death to a degree. He was able to laugh and joke with his friends during the day and pretend that all was okay. Getting through the nights, however, was not so easy. Over and over, he relived the sight of Jake Chavitz covered in blood—those large, dark eyes locked on his and pleading for help. Some nights he cried out and woke up, bathed in sweat and tears, and Mike and Nob were there to calm him until he went back to sleep. On other nights, the three wound up outside, smoking and talking until dawn. Daylight was a relief for Keil. He greeted it with a smile on his face, but the dark circles under his eyes, betrayed his nightly suffering.

Caruso was released from the hospital and returned to camp. He had lost some of his deep tan, along with a few pounds, but otherwise seemed fine. He blamed his weight loss on hospital cooking and said their cooks "couldn't hold a candle to Duane and his boonie stove." He had little memory of the frag grenades. His world had just exploded. He did remember Nob holding him and repeatedly yelling in his ear: "Yer not gonna die on me ya sonuvabitch! Yer not gonna die on me!" You had to love Nob. Otherwise, you might kill him.

Caruso knew quick action had probably saved his life and wanted to buy everyone a drink. First chance they had, the four troopers headed to one of the local bars and soon were feeling no pain. Some hours later, they staggered back to camp, arm-in-arm, singing a ragged chorus of "Blood Upon the Risers," a rather macabre (and often vulgar) song that is dear to the heart of every paratrooper from his first days at Benning.

> The risers wrapped around his neck,
> connectors cracked his dome;
> The lines were snarled and tied in knots,
> around his skinny bones;
> The canopy became his shroud,
> he hurtled to the ground.
> He ain't gonna jump no more.
> Gory, Gory, What a helluva way to die,
> Gory, Gory, What a helluva way to die,
> Gory, Gory, What a helluva way to die,
> He ain't gonna jump no more.
> (Sung to the tune of "The Battle Hymn of the Republic")

On July 2, two platoons of Alpha Company, 4/503rd, were loaded aboard choppers for a sweep of villages southwest of Tam Quan. The entire area had been a center of strong communist support since the end of World War II. Despite pacification efforts, no one expected any change in the hearts and minds of the local people. They seemed friendly enough during the day, but many were out planting mines and booby traps as soon as darkness fell.

Another cherry had been shipped in to replace Chavitz, so with Caruso's return, Keil's squad was back to full strength. The squad was happy to be back in the field and settled in that evening as Duane cooked dinner. Keil was joined by Blanchfield, Caruso, Daniels, Robles, and Hurley, the new man. Nob was taking the first guard shift. Duane would whip up a plate of his favorite "ham and muthas" later.

The platoons were up early on the morning of July 3. Intel had received a tip VC were holed up in a small village called Tân An. The troopers moved out before sunrise. An ROK unit had moved in quietly during the night to cordon off the area. The Korean soldiers, though large in stature, moved with surprising stealth, and nothing would get past them once they were in place. The airborne troopers would sweep the village and trap any Cong who might be found there.

The Alpha platoons moved in at first light and began to fan out through the village. Keil and his squad volunteered to take the western side of the small community, and they were followed by two other squads. It was still quite dark in the shadows of the thatched-roof hootches and difficult to see as the troopers moved from house to house, forcing the residents out into the narrow street and searching for weapons or signs of suspicious activity. The villagers were unhappy to be dragged out of bed and yelled loudly in Vietnamese, as if alerting others in the buildings ahead. Most of them were elderly men or women, and children who were wild-eyed with fear.

Hurley and Caruso had pushed on ahead, followed by Robles, with the radio, and Keil. Noblett and Blanchfield were next, with Daniels some ten feet behind them. As Hurley and Caruso crossed a narrow alley and moved toward the next row of huts, a small group of dark-clad figures ran from one of the houses firing AK-47s. Hurley and Caruso jumped behind a heavy wooden cart and returned fire as the other squad members dived for cover. The firefight continued for ten minutes, as the eastern sky grew brighter and the other squads moved forward to reinforce Keil's squad.

Some women and children had been standing behind Keil and Robles when the shooting began and had dropped to the ground. The gunfire tapered off and stopped. Keil rose up and began helping the women and children move inside. Without warning, a Chinese grenade sailed over top of the cart that had shielded Hurley and Caruso and exploded violently in a cloud of smoke and flame. Keil and Robles were both blown through the air and crashed into the side of an adjacent hootch.

Blanchfield and Noblett had taken shelter fifteen feet behind Keil, and both men were hit by shrapnel from the VC grenade. Mike was knocked to the ground with blood soaking his torn left sleeve.

"NO-O-O!" Nob screamed, and sprang to his feet to run to Duane's rescue. Mike tried to stop the boy, but Nob tore loose from his grip with a vicious swing and ran toward the smoke and dust where he had last seen Keil. Michael jumped up and ran after him.

As the two emerged from the thick smoke, Blanchfield heard something hit the ground. Glancing down, he saw a satchel charge had landed on the roadway between him and Nob. Without hesitation, he threw himself on top of the device.

The explosion was horrendous. Nob was thrown thirty feet through the air, crashing into a wall with his back and neck. Slowly regaining consciousness, he fought to get his bearings. He could see activity around him through the smoke and haze, but it all sounded far away. Blood from lacerations on his head was streaming into his eyes, and he wiped it away as he began to crawl back toward Mike and Duane. He had lost his helmet and weapon in the blast.

Nob saw Robles lying in the dirt, recognizing the radio strapped on his back, and he continued to crawl along the edge of the street. The boy was dimly aware of gunfire and people running by him, but his sole focus was on finding his buddies. His legs would not work, so he pulled himself along with his elbows, dragging his feet, until he found Duane.

Keil's body was lying crumpled against the side of the hootch where he had fallen. The front of his flak jacket was soaked with blood. Pulling himself up beside his friend, Nob realized Duane was still alive, barely.

"Medic!" he yelled. "Medic!"

Duane heard Nob's voice and his eyelids fluttered. He gave a slight moan and slumped over against the youngster's shoulder. "So tired, Nob," he murmured.

Slowly, Duane slid on down until his shoulder was across Nob's lap, and the boy was holding his head in his arms. "I'm so sleepy," he said softly—then he exhaled a long ragged sigh and was gone.

Nob's shoulders sagged as he continued to hold Duane. He laid his head back against the rough boards of the hootch and closed his eyes as tears streaked the grime and blood on his face. Rolling his head from side to side, he struggled to deal with the tragedy of losing his two best friends—the only people who had ever cared a shit about him his entire, miserable life—his brothers—his family. "Why them 'n not me, Gawd?" he cried out. "It should'a been me."

When the medics arrived a few minutes later, they found Noblett unconscious, still holding Kiel in his arms. Blanchfield's body was some distance away. The remainder of Keil's squad and most of the villagers in the immediate vicinity, though injured, had survived the explosion, thanks to Michael Blanchfield's courageous act.

David Noblett was medevaced to a local field hospital. He had deep lacerations to his back and abdomen and was bleeding from his ears and nose. He was then transferred to the 8th Field Hospital at Nha Trang for emergency surgery to relieve pressure on his spine. The youngster's back was broken in three places. Surgeons later implanted three feet of titanium steel cages, brackets and screws to hold his spine together. A general came by and pinned a purple heart on his pillow on the July 4, 1969, but Nob was barely conscious. Some months later, the same general came by and pinned a Bronze Star with "V" device on his chest. Nob did not think he deserved it. In his usual tight-lipped manner, he said, "Mah actions were'nt no better'n those of thousands a other guys that fought and died. They deserve this more'n me."

Sgt. Duane Richard Keil was buried with full military honors at Clark Lake, Michigan, in late July 1969. He was posthumously awarded the Bronze Star Medal with "V" device for valor and the Purple Heart. Duane was one month shy of his twenty-first birthday.

"I was jis' a boy, when Ah first met Duane," Noblett said, "afraida the dark in a silent jungle. On guard at night, he stayed with me, whisperin' what to listen for. Such warnin's were unfamiliar to me. He taught me the steps to follow that got me home. I wonder why fate touched him 'n not me."

Funeral services for Spc. 4 Michael Reinert Blanchfield were held on August 2, 1969, at St. Joseph The Worker Catholic Church in Wheeling, Illinois, and he was buried with full military honors at All Saints Catholic Cemetery in Des Plaines, surrounded by a host of family and friends.

On April 22, 1971, Jeanette Blanchfield and her four remaining children flew to Washington, DC, and in private ceremonies in the White House Blue Room, Pres. Richard M. Nixon presented her with Michael's Medal of Honor "for conspicuous gallantry... above and beyond the call of duty." He was also awarded the Purple Heart. Michael Blanchfield was nineteen years old.

David Noblett's eyes welled with tears. His voice quivered and rose in pitch as he said, 'When Ah think a Mike, who was nineteen n' threw his body on that bomb to save me and I think a Duane—shrapnel caught him in his lungs. After Ah woke up, I picked Duane up in mah arms, and he died in mah arms, drownin' in his own blood. And those two young guys were never gonna go on through life like Ah was. It jis' breaks mah heart."

"The thunder of the silence
Soothes my soul
As I drift in laughter's wake,
And I dance on the air
With the earth my goal,
All for my country's sake."*

"Out of the Clouds"
—Esther B. (Campbell) Gates

Composed in memory of her son, Spc. 4 Keith Allen Campbell, 173rd AB, KIA Biên Hòa, RVN, February 8, 1967

Distinguished Service Cross, Bronze Star Medal w/"V" Device & Oak Leaf Cluster, Purple Heart

On September 11, 1971, the Wheeling American Legion Post, Wheeling, Illinois, changed its name to the "Michael R. Blanchfield Post 1968 American Legion."

On December 1, 2010, a stamp collector's "First Day Cover" was issued featuring: "Medal of Honor, SP4 Michael Blanchfield, U444 Army Memorial." The cover was postmarked Washington, DC, and featured a color portrait printed on cachet #4800 by Alvin Eckert USCS #9964—Franked by a forty-four-cent Flag forever stamp and a fifteen-cent Vietnam Campaign Ribbon stamp.

On May 11, 2011, Wheeling High School, Wheeling, Illinois, presented Michael Blanchfield's family with his honorary diploma and a plaque signifying his induction as a distinguished alumnus.

Epilogue: *NOB'S Final Fight*

David "Nob" Noblett

For David Noblett, life was never easy. From his days as a teen-aged delinquent to the heartbreaking loss of his "brothers" at Tân An, his life was a series of battles, and many of them were fought alone. His devastating injuries on July 3, 1969, led to months of hospitalization and numerous surgeries. He most certainly endured bouts of severe depression and loneliness, and it is doubtful he ever received any kind of counseling. The concept of "PTSD" was unknown in those days. When his enlistment was complete, he left the Army with the rank of Sergeant. He was a decorated veteran of an unpopular war and was nineteen years old.

After the military, Nob knocked around for a while. He got married in September 1971. He was twenty—his bride, Wendy, was fifteen. They divorced in April 1974 and he married his second wife, Marcia, two months later. How long the second marriage lasted, no one knows. He enrolled in a Bible college, graduating in 1976 as an ordained minister and later worked as an EMT. He suffered from acute pain for the last forty years of his life due to the injuries he incurred in Vietnam and also developed skin cancer from exposure to Agent Orange.

Nob was always a fighter, though, and in his last years, he found a new battle: leading the fight for his fellow Vietnam vets suffering from chronic pain. In the view of Nob and his supporters, the Texas Medical Board was denying Texas physicians the right to treat patients with long-term chronic pain as they saw fit. In the early 2000s, the Board was forcing doctors to drop such patients, considering them drug addicts and denying them the medical treatment they had a right to expect.

"These 'r things mah friends Mike and Duane died for," the old warrior said. "That's why Ah'm doin' what Ah'm doin'."

He was so determined to carry on the fight; he dug out his old 173rd Airborne fatigue jacket for a public meeting at Texas Christian University.

"Ah've always had a fear a talkin' 'bout my service in 'Nam," he said. "Ah've seen so many claim ta be 'Nam vets n' really weren't or claimed to do things in the war n' really didn't. Ah've always kept mah mouth shut 'bout it. I'm tellin' you so you'll understand how much this issue meant ta me. Fer the first time since I got back from 'Nam, I got my old fatigue jacket outa mothballs, an' I got out all mah medals and decorations n' covered the fronta the jacket, hung 'em on there, n' I wore that down to the meetin'. I know people were prob'ly lookin' at me lahk I was some kinda nut or a 'Nam vet with PTSD."

As Duane Keil might have said, "Nob would take on the devil himself, as long as he could see him, especially if it would help his cause."

"Ah wanted to make a statement," Noblett drawled.

In spite of his inherent shyness, Nob turned to the news media to tell his story and continue the veterans' fight. He was organizing a patient class-action law suit and was interviewed for a major story by the *Ft. Worth Weekly*. The reporter, Jeff Prince, asked Nob if he would wear his fatigue jacket and medals for a cover photo. He was not comfortable doing that; however, he did agree to be photographed holding the jacket.

Nob was sitting at his desk waiting for Prince to arrive, when he died of heart failure in 2008. He was fifty-eight years old. The State of Texas could find no next of kin to claim his body, so after two weeks it was released to a friend. Other friends raised funds to purchase a burial plot, casket, and headstone.

David Noblett was buried at Greenwood Memorial Park in Ft. Worth, Texas, on October 9, 2008—laid to rest next to his father, whom he had barely known. The US Army provided a color guard and a flag for his casket, and he was buried with the full military honors befitting a hero.

Among Nob's most prized possessions were his engraved, silver lighter and a scrapbook filled with photos of a scrawny Noblett during his time in Vietnam. He was wearing fatigues, with a full head of blonde hair, bleached white by the tropical sun. In some of the photos he was smiling, posing with other young men putting on brave faces, and he looked happy. There were photos of dead VC and photos showing Noblett talking to Vietnamese children. They were wearing big conical hats and smiling broadly at whatever he was saying.

There was also a citation for the award of Nob's Bronze Star for valor in ground operations against hostile forces in 1969. "His loyalty, diligence, and devotion to duty reflect great credit upon himself and the United States Army," the certificate reads. For Nob Noblett, that was true all the days of his life—devotion to the ideals he believed in and complete loyalty to those whom he loved.

> Poor is the nation that has no heroes,
> but poorer still is the nation that having heroes,
> fails to remember and honor them.

—Marcus Tullius Cicero

Notes and Acknowledgments

As always, thank you to my wife, Myra Meadows Blackburn, for her editing skills, her advice, her literary suggestions, her support, and most of all, her love. During her thirty-eight-year career teaching English and Creative Writing, she taught thousands of young people from all over the world. She remains an inspiration to many of them and to all who know her.

And thank you to my former co-author, military editor, and old friend, Lonnie Long. He was not sold on the idea of this book at the start. Me writing a book in which most of the heroes died did not appeal to him. One of his first comments was, "This is not going to be a happy book." My response was, "*Romeo and Juliet* was not a happy book!" However, being the loyal friend he is, he supported me, wrote the introduction and served as my invaluable technical advisor on all things military.

GBB

Sources

Foreword
Heroes of the Vietnam Generation by Senator James Webb

Introduction
Unlikely Warriors: The Army Security Agency's Secret War in Vietnam 1961–1973 by Lonnie M. Long and Gary B. Blackburn, iUniverse, Inc., Bloomington, Indiana, 2013
Enduring Vietnam, An American Generation and Its War, by James Wright, Thomas Dunne Books, St. Martin's Press, New York, New York, 2017

1
John Francis Link
Notes from Terry Link and friends
"Johnny We Hardly Knew Ye" by Joseph B. Geoghegan, 1867
Unlikely Warriors: The Army Security Agency's Secret War in Vietnam 1961–1973 by Lonnie M. Long and Gary B. Blackburn, iUniverse, Inc., Bloomington, Indiana, 2013
War Story by Jim Morris, Paladin Press, Boulder, Colorado, 1979
Mike Force by Lt. Col. L. H. Burruss, iUniverse, Inc., Bloomington, Indiana, 2001
The Ether Zone by R. C. Morris, Hellgate Press, Ashland, Oregon, 2009
Distinguished Service Cross Certificate
"Requiem" by Lonnie M. Long

2

Larry Leonard Maxam

"Larry L. Maxam: An American Hero" by Duane Vachon, *Hawaii Reporter*, August 23, 2010

"Larry Maxam: The real meaning of Memorial Day" by Dennis McCarthy, *Los Angeles Daily News*, May 21, 2015

Lindasburbankhighschool.blogspot.com

Individual notes from high school friends

www.mishalov.com

"Jack's Flash" Observations by Jack McLean, May 31, 2011

"Larry Maxam Avenue" by Dick Moskun, November 10, 2012

"Through Blood and Fire at Gettysburg" by Gen. Joshua Lawrence Chamberlain

3

Leonard Ray St. Clair

Notes from friends

Amazing Spider-Man, by Stan Lee, July 1967

U.S. Marines In Vietnam: Fighting The North Vietnamese, 1967, by Maj. Gary L. Telfer, Lt.-Col. Lane Rogers, Dr. V. Keith Fleming Jr., Pickle Partners Publishing, Aug 9, 2016

ec47.com/supporting-the-marines-january-june-1967

"OPERATION DESOTO After Action Report" Pentagon

"US Marines Combined Action Platoons (CAC/CAP)"

combatwife.net/desoto.htm

"The Spiders of Weariness" by Robert Ervin Howard, Unpublished, Public Domain

4

Dale Eugene Wayrynen

"Vietnam vets remember Dale Wayrynen's sacrifice" by Mark Steil, Minnesota Public Radio News, 2007

"The Road to Remembrance" by Kathleen Pakarinen, *Aitkin Independent Age*, 1996

"McGregor veteran Dale Wayrynen's actions remembered fifty years later" by Lisa Kaczke, *Duluth News Tribune*, Duluth, Minnesota, June 14, 2017

"Another name on the wall" by Wick Fisher, *Moose Lake Star Gazette*, Moose Lake, Minnesota, July 24, 2014

Department of the Army General Order #66, October 27, 1969

"For The Fallen" by Robert Laurence Binyon, 1914, Public Domain

5
John C. Borowski

"Afternoon 10 July" by Lt. Mercer Vandenburg

Theirfinesthour.blogspot.com

Distinguished Service Cross citation

History of the 503rd

Evergreen Park Community High School—Class of 1965- Individual notes

"GI Volunteer Loses His Life in Viet Attack" by William Jones, *Chicago Tribune*, Chicago, Illinois, July 20, 1967

"Stanley J. Sak Obituary," *Chicago Tribune*, Chicago, Illinois, February 22, 2000

"The Grave of Keats" by Oscar Wilde, 1881, Public Domain

6
Harold Ray Reeves

Notes from friends and family

Steve McDonald's Diary by Steve McDonald, December 1968

Permian Basin Vietnam Veteran's Memorial

www.minwest.com

"Odessa Infantryman Dies In Vietnam," *Odessa American*, Odessa, Texas, December 21, 1968

redcatcher199lib/bmb

2buds.com

dod.mil/pubs

A 5/12 Database

The Senior by Mike Flynt, Thomas Nelson Publishing, Nashville, Tennessee, 2008

199armytour.com

The Killing Zone: My Life in the Vietnam War by Frederick Downs, W. W. Norton & Company, New York, New York, 2007

"In Texas, down by the Rio Grande" by Frank Desprez, 1882, Public Domain

7
Kenneth Alan Luse

Notes from friends and family

Unlikely Warriors: The Army Security Agency's Secret War in Vietnam 1961–1973 by Lonnie M. Long and Gary B. Blackburn, iUniverse Publishing, Bloomington, Indiana, 2013

bullwhipsquadron.org

airvectors.net

warrelics.eu

U.S. Army AH-1G Cobra Units in Vietnam by Jonathan Bernstein, Osprey Publishing, Oxford, United Kingdom, 2003

blueberet.org

"Questions About Helicopters in Vietnam," ar15.com

"High Flight" by John Gillespie Magee Jr., 1941, Public Domain

8
Ralph Judson Mears Jr.

Individual notes and interviews with family and friends

Paratrooper: My Life with the 101st Airborne Division by Michael B. Kitz-Miller, Page Publishing Company, New York, New York, 2015

"Operational Report, Lessons Learned, Headquarters, 3rd Brigade 82nd Airborne Division," Department of the Army, Period ending 30 April 1968

"Dedication: 100th Anniversary Celebration, Tidewater Council, Boy Scouts of America"—Dedicated to Eagle Scout Ralph Judson Mears Jr., October 16, 2010, Virginia Beach Virginia

The Eastern Shore News, Onancock, Virginia

Danville Register, Danville, Virginia, June 5, 1969

"Obituary of Ralph J. Mears Sr.," *The Virginian Pilot*, Norfolk, Virginia, Oct. 1, 2017

"The Healers" by Robert Laurence Binyon, 1917, Public Domain

9
Christopher Joseph Schramm

Notes from friends and family

Unlikely Warriors: The Army Security Agency's Secret War in Vietnam 1961–1973 by Lonnie M. Long and Gary B. Blackburn, iUniverse, Inc., Bloomington, Indiana, 2013

The Philadelphia Inquirer, May 18, 1968

10
Oscar Palmer Austin

Notes from friends

"A Look at Black History and Segregation in Phoenix" by Brandon Lee, azfamily.com, November 22, 2016

"African American Historic Property Survey" by: David R. Dean & Jean A. Reynolds, Athenaeum Public History Group, phoenix.gov, October 2004

"As Navy commissions its newest guided missile destroyer, Vietnam Marine recalls its namesake saving his life" by Sgt. Chet Decker, leatherneck.com

"Day of Remembrance in honor of Oscar Austin" by Danny L. White *Arizona Informant*

marzone.com/7thMarines/MOH0DDG794

"An Anchor in the Prairie: The Life and Times of Bill Forbes" by Bill Forbes, BookBaby, September 2016

Public domain material from websites and documents of the US Marine Corps

"A smile or a tear has not nationality," by Frederick Douglass, *Composite Nation*, Public Domain

11
Joseph Andrew Matejov

Interviews with John Matejov

Time on Target: The World War II Memoir of William R. Buster by William R. Buster, University Press of Kentucky, Jan 13, 2015

www.mindinvasions.com/vietnam-pows-betrayed.html

"'Run to the Wall' honoring Vietnam Veterans" by Ashley Anne, May 24, 2018

"Vietnam War Airman's death reexamined after decades of controversy" by Travis J. Tritten, *Stars and Stripes,* April 11, 2016

"Still seeking answers about Joseph Matejov and many others missing in war" by Mike Francis, *The Oregonian,* Portland, Oregon, January 11, 2014

taskforceomegainc.org/m194.html, Task Force Omega, Inc.

"Mystery of the Last Flight of Baron 52 Solved" by Thomas W. Lippman, December 10, 1995

"Grieving Family Says '73 Laos Crash Didn't Kill Son" by Lynn Smith, *Los Angeles Times,* May 28, 1990

"Prisoners of Not Knowing: The issue of MIAs and POWs in Southeast Asia" by Karen Tumulty and Dan Weikel, *Los Angeles Times,* July 31, 1991

"No Closure For Kin of Missing Airmen" by Tom Topousis, *New York Post,* April 25, 2000

"Intelligence Squadron Honors BARON 52 Vietnam Veterans" by Staff Sgt. Alexandre Montes, 70th ISR Wing Public Affairs, May 15, 2017

Is Anybody Listening?: A True Story About POW/MIAs in the Vietnam War by Barbara Birchim, AuthorHouse, May 23, 2005

"Their flight was supposed to be a secret. Their fate was not" by Alfred Lubrano *Philadelphia Inquirer,* January 11, 1998

"Abandoned in Place" by Mary Ann Reitano, *The Newsletter,* POW/MIA Information Center, Norman A. Todd Chapter 41, March 18, 2016

The Listening Post, Vietnam Veterans of America, June 2016

"Air Force denies MIA status for Airman in Vietnam-era Baron 52 case" by Travis Tritten, *Stars and Stripes,* November 10, 2016

"For MIA Families, Grief is Greatest When U.S. Lies" by Karen Tumulty and Dan Weikel, *Los Angeles Times-Washington Post* News Service Aug 3, 1991

The Spokesman, U.S. Air Force, September 1997

"Remembering Joe Matejov, He didn't deserve what he got" by John Matejov as told to Marilyn Grote, *The Moonduster Chronicles*

"Mother Believes Mia Son Survived: Dogtag At Laos Crash Site Not Convincing Proof For Her" by A.J. Plunkett, *Daily Press,* Newport News, Virginia, September 14, 1993

US Army Border Operations In Germany, 1945–1983 by William E. Stacy,

www.usarmygermany.com

Leave No Man Behind: Bill Bell and the Search for American POW/MIAs from the Vietnam War by Garnett "Bill" Bell and George J. Veith, Goblin Fern Press, March 31, 2004

The Katy Rancher, Katy, Texas, Leslie Williams- Dennis, March 10, 2015

"GIs Leave Behind The Vietnam War In 1973: But Not Before Sacrificing 34 KIA" by Richard K. Kolb, *VFW Magazine*, February 2013

"M.I.A. Hunter in Hanoi Chains Himself to Gate" by THE ASSOCIATED PRESS, *The New York Times*, June 5, 1995

"Vietnam Ousts American Over the P.O.W. Issue" by REUTERS, *The New York Times*, June 9, 1995

"The Men Who Never Came Back—New Report Suggests U.S. Disowned POWs" by Monika Jensen-Stevenson and William Stevenson, *Washington Post,* November 11, 1990

Kiss the Boys Goodbye: How the United States Betrayed Its Own POWs in Vietnam by Monika Jensen-Stevenson and William Stevenson, Skyhorse Publishing, 2014

"Claim of P.O.W. Cover-Up Rends Senate Decorum" by Adam Clymer, *The New York Times*

The War Against Trucks: Aerial Interdiction in Southern Laos 1968–1972 by Bernard C Nalty, Air Force History and Museums Program, May 27, 2012

"Unattended Ground Sensors and Precision Engagement" by
    Eric D. Haider, Master's thesis, Naval Postgraduate School,
    Monterey, California, December 1998
"Disappearance" by Gints Bija

12
Patrick Michael Corcoran
The USS *Frank E. Evans* (DD 754) Association, Inc.
"A Survivor's Account" by Andrew (Joe) Mulitsch, ussfranke-
    evansassociationdd754.org
"Ignored losses of Vietnam War" by Louise Esola, November 11,
    2011
"The Fight Continues," *Press & Dakotan*, September 30, 2013
"Survivors recall the night USS Frank E. Evans was cut in two"
    by Alex Branch, *Fort Worth Star-Telegram*, Ft. Worth, Texas,
    September 29, 2012
"My Sunday Column: Getting Their Names on the Vietnam War
    Memorial Wall—'Lost 74' Sailors of the USS Frank E.
    Evans" by Ron Kaye, ronkayela.com
"He, Too, Was A Victim Of War" by Michael E. Ruane, *Philadelphia
    Inquirer*, Philadelphia, Pennsylvania, October 20, 1988
"USS *Frank E Evans DD754*—Her Story," johnjudyc.blogspot.
    com, October 13, 2007
"USS *Frank E. Evans:* Disaster in the South China Sea" by Phil
    Smith, *Vietnam*, August 2001
"Shipwreck survivors hold out hope for recognition" by Ben
    Bohall, KVNO News, October 5, 2011
"Ship cut in half 'like a knife through hot butter'" by Robert F.
    Orr, *Navy Times*, April 29, 2002
"Young Sea" by Carl Sandburg, *Chicago Poems*, 1916, Public
    Domain

13
Vernon Leroy Downs Jr.
Notes from friends and family
Letter from Bill Conger, USMC (Ret), popasmoke.com

3/9th Marines Records, February 1968
3/9th Marines Records, March 1968
"A Vietnam War nightmare: Purple hearts on Valentine's Ridge"
by Steve Luhm, *The Salt Lake Tribune*, Salt Lake City, Utah,
February 14, 2008
"The Young Dead Soldiers Do Not Speak" by Archibald MacLeish,
1940, Public Domain

14
Michael James Hatfield
Notes from friends and family
190thahc.com
fortwolters.com
obitsforlife.com
signal439.tripod.com/redcatcher199lib/190th-ahc-spartan-17
134thahc.com
"Trial by Fire" by Tom Pienta -187th AHC/187thahc.net
Essays on the Vietnam Conflict by Joe L. Galloway
"The Old Astronomer" by Sarah Williams, 1868, Public Domain

15
James Milton Warr
Letters and interview with David Warr
Notes from fellow soldiers
ruskfamily.com
tshaonline.org
"Veteran recalls serving as helicopter crew chief in Vietnam" by
Joe Todd, examiner-enterprise.com
240thahc.50megs.com
vhpamuseum.org
134thahc.com
River Assault Squadron Nine Operations Summary 1968 (USN)
Legend: A Harrowing Story of Green Beret Sergeant Roy Benavidez's
Heroic Mission to Rescue a Special Forces Team Caught
Behind Enemy Lines by Eric Blehm, Broadway Books, New
York, New York, 2015

militaryimages.net/threads/huey-cobra-pilot-crew-uniform.6700

9thdivisionlrrp.com/unitHistoryRick-3.html

"Do not stand at my grave and weep" by Mary Elizabeth Frye, 1932, Public Domain

Rusk, David—The Handbook of Texas Online, Texas State Historical Society

Thomas Jefferson Rusk, Sanjacinto-museum.org

16
Aldwin Aldean Ellis Jr.

Notes from friends and family

Letters from Sam Braaten

Letter from Roger Stowe

Letters from Linda Rasmussen Misterek

lzsally.com

"Screaming Eagles and The Battle for Mother's Day Hill" by Don Kochi, 327infantry.org

A Brief History of A Company, 2nd Battalion, 502nd Infantry Regiment, 1st Brigade (Separate), 101st Airborne Division, Republic of Vietnam, September-October 1967 by Charles P. Otstott/2nd502.org

What's Eating You? People and Parasites by Eugene H. Kaplan, Princeton University Press, Princeton, New Jersey, 2010

John 15:13

17
Thomas James Tomczak

Notes from Patty Tomczak-Verig

Letters from James Michael Alward

Letters from Dennis Foreman

Letters from Billy Frank Fuller

Letters from Vince Keeney

Letters from Tim O'Rourke

Letters from Jon Phipps

Unlikely Warriors: The Army Security Agency's Secret War in Vietnam 1961–1973 by Lonnie M. Long and Gary B. Blackburn, iUniverse, Inc., Bloomington, IN, 2013

asalives.org/ASAONLINE/sodhist.htm

specialforces78.com/in-memoriam/vietnam/

Top Secret Missions by John E. Malone, Trafford Publishing, Victoria, Canada, 2003

"Henry V" by William Shakespeare, 1599, Public Domain

18
Donald Sidney Skidgel

Notes from Tammy Skidgel-Russell

Notes from friends

Bangor Daily News, Bangor, Maine

newportmaine.org

usastruck.com

National Archives

Air Cavalry Squadron Field Manual—1969

"Dazed and Confused-Vietnam: January 5th through December 8th 1970" by Jim Cain, *The Bullwhip Squadron News*, November 2001

Absolute War, by Gen. George S. Patton, 1944

"A Mother's Whisper" by Lt. Col. Andrew J. Hudson (Ret)

19
Stanley Claus Campbell

Notes from friends and family

gia-vuc.com/MCB62.htm

seabee-rvn.com

Have Gun Will Travel by Raymond Cochran

mcb7.com/history.html

vietnam-era-seabees.org/Jim_Piccotti

Dirty Dozen by Raymond Cochran

msuweb.montclair.edu/~furrg/Vietnam/pbuncommon.html

mca-marines.org/leatherneck/1966/10/can-do

mcb121.com/MCB121.htm

Notes from MCB-7 veteran Jeffrey Caine CET2

SEABEE MAGAZINE, Issue No.3, 2004, "The Seabees in Vietnam," by The Naval Historical Center

"Requiem" by Robert Louis Stevenson, 1880, Public Domain

20
The Boys of Nui Vu

Notes from friends and family

homeofheroes.com

Small Unit Action in Vietnam Summer 1966: Howard's Hill by Capt. Francis J. West Jr., USMCR, History and Museums Division, Headquarters, US Marine Corps, Washington, DC, 1967

U.S. Marines in Vietnam: An Expanding War, 1966 by Dr. Jack Shulimson, Pickle Partners Publishing, 2016

Small Unit Leadership: A Commonsense Approach by Col. Dandridge M. Malone, Random House Publishing, New York, New York, 2009

Hill 488 by Ray Hildreth and Charles W. Sasser, Simon & Schuster, Inc., New York, New York, 2003

"Hill 488: A Fight to Remember" by John G. Hubbell and David Reed, *Readers Digest*, May 1968

leatherneck.com

projects.militarytimes.com

The M14 Battle Rifle by Leroy Thompson, Osprey Publishing, Ltd., Oxford, United Kingdom, 2014

1streconbnassociation.org

USS *Howard Hosts Vietnam War 'Battle of Hill 488' Survivors* by MCS2 Stacy M. Atkins Ricks, Navy Public Affairs Support Element West, June 21, 2016

"For the Fallen" by Robert Laurence Binyon, 1914, Public Domain

21

Blanchfield and Keil

Notes from friends and family

"Mother of GI Gets Highest US Medal" by Aldo Beckman, *Chicago Tribune*, Chicago, Illinois, April 23, 1971

"Adrian Soldier Killed In Combat," *Toledo Blade*, Toledo, Ohio, July 10, 1969

"Assault on Hill 875," US Army Records

US Army Medal Citations

Medal of Honor Citation—Michael Blanchfield

"Daily Staff Journal—173rd Airborne Brigade," July 3, 1969

"Out of the Clouds" by Esther B. Campbell Gates

Ironwood Daily Globe, Iornwood, Michigan, July 11, 1969

Roselle Register, Roselle, Illinois, August 1, 1969

"He Saved Lives, Didn't Take Them" by Patrick Joyce, *Buffalo Grove Herald*, Buffalo Grove, Illinois, May 3, 1971

"Wheeling Legion To Name Post To Honor Dead Hero," *Daily Herald,* Chicago, Illinois, September 10, 1971

"Medal of Honor winner gets Wheeling High School degree post-humously thirty years later" by Rachel Levin, *The Daily Herald*, Chicago, Illinois, May 27, 2011

"His Last War, David Noblett and dozens of other patients just wanted their doctor back" by Jeff Prince, *Ft. Worth Weekly,* Ft. Worth, Texas, October 1, 2008

Photographic Sources

1a-Link—Link Family
1b-Link—Link Family
2-Maxam—U.S. Marine Corps
3-St Clair—Photographer Unknown
4-Wayrynen—Laverne Wayrynen Malinen
5-Borowski—U.S. Army
6a-Reeves—U.S. Army
6b-Reeves—Reeves Family
7a-Luse—Luse Family
7b-Luse-Babyak—Grant Curtis
8a-Mears—Don McPhail
8b-Mears—Rick Tagaolaga
9-Schramm—Lori Ann Rapanaro-McCormick
10-Austin—U.S. Marine Corps
11a-Matejov—John Matejov
11b-Matejov—John Matejov
11c-Matejov—John Matejov
12a-Corcoran—U.S. Navy
12b-Corcoran-Gary, Kelly Jo, Gregory Sage—U.S. Navy
13-Downs—U.S. Marines
14-Hatfield—Shelly Hatfield-Rioux
15a-Warr—David Warr
15b-Warr—David Warr
16-Ellis—Ellis Family
17-Tomczak—James Alward
18a-Skidgel—Skidgel Family
18b-Skidgel—U.S. Army
19-Campbell—U.S. Navy

20a-Nuivu-Marines—U.S. Marine Corps
20b-Nuivu-Howard—U.S. Marine Corps
20c-Nuivu-Carlisi—Photographer Unknown
20d-Nuivu-Hildreth—U.S. Marine Corps
20e-Nuivu-Glawe—U.S. Marine Corps
20f-Nuivu-Holmes—Holmes Family
20g-Nuivu-McKinney—U.S. Marine Corps
20h-Nuivu-Mascarenas—U.S. Marine Corps
20i-Nuivu-Adams—Photographer Unknown
20j-Nuivu-Thompson—U.S. Marine Corps
20k-Nuivu-Victor—U.S. Marine Corps
20l-Nuivu-Meyer—U.S. Marine Corps
20m-Nuivu-Redic—U.S. Marine Corps
20n-Nuivu-Indians—Photographer Unknown
21a-Blanchfield—Gary Holcomb
21b-Keil—Toni Weaver
21c-Nob—Photographer Unknown
21d-Nob2—Jeff Prince, *Ft. Worth Weekly*
21e-Nob3—Photographer Unknown
"The Author" photograph—Connie Blackburn Futrelle Robinson

About the Author

Gary B. Blackburn is a native Iowan and served with the US Air Force Security Service from April 1961 to November 1964. He studied Chinese at the Institute of Far Eastern Languages–Yale University and Technical Chinese at Goodfellow AFB, Texas. Overseas assignments included the Joint Sobe Processing Center, Torii Station, Okinawa, working for NSA, and the 6987th Security Group, Shu Lin Kou Air Station, Taiwan. After his duty in the Far East, Gary returned to Goodfellow AFB as a member of the elite 6948th Security Squadron (Mobile), USAFSS, to fulfill the last year of his military commitment.

Gary is a graduate of John Wesley University in High Point, North Carolina, and is retired from Eastern Air Lines and the US Department of Homeland Security. He served as commandant of cadets and vice-president/director of Public Relations and Alumni Affairs at Oak Ridge Military Academy, Oak Ridge, North Carolina, for a total of ten years. He is a published author and photographer.

CPSIA information can be obtained
at www.ICGtesting.com
Printed in the USA
FSHW011153020421
80004FS